The Wild White Man of Badu

MABUIAG

I ON IDRIESS

'Jack' Idriess was born in 1891 and served in the 5th Light Horse in the First World War. He returned to Australia to write The Desert Column, which was published following his huge success with Prospecting for Gold. He went on to write 56 books and was largely responsible for popularising Australian writing at a time when local publishing was still not considered viable. A small wiry mild-mannered man, Idriess was a wanderer and adventurer, with a vast pride in Australia, past, present and future.

ETT IMPRINT has been publishing Idriess for over 25 years, including:

Flynn of the Inland
The Desert Column
The Red Chief
Nemarluk
Horrie the Wog Dog
Prospecting for Gold
Drums of Mer
Madman's Island
The Yellow Joss
Forty Fathoms Deep
Lasseter's Last Ride
The Cattle King (audio)
Sniping
Shoot to Kill
Guerrilla Tactics
The Wild White Man of Badu
Gold Dust and Ashes
Headhunters of the Coral Sea

The Wild White Man of Badu

A Story of the Coral Seas

Ion Idriess

ETT IMPRINT
Exile Bay

ETT IMPRINT
PO Box R1906
Royal Exchange NSW 1225 Australia

First published by Angus & Robertson 1950.
Reprinted 1951 (twice), 1966 (twice).
First electronic edition published by ETT Imprint in 2019.
Published by ETT Imprint 2020. Reprinted 2021, 2022.

I experienced considerable difficulty in securing photographs to help illustrate this book. Captain Frank Hurley and Colin Simpson came to the rescue; and to these good-natured travellers I tender thanks and a cheerio. Ion Idriess

ISBN 978-1-922384-93-5 (pbk)
ISBN 978-1-922384-94-2 (ebk)

Cover: Original cover by Quinton F. Davis, 1950.
Design by Tom Thompson.

AUTHOR'S NOTE

It is only due to a combination of circumstances that this book is written. For by now even the "threads" of the story are vanishing—probably *have* vanished. Just one more page absorbed by Time in the fascinating book of Australian history.

Years ago, ah, time dreams by!—when I was a lad in a strange new world sailing the Coral Sea in a cockroach infested cutter. Dallying from island to island, among the three little groups of Torres Strait.

Again and again, under the palms, in village or on seashore, in canoe or lugger, the greybeards would refer to, then on inquiry murmur a story of Wongai, chief of chiefs of all Badu and Mabuiag, conqueror of Moa. Reincarnated from the skies to teach them how to. make gardens, how to make war. The young fellows would silently listen, bashfully so. For even then, under the contact of civilization, each succeeding generation wished more and more to forget the stories of the "old times", to break entirely from their traditions of the past, to rapidly become "civilized".

In succeeding. cruises, before I imagined I should write books, I heard story after story of this great Wongai on Badu, Moa, and Mabuiag, "away across", too, on the Eastern Group—Mer, Eroob, and Ugar. And at Yam and Warrior Island, renowned as once the home of the great chief Kebisu. His son, known to the Strait and early Papuan history—he constituted himself the personal bodyguard of that great man Sir William MacGregor—as "Old Maino", told me many a story of his father, the sea-rover Kebisu. And again and again introduced "the great chief Wongai" into these reminiscences.

These adventure stories fascinated me, as they would any lad. But it was not until later, at Thursday Island, the pearling port, that it dawned upon me that Wongai, chief of chiefs, beloved of Sida, God of the Crops, beloved of Kwoiam, God of War, had really been a white man.

For a few of the old-time pioneer pearlers were still above ground and sea. And ever and again in their stories, at the boatshed by the wharf, under the palms at the Waterfront, or in the easy chairs at that palace of story-telling, Jack McNulty's pub, with pipes alight they would refer to "Wani, the Wild White Man of Badu".

A renegade from their point of view, to the Islanders but little short of a god.

Eventually, I came across references to him in a few old records of the times. Particularly in MacGillivray's *Narrative of the Voyage of* H.M.S. *Rattlesnake* and in Dr Logan Jack's *Northmost Australia.* And in an occasional old record haply saved from the past by Jack McNulty, one of the enthusiasts of the tiny Thursday Island Historical Society.

I began to make notes, determined on my next wandering among the islands to visit the greybeards again and nail them down to details of what each could tell.

A stroke of luck happened first. For on Cape York Peninsula I lived for some months at the old Residency, home of Frank Jardine. And came across some of his huge journals, his correspondence, over years, to the Colonial Secretary of the day, and many fascinating records of that pioneer settlement, in Jardine's time proudly believed destined to become a "second Singapore". Alas, nothing remained but portion of "the Residency". Nature had overgrown all else. Nature was even then busy blotting out the very records-white ants were eating Jardine's journals.

How often since I have wished I'd "souvenired" those priceless journals! Priceless, because they were the written record of one of the most colourful epics in Australia's pioneering history.

In Jardine's journals again and again I came upon records of this "Wani, Wild White Man of Badu", one of "the most fiendish renegades that ever terrorized the seas". So that yet again there appear to be two sides to every question.

So, here at last is the story of Wongai, Wild White Man of Badu. It is the best I can do with the scanty scraps of material. But to delay longer would mean it would never be printed. Not that that would matter one iota, of course. However, the book may prove of passing interest to those interested in "Hashes" from our Australian past. And to those interested in a tiny but colourful race of islanders, a race whose descendants today have reached the full climax of their ambition, to become "civilized" enough to even don uniforms in a "white man's war".

But Time passes, like Wongai, like the islanders' culture of a thousand years, like history, like-everything.

ION IDRIESS.

CONTENTS

MOA AND BADU

Garainju ogur
Usar
Tipapulaizi kula
Murarad
Balbul
Iit
Gudalu pad
Wonai
Daudar
Soxau
pad
Belasanmaulunga
Oranikuik
Daudan
Ou
Kwail
Giwaio
Vour
Damu pad
Sarbi
Totolai
M O A
Widui
Boigu
Tabunaihai
Porbar
Dabu
Ir
Seseenegegat
Kwaikitaa
Baigua rock
Adaru
Kota inab
Koted
Kubikia
Tulu
Baiit
Kulkai
Iki
Waira
Zuzur
Dungo ngur
Muid
Gud
Zauma
Baigoa
Ngur
Ulamain
Wadauibad
Dualud
Mipa
Kubin
Bobuauikiai
Gurl
Dorgai
Wabait
Upai
Zagnu ngur
Karbai
Ubulag
Zunag
Idumaab
Marpaiil kuau
Kaialag
Aiia
Zarni
Kusa
Samun
Karbai bau
Wia
Kuta aiia
Autai nab
Samun
Graz
Tun
Takomolai
Kulewai
Gaimuni
Abaruduab
Bugul nguki
Graz
Ngulu
Kulal sabi
Moktan
Ngurtai
Kanig
Argan
Graz
Tupukuai
Karmalogab
Dumaui
Gauobuut
Gub
Mug
Tagalkau
Kuteal
Kai akulman
Mugi akulman
Warubungai
Au
Mekenakausai
Ilabnab
Nguru
Brabras
Marti
Waru
Damu pad
Kumat
Butai pad

CHAPTER I

KILL!—OR BE KILLED

Two men—*such* men. Repulsive in repose. Implacable. Blood-shot eyes simmering to blaze into animal fury—now veiled by a cold wariness pretending utter lack of interest in the other. Grim, deep-lined faces shadowing brutal mouths, beards matted with salt spray. Protruding bones made wretched the near-naked bodies seared with wounds from the cat-o'-nine-tails, wounds festering under sunburn, wounds hellfire torture from salt spray.

One man *would*—*must* kill the other.

Both were determined to live. Once there had been *five* in the boat. Now there were two.

A sip of water remained in the keg. But—no food.

A man must eat to live. *Both* were determined to eat!

He who crouched in the stem with gaunt arm across the tiller half turned his head to gaze indifferently over the sea. He who sprawled with his back to the bows could *feel* the other's thoughts. Both had shammed sleep for-how long now! The very boat seemed to *know,* had absorbed the blood and terror of these nights and days; it felt a living thing gliding along with suppressed shudder and sigh of spray, pretending it did not know that of these left one must kill and-eat the other.

To live.

Both knew so much of death. Neither meant to die.

He in the stern was actually a young man—surely not! This gaunt fiend escaped from hell. The hell of Norfolk Island. Back there, his fierce eyes hooded by a terrible wariness—wary to the sneaking footfall, to the coarse laugh that might disguise betrayal, to the hiss of the lash, to the thump of the musket butt that could smash against mouth—could herald death! Once, this wild thing had been human, had had a strong, intelligent face. Now brutalized, scarred, craftily cruel. His matted beard, black as coal, partially hid a mouth whose iron jaws and teeth looked capable of tearing out an enemy's throat—were destined to do so. That battered body had been noted amongst strong men for its strength—with maniacal laugh he flaunted it when, urged by the lash, he had toiled at the breakwater. No maddened slave amongst the hundreds of despairing wretches could handle as large a rock as he. In a gruesome way his emaciated body caricatured that strength now, in the horrid bones, the taut sinews, the knobbly, contracted lumps of muscle. The bones of his big hand, with clawed fingers loosely clenched round the tiller handle, looked horrible. The hairy brute could well have been a club-man of ages past. He gaped famishing over a cloudless sea as to a light breeze the boat just glided along.

That other one, that shapeless bundle of bones slumped back in the bows facing the other crouching in the stern, was staring out past him with deceptively unseeing eyes. He *too*, had a knife. He too was scarred by the lash, though not nearly so cruelly as the other; he too bore the imprint of fiendishness yet more horrifying now in desperation. He was small, weedy as the other brute was big. Back in the hell he had been known as "the Weasel". His cunning, his slinking ways, his mean, shifty eyes, his knowing whisper had shielded him in tragic times where strength had not availed others. That craftiness had saved him so far during this last desperate venture in the boat. The other three had been merely strong men.

He was cornered now. But the weasel when cornered can bite.

Not for an instant did he show he was in despair. Not of death, it was of life he despaired. He was certain his knife-thrust would be swifter than the other's. But afterwards—!

He would be alone in a boat, sailing—where? That other devil understood a boat, understood this accursed sea, understood where he was going—to be a king among the savage islands! But he, the Weasel, did not understand a boat, feared and hated this vast loneliness of sea, could not think what he could do even if he did reach those islands—how far away!

For all that, he was determined not to die—yet.

The boat crept eerily along. Broad daylight, yet not a sound but the gurgling at the bows, a sigh from the cordage. Nor a call from one solitary sea-bird. Not a sail in sight—there never bad been.

He in the stern was thinking that soon now he must strike. For that cursed Weasel could cling to life night after night after night without sleep.

Yes, he *must* strike soon, otherwise he would sink into sleep and-never wake.

But what a thrill—this looking back! He took a deep breath. Free for ever, aye, for ever from those accursed chains, from those snarling commands, from the lash, from those cells black as the depths of hell— free from the soul-searing hatred of that hell on earth. The deadening misery of isolation far away for ever from home and fellow men, the irony of the beautiful island turned into hell by man. Always there, under the sighing pines sweet with singing birds writhed the wretches perishing of dysentery, happily cheating Authority by dying. Alone in the cells they had quarried themselves, in darkness with rats and horror that drove men mad. Aye, they made demons of men, that they did. Like demons they lived. Demons they died.

He glared out over the sea, his memory a nightmare of phantoms of the near past. His mind could never rest. Clank of chains. Dull tramp of feet shuffling to gallows or, firing squad. Groans, bitter curses stifled in stench of sweat and heat, slaving in the quarries. Hiss of the lash, agonized screams—the dreadful writhings at the Triangle. Bestial roar of the mutinies, thunder of musket volleys.

His eyes glaring, teeth clenched, hand gripping the tiller as if the throat of a taskmaster. He shuddered, relaxed. He was free—free.

Breathing deeply, he almost smiled. Thoughts drifted again, the wild beast faded from his eyes, cunning masked the murder in his face, gloating now in pitiful self-praise. *His* was the plan to seize a boat and sail away. Oh no, not to the Australian coast and the bush and starvation or spear of wild blacks, or far worse of recapture! *No!* to the New Zealand islands to take their chance amongst the whalers or warlike Maoris. Oh no! But his the plan to sail a thousand miles just west of north to the "Isles of Terror". That was what the whalers called them, and the sandalwood getters and the sea-dogs who sailed to the Chinas and Indies, scurrying across the Coral Sea in fear of their miserable lives. Escape away to those far distant, unknown Torres Strait islands, so dreaded by all mariners.

He chuckled grotesquely. The "Terrible Isles", they called them.

Ah, but there was no lash there, no soldiers, no "civilization"! Just the untamed islands and savages with food in plenty under a free blue sky. He had whispered to the others that they take a boat and sail away and seize an island and be kings among the savages and be free for ever.

It was the cunning Weasel who had spied out the rest. The whaler had come, a whaler from distant Hobart Town. They and American whalers fairly often came to the Norfolk hell and anchored a few days and traded oil and food. It was the Weasel who noted how careless this ship was with the boat.

They had escaped during the night. Had swum to the boat, had got clean away.

He had steered by sun and stars, the way in his mind only by the stories of sailormen. Hundreds of miles just west of north, so they said, a great coral reef ran north a thousand miles and more parallel with the wild Australian coast. It ended in a little sea of coral reefs and islands.

And he had thought that if he could reach this great reef and sail up beside it it must at last lead him to the islands. Much safer if from the open sea he could only find one of the few entrances through the reef. Then he could sail up north between it and the Australian coast, in calm water, seeking fish and water among the reefs and islands. And to do this he had tried to steer by his mind to one particular such entrance that sailormen called Entrance Passage.

Miracle of miracles, he was steering right there now. Over a thousand miles of sea, against varying winds and tides and currents the boat was heading directly for a tiny entrance in a reef twelve hundred miles long.

But he did not know it. He had been very anxious as day followed day and still no sign of this Great Barrier Reef.

And now —

He glanced up at the masthead, something beautiful was fluttering there, an enormous butterfly with pulsing wings of gold and peacock blue. It hovered awhile, a delicate thing of loveliness far away out at sea.

He staggered up, hand shading questing eyes as he stared towards the horizon. No sign of land.

Butterflies sometimes drift seaward an unbelievable distance from land. He crouched down again in dull disappointment, staring up at the butterfly now settled on the masthead top. They *both* were staring up at this fair visitor from land. He leapt towards the bows and his knife slashed down as the Weasel's slashed up. He snarled to the stab ripping his thigh but the Weasel's throat was gurgling blood, his eyes all startled horror.

The butterfly flew away.

The Weasel relaxed, gurgled backward.

He panted, with the knife shivering in his hand, then staggered back to the stern. He crouched down, panting heavily, he was done, he had left it almost *too* late.

He lashed the tiller, stretched out in the boat and — was asleep.

He awoke in a dream of birds, a riot of birds, a din with their cluckings and squabblings. Millions of birds. A pleasant dream, staring up at a starlit sky through still, dark night. Just gliding along, gliding through a world of birds, birds down on the land, not birds on the wing, but birds that did not fly away, countless birds, millions of eggs upon the coral sand crunching under his feet as he walked along gazing down at innumerable fat baby birds squawking up at him. He licked famished lips, his fingers clawed to bend down and wring their necks and eat, eat, eat. Then he gazed starwards in disappointment — it was only a dream! The stench as of a vast fowlyard disgusted his nostrils, he wondered that a dream could be so overpoweringly convincing. He sat up, yawning.

Right beside him a long, black "something" was spread upon the sea—a swift tide carrying him straight towards an end of it. He snatched at the tiller to steer clear, leaping up as he did so. And the long, black thing was silhouetted by sky and a million stars. A wall! He was sailing straight past the end of a wall! He was awake now, horror-stricken—carried by an irresistible tide straight past the end of a breakwater.

Where was he? When he had thought there was not a living white man within a thousand miles!

He stared in despair, felt the searing toil, the muscle-breaking labour of struggling to manhandle huge stones into position—he had helped build others such as this. The night was filled by the heavy murmuring of the tide upon rocky ramparts, a tide carrying him through a narrow passage-way, sweeping him straight into some harbour back to the chains and the lash—aye, and the noose this time!

With a snarl he leapt to the bows and lifted the thing there overside, lifted it down to the water and let it go gently as a babe. The night filled with the squawkings of countless birds—that cursed dream that had stupefied him while the tide carried him straight back to the chains.

He sprang aft to the tiller. When he had cleared the passage he would lower sail and turn about and paddle back and beat the tide. He still had the oars.

Only when he was gliding past did he become really conscious of the birds, though at night their din seems to fill sea and sky. For he was creeping past low-lying Raine Island, a mere sandbank a few feet above the sea enclosed by coral. The breeding place of tens of thousands of boobies and frigate birds, of gannets and noddies and terns. If he had set foot on that desolate spot he would in truth have walked upon thousands of birds' eggs, seen thousands of baby birds squawking up at him.

He glided past the islet without challenge, just the boom of the tide upon the Great Barrier Reef, and the noise of the birds. He was beginning to breathe again when a fire lit up. Flamed up, illuminating a tent—and a marine bending over the fire.

In shuddering fear he crouched low, pushing gently on the tiller. That sailor now standing by the fire was a man-o'-war man.

Expecting a musket shot, he glided past into the night, prepared to leap overboard. No chance now of beating back through the passage-way, for the growing fire was throwing a rosy lane of silver across the channel. He glided on unchallenged, staring back at the fire growing smaller, at the sailorman beside it. Presently the fire was only a little rosy ball. He sighed heavily, relaxed, then almost collapsed—at the dark outline of a vessel!

He slipped past unchallenged. And then, an hour later, crept past another ship. Just before dawn he thought he was done—a man-o'-war loomed up, there was no mistaking her.

She actually was H.M.S. *Fly,* Captain Blackwood.

There was no escape, his choice was to drown or swing at the yard-arm.

The Watch was never quite certain. Peering from the lookout, he could almost swear he sighted a small boat bearing down upon them. Just when the mist came. And then the white squall came howling, blotting all from sight. He must have imagined it, for what would a small boat be doing out here in this unknown, uncharted sea!

What was the extraordinary fortune that guided this man from the moment of his escape—from the perils of the unknown, of the elements, and of white men, black, and brown throughout many bloody years?

As the swiftly driving mist pressed a ghostly shroud round the man-o'-war his heart thumped violently, he dared hardly breathe. To an icy breath the boat trembled, then began to surge ahead as the white squall with its hissing rain blotted man-o'-war and outcast from the sea. He jumped up and shook his fist astern, his maniacal laugh howling with the wind.

He was in no harbour, as he imagined, he was now on his right course between the Great Barrier Reef and the Australian mainland, heading directly north towards those savage islands on which he had sworn he would become king. Surely it is one of the strangest flukes of sea history that this hunted outcast should sail the vast, turbulent Pacific in a tiny boat with sea and tide and wind gently pressing him across a thousand miles to one tiny opening in a mighty reef. That through that opening he should dodge a naval party and three of Her Majesty's ships, that he should then sail on, on his right course, and survive the most dangerous sea in all the world, an uncharted sea already littered with a hundred wrecks, a sea feared above all others by mariners, some of its islands peopled by warlike savages a hundred times more dangerous in that they believed white people their implacable foes. And he was not only to survive, but would become an "island king". But such is fact.

The first two vessels he had passed were the pinnace *Midge* and the schooner *Bramble,* tender to H.M.S. *Fly,* which was on survey work, in particular along the Great Barrier Reef. And here, on Raine Island, on a later cruise Commander Blackwood intended to erect a beacon as a guide to shipping coming from the east, to mark a passage-way through the great Reef that as a mighty rampart walls off the Pacific from the Australian east coast. For as the Australian colonies to the south were developing, more and more shipping was beginning to use this lonely, particularly dangerous, uncharted sea.

All this he in the boat did not know as he fled into the shielding heart of the white squall. He felt the boat and he were mates; he patted the gunwale encouragingly; both he and it were straining all to race away from that hidden terror astern.

An hour later mist and squall cleared rapidly before a rising sun. He stared anxiously astern, sighed deeply, then chuckled in nervous relief. He had beaten them again; there was no sign of ships, only a choppy sea, a hazy line of hills far to the left, a line of foam and thunder as of distant guns to his right.

He was in no harbour. Standing in the stern he stared incredulously; afraid to believe it true. Then laughed to the skies as truth dawned upon him. He was within the Great Barrier Reef, that was it to the right, that line of foam and spray stretching north and south far as the eye could see. In delight he listened to the thunder, out there, where the rollers from the open Pacific were breaking upon the mighty coral rampart. It was just as the whalemen had said. He was in calm water, safe from the open sea, safe from pursuit, and upon his true course.

Distantly, he saw islands ahead. The whalemen had told him that the island shores were sometimes thick with shellfish, the mangrove tidal creeks held fish that might be caught with a pronged stick in the shallows when the tide went out.

Only then he again felt himself ravenous.

He glanced at the bow, at the dark stain there—he had not bled much. He would not need the Weasel now.

CHAPTER II

LIVE—OR DIE

Before midday he thrilled to the pleasure of landing on his first island, just a granite knoll supporting a few wind-blown trees, a patch of scrub, coarse grass, and creepers. But—his ravenous glance saw the shore rocks grey with oysters. Seizing a stone, he smashed at the oysters, his fingers clawing at the broken shells.

He ate and slept on that islet three days and nights, building up his strength as would a famished wolf, soon desiring heavier food than shellfish. He was safe from natives, seldom would they visit such an inhospitable spot as this. One distant sail he recognized as a Yankee whaler.

At dawn on the fourth day he was at sea again, immeasurably refreshed. Brilliant sunlight, cloudless sky, a light breeze, the glorious weather of the Great Barrier towards the close of the sou'-east season. Slap of lazy sea at the bows, trilling gurgle of the tide. Sailing along, deeply he filled his lungs that so often had panted for breath, turning friendly eyes to the seagulls whose freedom he had so often envied. Far behind him now was hell, behind him for evermore. Every league ahead carried him nearer to the heart of a sea of savage islands, lands unknown to white men, the seas sailed only by occasional venturesome craft that gave the islands a wide berth. Other islands stretched for a thousand miles and more, and no European, no flag at all flew here. He would take an island and make of himself a king, far from the accursed injustices of civilization.

How could such as he foresee that he was sailing but a few years ahead of a new era in the Pacific? Soon explorers would be toiling through that unknown mainland on his left. Rapidly increasing shipping would warily sail this very water. Small craft, daring all for riches of sandalwood, bêche-de-mer and pearlshell, would press into the dreaded Coral Sea. The struggling Colonies would grow into States—into the Commonwealth of Australia, a nation.

But now around the man was a vast loneliness of sea and land with a feeling of impenetrable isolation that was joy.

Steering clear of the mainland he sailed on to yet another island, one blessed with fresh water. He filled the cask. No food. Not worried, he gazed out from a low hill at several other islands visible to the north. He set sail again, envying a school of sharks shepherding a shoal of mullet towards the mainland. In some quiet, shallow bay they would wheel.

them into a panicking mass then rave into the slaughter with clash of jaws in flurry of foam. How he, too, would like to feel his teeth in those fat mullet.

By late afternoon he steered to an islet little more than a sandbank fringed by mangroves and encircled by a coral reef. If he could find anchorage he would camp here, for he wisely desired to sleep soundly ashore when possible. Under a dying breeze the boat glided over the reef into the placid water of a tiny lagoon. He ran her up on to a miniature beach and stepped ashore. And stood still in his tracks.

At his feet were the ashes of a fire, round it burnt shells from freshly roasted shellfish.

He peered among the mangroves, hand on knife, staring at the marks of a canoe upon the beach. It had been launched, had sailed away.

To make sure he ran through the mangroves and up to the sand mound, glaring all around. He could see everything, he was the only man here. With a sigh of relief he hurried back to the beach. He felt the ashes, they were warm! Brushing away the centre he knelt down and blew. Fiery sparks flew up. Urgently he ran back to the sand mound, grabbed an armful of dry grass and twigs, and hurried back. He threw on a little of the grass, knelt down and blew carefully. Soon the grass smoked, caught alight, a wee flame sprang up.

He had a fire to cook his food. His haunted face grinned in delight.

He threw on twigs, then mangrove sticks. Soon he was talking aloud, praising himself and the fire that had answered so companionably.

He now had company, too.

With a glance at the sun near vanishing over the mainland he examined the burnt shells. There were only three sorts. With one of each he hurried to the reef. There was an abundance of shellfish there of all sizes and shapes and colours. But the like of those he held in his hand took finding. Presently he distinguished one; it was easier then. By dark he had gathered quite a small pile. Smiling all over his gaunt face, he carried them to the fire. He had been uneasy lest the day should come when he would eat poisonous shellfish. But he would always know these three sorts now. He would soon learn. Yes, learn and master not only things of the wild but—wild men, too.

By the fire that night, his belly full, he felt a king. Ah, far better—a free man. The very air he breathed was freedom.

He, who had breathed the foul air of dungeons packed with beasts filthy as he, filled his lungs with this sweetest of air. His ears that so long had listened to groans, to bitter curses, to the scurrying of rats, now drank in the music of insects, the tinkle of ripplets upon the shelly beach; his eyes that had glared into the darkness of the solitary cell now gazed up at the stars.

He stayed on the islet three days, eating, sleeping, resting. And sailed richer in knowledge, strength, and comfort. He knew he would never starve now, even that first barren islet had taught him that. And he would soon learn to catch the fish he saw so plentifully, even though he had neither line nor hook. Sitting hand on tiller, with a pleasant breeze astern, his eyes gleamed at thought of unknown islands far ahead—"isles of paradise" the sailormen had called them, islands on which grew everything that heart of man could desire. Fiercely he swore again he would take an island for his own.

For his comfort and use now he had fire, and all that fire could do. In the boat was a large clam-shell he had half filled with sand. On it a fire smouldered, with beside it a little heap of the tough, slow-burning mangrove wood. Wherever he landed now he would have a fire for his cooking, for warmth, and for company.

Confidently he sailed on and his eyes were keen with interest as he gazed towards the haze of the mainland hills always to his left, the lazy blue sea stretching ever ahead, the dots of distant islands, the Great Barrier Reef a line of murmurous spray on his right. With brutish confidence he felt his island was near within his grasp.

And two days later came within an ace of losing all. Jumped ashore, walked in among the sighing casuarinas. And stepped face to face with a savage.

In chilled silence they stared he sprang forward at the backward jerk of the spear arm and plunged his knife straight to the aboriginal's heart. He glared down at the dying man, panting as sweat oozed from his forehead. It had been icy surprise, breathless shock. But for the grace of he knew not what it would have been he lying there all twisted up with scarlet blood slowly staining the sand. He leapt round to an inhuman scream to glare into fiendish eyes, devilishly bared teeth. She sprang, but missed his throat as her teeth fastened in his neck while her claws were gouging his eyes and her legs whipped round his waist. Plunging like a hunter with a panther at his throat he tore at her in a roaring fury— afterwards he wondered why he had not plunged the knife into her. But he did not, he fell to crush her to the ground but her body was a rubber ball while she bit him deep. With a yell he leapt up, tearing at her hair, and felt her grip slip. Convulsively he locked his arms round her neck and clenched her tight, sensing her fang seeking his stomach to gnaw into his entrails. Racing across the beach, he leapt out into the water and fell into it, her head locked to his body. Agonizing moments as slowly those terrible teeth ate less into his flesh while her air-bubbles rose up to play round his face. When he felt her no more he still was captive, had to grope under water and wrench her jaws apart. With a shuddering heave he cleared himself of teeth and claws and legs. He stood up, groaning with shock.

His neck and chest were a bloody mess of chewed flesh. In livid fear he glared down. Were her teeth poisoned?

She lay there, a little, twisted black body, in the water at his feet. Gingerly he bent down, lifted her up, carried her back to the beach and threw her down above high-water mark. As he launched the boat he wondered why he had bothered to lift her from the water. He must sail from this accursed place before others came.

He had been lucky again, there were *no* others. The aboriginal and his woman had but paid this islet a chance visit. Alas, chance often holds the trump card in the game of life and death.

He hurried, urged by fear.

And was lucky again. And stared amazed as towards sunset his tiny vessel neared an island, its foreshores fringed with snow that here and there appeared to move in waves. The snow of birds' plumage, countless thousands of plump Torres Strait pigeons turning creamy-white the dull green of the dwarf mangrove-trees. The noise of their cooing was a murmur out to sea, deafening as he drew close inshore. A black cloud appeared, a swift travelling cloud that whirred over the lonely boat and rained down upon the trees to a deafening hubbub of protest and swaying branches. In amazement he gazed, wondering how the sagging branches could support such numbers. Half-crazed from pain and fear of poisoned wounds, he ran the boat up on a crinkly coral beach. And at his feet was a bailer shell—he snatched it up with joy. It was large as a billycan. If only he could boil water in it! For hours he had been praying for something in which he could boil water to wash his wounds. In feverish haste he made a fire, filled the shell with fresh water, put it on to boil.

He need not have watched it so earnestly, for it was a natural cooking pot; he was to see similar shells put to such use for years to come.

Night fell to a riot of pigeon sound, swishing of branches like continuous wind as they quarrelled for room. And the noise of their droppings was like rain.

As the water boiled he bathed his neck and chest, throwing hot water into the wounds until he felt he was cooking his own raw flesh. But it brought relief and a thankful ease to his mind. To have died from a wild woman's teeth would have been irony indeed.

He filled the shell again and set it on the fire, resolved to bathe his chest throughout the night. Then hungrily he grasped a stick. No need to search for food, the night was alive with it. He sneaked below a branch, then struck out. Five pigeons he knocked with one blow to hubbub from above. He sneaked to another tree and struck gingerly, for the first blow had torn his wounded chest and drenched it with droppings.

He soon desisted, seeing that by night at least he need but reach out a hand for what pigeons he needed. He collected some and, returning to the fire, plucked them and threw them on the coals. Ravenously he ate the first, only half grilled. It was the first meat, apart from human, that he had tasted for a long, long time.

Before dawn he had fallen asleep. He woke confusedly and leapt to the sails that were not there, believing a tornado had struck him in the boat, a roar of sound, swishing of violent rain, a rushing wind. But it was the branches that were moving, swaying to waves of sound as cloud after cloud of pigeons soared up in flight. He was splashed with bird refuse, it sounded like rain upon the water as he gazed up into a soft snow of falling down and feathers. In amazement he stared, his ears filled with sound.

Then snatched a stick and with a dismayed cry ran in under the trees.

The pigeons were going! The pigeons had gone.

He gazed after the vanishing clouds. What a fool he had been not to have killed and killed all through the night before!

He rested that day, bathing his wounds.

Towards sunset he was gazing over the sea towards the mainland. A tiny cloud appeared, idly he watched it, apparently it was growing larger, moving fast. Soon it was a fair-sized dark cloud. It grew into a large black cloud swiftly approaching. And now he saw other dots of clouds far behind. The cloud grew into a rushing wind, all white and black, of thousands upon thousands of pigeons that swooped down on the island to settle in balls of snow upon the swaying branches. Instantly the solitude was a riot of bird noises. Other clouds were swiftly approaching.

It was the pigeons come back to roost at sunset, as they always do at this season of the year. At daylight they fly back to the mainland to gorge upon the wild nutmegs on the highest trees of the jungle mountains.

The man stayed a fortnight upon the island. It was only a small, low-lying islet fringed by a coral reef, there are plenty such. Three parts surrounded by mangroves, in its centre a low, sandy hillock. And here grew grasses. He dug up the roots of these grasses and boiled and ate them to purify his blood. He mixed the tender breasts of the pigeons with shellfish, and later with small fish that he learnt to catch with a pronged stick in coral pools when the tide went out. Just inside the mangrove fringe under a clump of scraggly pandanus palm a wee carpet of emerald-green grass caught his eye. He pulled some of this to boil it. He noticed that the earth was wet. He dug with stick and hands and to his amazement found fresh water, though the spot must have been almost within reach of the big tides. He was learning fast.

He slept aboard the boat, ready to cast off at any alarm. By day he searched the sea from the hillock for any sign of canoes before he went into the mangroves or out on to the reef to search for food. And every hour he climbed the hillock again, shocked back to the realization that in his new-found freedom he lived but under the pitiless law of survival of the wariest.

From the hillock one day he saw a small schooner and two ketches in company sailing south, possibly loaded with bêche-de-mer. These venturesome fishers of the sea-slug were bound for Sydney Town before the cyclones of the nor'-west season should lash these calm waters into fury. The gaunt, bearded brute squatting on the hillock watched the distant vessels through scowling eyes. A wavelet washed together some clinking corals on the beach and he heard again the clank of chains, hiss of the lash. He spat a bitter curse. Even in this wilderness the horrors of civilization as he knew it haunted him. He would sail on and on.

When he did his wounds were partly healed, but he would never lose the scars. He had gained considerably in weight and strength. And in a confidence now tempered with caution.

With big brown arm lightly across the tiller he sailed on to a breeze that made hardly a ripple on the blue waters of the inner Barrier. A beautiful sea at this time of the year—soon to be treacherous. His beard had grown to a black riot.

His chest was still a misery, for the hairs had been chewed into the wounds and he winced daily as he pulled them out. His face had filled out, the broad hawk nose broken by a musket butt had filled out, too, as had his cheeks. The scowl still hung about the grim mouth, but the eyes showed less of the defiant terror of a hunted animal. Fierce eyes under shaggy brows, deeply suspicious eyes, but now expressive of the hunter more than the hunted. He was soon to learn, to his impotent rage, that he was still a hunted man.

CHAPTER III

EVERY HAND AGAINST HIM

He was sailing past two long, low-lying islands between him and the Great Barrier Reef, glad to see a small islet about an hour's sail ahead. He would make it before sunset. The smaller the islet the sounder he would sleep—he would walk over it first to make sure he slept alone. No telling what that mangrove forest on those larger islands might conceal.

He had cleared the islands when a distant yell startled him. Away behind the islands lay the wreck of a brig silhouetted upon a reef, dark figures swarming over her, canoes massed round her. Faintly the wind brought him the crash of cases, the howls as the loot was spilled upon the deck. No sign of survivors, no fleeing boats. Probably they had escaped before the natives boarded her.

He sailed on, using all his skill, praying the breeze would strengthen. They were so engrossed at their task they might not notice him. He gazed back towards the wreck with bitter chagrin. If only he had found her first he would have found muskets aboard, and knives and axes and ammunition that would have made him invincible. A thousand things, too—he could have loaded the boat, towed a raft with priceless articles to stock his island-to-be. Whatever that wreck contained, even down to old scraps of iron, would have proved of far more value to him than a ship loaded with gold. And now every priceless thing was but to be a wasted orgy for savages.

They saw him! A yell! He could distinguish pointing arms as they turned to stare. With a howl they leapt overboard into the canoes.

He snarled defiantly—let them catch him if they could! They never would—if only the breeze held.

They very nearly caught him. As their light dug-outs skimmed the water to perfect paddle play uneasily he watched them gaining, never dreaming that canoes could travel so fast. They got to almost within spear-throw, the leading canoe with a naked spearman in the bows balancing his weapon with body swaying to violent hissings as he urged the rowers just a little faster. He in the boat sailing with desperate skill, near weeping bitter curses for just one musket. If he had only one musket!

The breeze strengthened with an encouraging gust right at the critical moment, he laughed to the smack at the bows as the little vessel strained ahead. He was passing the islet he had intended to camp on, it was near sunset. The breeze brought him a howl of baffled anger, he howled back a curse in reply. The canoes gave up the chase, turned about, anxious now to return to their loot.

He sailed on into the night. For a time he wondered whether he dared hide behind that islet and return to the wreck after the savages canoed back to the mainland. Common sense told him to sail on. He did, cursing now and then that naked savages had the power of making him a hunted man.

Late at night a glow far astern attracted him. The natives had fired the wreck. In his sullen regret he wondered what she was.

No one would ever know. She might have been a sandalwood getter from the Bloody Isles, far off her course. She might have been a gatherer of bêche-de-mer, a trader from Noumea, maybe a wanderer from the South Seas. Whatever she had been she now was but a moment of flames, one of the hundreds of wrecks that have vanished upon the Great Barrier Reef.

He in the boat sailing on into the lonely night was to see other such wrecks. A wreck at sea is tragedy. But then, he was born to tragedy.

The weather changed. Hot days brought calms, the seas green and clear as transparent glass. Gradually came a wind, it changed to the nor'-west, blew strongly for a day dead against him. Died down, changed again to the sou'-east, and the boat forged cheerily ahead. Then he ran into a white squall, it bore down against him with hissing rain driven by a wind that lashed the water into vicious waves smashing upon the bows. The boat heeled over, then plunged forward as he clung to the tiller, staring into the stinging rain. The sea, the air, this dense grey world an inferno of hissing sound—a chilling experience to a man alone in a boat. Half an hour later and the boat burst through the squall out into brilliant sunlight under a clear blue sky smiling upon a lazily rolling sea. He breathed in surprised relief.

This changeable weather caused him growing uneasiness as day by day he scanned the sea for the island of his dreams. He knew it was not here, not among the low-lying mangrove islands, nor the hillocky islands so barren and windswept, nor these occasional rocky islands, rugged and desolate.

He was really sailing through the change of the seasons. A few more weeks of this uncertain, varying weather, then his favouring wind would vanish while the howling nor'-westers would turn this quiet water into a treacherous fury of foam and tide and cross seas such as have smashed many a staunch craft upon the hidden reefs. Maybe cyclones would rage this season, then pity help any ship at sea. Certainly the rains would come in earnest. But he did not know this.

One night he sailed through his first tropic thunderstorm, a rolling, crashing of thunder as if the heavens were bursting asunder. He clenched the tiller as blackness vanished in quivering light spread far as eye could see in blinding curtains of lightning splitting sky from sea. He thought the sail, the boat afire, for it was glowing in green and pink and yellow vapours like quivering ghosts of flame. Around the trembling vessel eerie wisps of light were dancing and vanishing and dancing upon water that hissed into a lake of bubbling phosphorus. Those tropic electric thunderstorms can be as beautiful as they are terrifying. The hair and beard and hairy chest of the man were filmed with ghostly light. He was a scared man in a sea of loneliness now thundering with lightning flaming to a sea plunging in waves of brilliant phosphorus. A wave smacked the boat and sprayed the sail, and man and sail were dripping bubbles of phosphorus in vanishing greens and purples and reds.

A week after the storm he was drawing near the tip of Cape York Peninsula. Never did he dream that along that unknown coast a few years later the Kennedy Expedition would be trudging to disaster and death. He passed Newcastle Bay, near where Kennedy was soon to be speared to death. A brown, hilly island loomed up, Albany Island, a narrow passage between it and the mainland. Cannily he steered to pass it on the seaward side, kept to the open sea again when Mount Adolphus Island towered ahead. This man was to live long only because of his determination, his ferocious bravery, his alert suspicions, deep cunning. Had he sailed between those islands and the coast then canoes would have attacked him from both islands and mainland, impossible for him to have escaped such a natural trap. Later he was to learn that he had been seen and the trap set. Lucky for him that the canoes of these numerous tribes were not the big, swift-sailing war canoes of the Torres Strait islanders.

It was dark when he cleared Mount Adolphus Island, the stiff breeze fell away with sunset. The boat crawled along through the warm night growing breathless and hot. Anxiously he glanced at an overcast sky—he had had enough of storms in an open boat at night.

Unexpectedly a light pierced the darkness directly ahead. It darted up, then spread into a glow, another glow flared out, yet another flamed up. They spread in a hazy cloud gleaming brighter to blaze and swiftly illumine rigging, then deck, then towering masts and motionless sails of a ship. He stared amazed.

She was a whaler. They were trying out, boiling down the blubber, converting it into oil in the great iron pots. But how strange that they should light up now! He was almost upon the ship, but she carried not one solitary light until suddenly they had lit the pots. What could they possibly have been doing in total darkness? Instinctively he felt something brewing as cautiously he drew closer, for the breeze that just pushed him along was useless to the idle sails of the ship. Against the now flaring lights were silhouetted a few dark, furtive figures, not nearly enough for the number of men who should be engaged. The network of rigging above them was brightening into a fairy tracery from the flares, distinctly outlining the shape of the dark sails towering above. Under the steadily growing reflection he could see much of the planking of the big old wooden ship, but not a man was visible except those few momentarily crouching round the pots.

What was she doing here at this time of year with blubber still in her pots? What had gone wrong with her lights? And—yes, there was something wrong with her sails!

But his questions would for ever remain unsolved, like many another mystery of the Coral Sea. As he gazed, a stab of flame shot from her deck, a musket report answered by a roar of animal-like rage to which he in the boat instinctively responded with a snarl.

Figures in black silhouette leaped upon her deck as the sea echoed to musket reports, hoarse shouts.

Mutiny! A fighting mutiny.

He had drawn quite close, saw the stab of flame directly at him, leapt up and roared a curse as a musket ball came singing through his sail. Another came whining to smack the water beside the bow.

Some were firing at him—at him whom they did not *know*, who had never done them harm. They were fighting among themselves, but spared time to fire at a strange boat that glided within the reflection from the fires.

Probably the truth was that either one side or the other fired on the boat believing it to be filled with deserters from the ship. He pushed the tiller over to draw away, snarling curses upon them and their ship. To think that even during a mutiny upon the open sea every man's hand should be turned against him!

Neither ship, crew, nor outcast had noticed the chill creeping through the inky blackness. A thunder-clap that shook the seas brought some to their senses.

"Reef topsails!" came a bellow across the water.

But no willing hands jumped to rigging and yards.

"Fools of hell!" roared the voice. "A squall is upon us—reef topsails! Or do we all go down together?"

Five dark figures now leaped to obey; to musket shots two fell back to the deck.

And now the first breath of the squall came in a blast of icy wind. The little boat heeled over, the big old whaler trembled to a rattling of blocks, creak of yards. Too late, men now sprang to trim her to the storm already upon them, in a flash of lightning monkey figures were leaping for the rigging. To a howl of wind came a rolling crash of thunder, then lightning flashed straight down upon the ship. As she heeled over came a cracking of timbers as livid flame engulfed her in a blinding white light. It vanished in darkness immediately lit by fire as the cauldrons boiled over and flaming oil spilled upon the decks. To a howling wind flame was blown into the rigging and the ship was afire, heeling over there with a flood of boiling oil bathing her decks in leaping flame to screams of men—a whaler afire in a shrieking wind with her holds stowed full of oil!

Even the man in the boat ceased his curses as he strove to race from that inferno. The wind licked the ship with tongues of flame as men leapt overboard. Then came a rumble, a terrifying roar as the oil in the holds caught alight and turned the ship into a volcano. The end came in a pillar of flame as she burst apart in a fury of blazing oil spilling over the sea, while overhead sped terror in sheets of wind-blown oil fiercely burning. In stark fear the man in the boat clung to the tiller. He had sailed fast, but wave-crests of burning oil chased him, ragged sheets of blazing oil were blown after him by the wind, thunder crashed in lighting flashes that hissed into the burning sea. He survived—with Death ever grinning at his elbow, he was to survive long years to come.

Morning dawned to a clear blue sky, a strong breeze again from the south-east. Difficult to believe on this beautiful morning the fury of the night before.

He stood up and gazed around. Except for one small, low-lying island there was no land in sight. Where was the coast?

He frowned, for latterly the coast, as before that the Great Barrier Reef, had been guide and companion day after day. He must have passed Australia, sailed on into some unknown sea. He was now in Torres Strait in the Coral Sea, a small sea, but the most fascinating in the world. Confined within the northern end of the Great Barrier Reef, it stretches from Cape York Peninsula to New Guinea. It washes a hundred islands and many thousands of coral reefs and subterranean gardens of the sea. Here play fish so beautiful as to outrival the colours of the rainbow, of the bird of paradise, of butterfly and flower. But here also dwell monsters of a devilish hideousness. There was great wealth in this notoriously dangerous, deceptively peaceful sea. But this wealth was unknown—as yet! Least of all to him in the boat, sailing now to a hillocky islet.

CHAPTER IV

THE THUNDER GOD REINCARNATES WONGAI

He landed on the isles, ravenously hungry. After the fears of the night he needed sleep and rest, too. His strength was returning fast. Soon he would be the powerful, cunning brute he must be to survive.

Satisfied he was alone, he began seeking fish in the pools and under coral ledges. He was learning.

Before lighting the fire he thought he had best glance round. He was distant from other islands but—one never knew!

He strolled up on to the higher ground and ducked down.

A flotilla of war-canoes was sailing past.

If he had lit that fire, they would have seen it.

If they had passed by on the western side instead of the eastern, they would have seen the boat.

Crouching under cover, he gazed at the canoes sweeping by. The leading canoe was almost a small ship, to his amazement it was seventy feet in length, could carry a hundred men. Two-masted, with huge mat sails catching every breath of wind, she seemed to be flying over the water. The crouching man stared at his first sight of outriggers, light logs shaped like long torpedoes some twenty feet out on each side of the vessel, connected by poles to the bulwarks. These outriggers skimmed the water, adding buoyancy and helping in speed, prevented capsizing, too, in heavy weather. Across the centre bulwarks extended a platform of planks away out over the water on each side. This was the fighting platform and on it, amidst a group of befeathered warriors, a commanding figure, a tall, bearded, dark-brown warrior with massive shoulder muscles. Coal-black ringlets fell upon those shoulders, but neither they nor the beard could hide the grim jaw and broad, savage cheeks. On his chest gleamed the pearlshell "mai", insignia of the Mamoose, the chief of chiefs. Adorning his head a brilliant headdress of bird of paradise plumes, round his waist a short, black skirt of cassowary plumes. His weapons a wooden sword cruelly edged with shark's teeth, the "gaba-gaba" disk-headed club, and a dagger of cassowary bone.

Thus leading the flotilla sped the *Skull Chief*, war-canoe of Kebisu of Tutu, Warrior Island. Most powerful Mamoose in the Coral Sea, arrogantly he believed the world his own, unaware that the shadow of the

White, Man had already fallen upon these waters. He was destined to be the last great chief of the Coral Sea.

He who hid in the bushes stared down as the big canoes sped by manned with their hefty warriors, noted the seven-foot bows and sheafs of arrows. He warmed to these men, real fighting men, these were the men he'd thrill to lead upon his island-to-be. He watched as rapidly the canoes grew smaller, hesitating as to whether he should follow. Best not, they were on the warpath, safer for him to come upon them on some peaceful occasion. He walked thoughtfully back to the beach to cook his food. Thus Destiny again shielded him. Had he followed Kebisu his skull for a certainty would have been sun-dried at the mast-head of the *Skull Chief*, a prize to adorn the Zogo-house of Warrior Island.

Not two days later he drew near an island he thought might be his heart's desire. A lazy blue sea broke in creamy foam upon a reef that enclosed a pretty lagoon, a tracery of palm fronds lined a golden beach.

But when he drew near he saw it was a very small island. No interior, no sheltering hills and valleys to which a hunted man in a crisis might escape. As a tiger seeks a den, so he might need a hiding place.

As regretfully he realized how small the isle was the wind abruptly changed, a squall came hissing in driving mists pressed by a strong blow directly nor'-west. He accepted destiny—he had to—and changed course as the squall blew him nearly due west.

Yet again Fortune had smiled upon him. For that pretty isle was Parremar, later to be called by white men Coconut Island. And on it lived a small tribe of handsome, brown-skinned folk, wary of their lives day and night, ever ready to race to their canoes and hurry to sea and stay there until raiding head-hunters had burnt their village, ravaged their gardens, and sailed away.

Not an isle to hide an escaped convict not in danger of head-hunters alone.

The blow died down, came a calm, and he drifted until late afternoon, sunlight burnishing a sea still as glass. Curiously he watched the sea-snakes making love, he thought in their writhings they were fighting, for they were tying themselves in knots. A Long Tom broke surface, smacking it now and then in gigantic leaps. In deep pleasure he thought of this strange sea he was entering. Savages that seemed no more than man-animals. Other savages, keen, cultured, virile—fighting savages of no mean order. Snakes upon the sea, arrow-like fish that skipped over it. The fantastic mysteries in the coral gardens. Unknown islands on the horizon. Into what strange happenings was his life to be cast? Eagerly he awaited a breeze to start him off again to work out his fate.

A breeze came rippling the water. He steered for a low, woody island clearly visible. It was cool night when he reached it, clouds hid the stars. No sound from the black mass of the island. He was about to run the boat ashore when a light appeared there, blazed into fire. Dark figures leapt up and a wild dance started, chant of warriors' voices. From outer darkness flares came gliding—blazing torches carried by unseen men.

Hastily he turned the boat about, gazing back as other figures leapt to the dance, the chant swelled in volume. To thundering stamp of feet came a roar in unison.

"Wongai! Wongai! Wongai!"

Again they joined in dance, again as he sailed farther away came thud of stamping feet, roar of "Wongai! Wongai! Wongai!" As he sailed farther away the fire grew smaller, there came now faintly but clearly, "Wongai! Wongai! Wongai!" He was certain they were dancing a war-dance, that "Wongai! Wongai! Wongai!" was the signal to charge.

The reverse was the truth. For this was a dance of peace, a festival dance. Now was the Wongai season, the time when the wongai plums are ripe—the rich red and purple plums, eagerly esteemed luxury of the Torres Strait islanders. The wild plum-trees only grow on a few of the islands, such as the one he was leaving astern. And there the people were dancing to Wongai, lieutenant of Sida, God of the Crops—Wongai the super-man, who in their mythology had long ago come down from the skies to plant the Wongai-trees that his beloved islanders might eat their fill in season.

Like a whisper carried on the breath of the breeze, came to the man in the boat, "Wongai! Wongai! Wongai!"

Such strange destiny for this nameless outcast, whose back was scarred for life with the weals of the lash, a destiny that seemed purposely to protect him again and again—maybe in recompense for the years of hell he had been forced to suffer,—perhaps unjustly—who can tell? That this one word now be firmly implanted upon his mind as a war-cry. That soon he should use it as such. And yet its true meaning—and what that meaning was to mean to him!

Several days later, across a lazy sea a distant peak seemed beckoning like a finger of Destiny. The Peak of Moa, tallest peak in Torres Strait. Gradually the island coastline took shape in wooded hills light-splashed with forest, dull-splashed with scrub. Then here and there a little beach showed white and gold. Presently the peak seemed to tower above the sea, its crest dark with sombre scrub. Many a raid, many a scene of savagery, of terror and rapine had that grim peak witnessed by land and sea. In the years fast coming it was to witness yet more. Scenes of native conflict, ruthless raids by crews of white men's ships seeking both men and girls, scenes of shipwreck, of castaways sailing for their lives, of other castaways clubbed and beheaded. Perhaps it was some malign influence in the powers of the universe that irresistibly drew the boat towards that sinister peak.

Gradually the breeze died away, the heavens darkened, a stifling, breathless stillness settled upon sea and land. Anxiously he glanced round. Fast-gathering. black clouds showed a storm brewing, he was hemmed in by coral reefs with the big island directly ahead. He wondered what fate might await him there—one lone white man to land on an island certainly peopled by warlike savages. He did not falter, he was in for it now. But he was not to land there—not yet. Had he succeeded in doing so he never would have been heard of again.

The destiny that drove this man on was uncanny. Seas, tides, winds, storms, thirst, hunger; not man-controlled happenings but even the forces of nature drew him on inexorably over great distances and through many perils to the one spot, in the right time, and under almost magical circumstances to where he could take his island—the *right* island.

The boat lay still with moveless sail, the sea still as a lake of oil reflecting stifling sunlight. He cursed his luck, for before him now had opened out the broad mouth of a river, or so it seemed. If only he could get in there he would be safe from the storm.

Distantly, from away up the "river" sounded a long drawn out, hoarse bellow. Tensely he listened. Defiantly the blast was answered, booming out through breathless air, off moveless water. From the Peak of Moa rose a dense black column of smoke, immediately answered from craggy Butai Pad across on Badu.

Hoarse as a foghorn is the challenge of the boo shell, blown by the lungs of a deep-chested warrior.

The war-boo. Moa and Badu were at war.

The man in the boat sensed violence, sensed, too, the brazen menace was not meant for him.

Sky, sea, land darkened as if inexorably being compressed into night, Nature in breathless suspense. Lightning turned livid the horizon, thunder crashed upon the sea followed by roll upon roll of thunder hurtling through the skies now quivering in lightning flashes. An icy breath came, the water turned grey under a fast-advancing squall before which the sea heaved as if pushed by an irresistible hand. That squall shrieked past in icy wind as seas rose up in angry motion.

The boat raced ahead with the wind screeching astern, there was no turning back now. He laughed in defiant abandon as the boat raced for the river mouth. A glimpse of wooded shores, of lanes of palms, of canoes drawn up on tiny beach by a village of beehive huts. Then sheet rain blotted out the "river" and all as a boo harshly blared, drowned in roar of thunder, howl of wind and rain.

He had been seen, he sped on up the "river" now surging with waves, to the moaning of wind-lashed trees.

It was no river. It was the seaway dividing the two large islands of Moa and Badu. About a mile in width, this sea causeway appears to be a beautiful river with its banks the hills and dales of Moa lining the one side, the palms and hills and dales of Badu the other.

To thunder that made the very islands tremble, the worst thunder the crouching villagers had ever heard, the boat sped wildly on, illuminated by dancing lightning. A phantom thing she appeared, thrown there by the Thunder God in the eyes of the superstitious villagers peering from their huts as boo after boo gave warning of the passing of the spirit craft. The wind blew aside the rain to a shaft of sunlight as the dancing boat was about to pass the large village of Badu. Then her nose turned inshore and she was racing swiftly for the landing. She ran straight up on shore and out of her stepped a shaggy giant in a robe of lightning crowned by a thunder-clap. He stood blinking a moment, surveying those rain-drenched houses under a thousand swaying palms. Then he came mistily forward, squelching in the running water.

Down the platform of the largest hut leapt a powerful savage whose headdress and crescentic mai proclaimed him the Mamoose, chief of Badu. He swung his dub and shouted "Lamar! Lamar!"

A hundred voices roared "Lamar! Lamar!" as out from the huts poured dark-brown warriors fingering lances, fitting arrows to great war-bows.

But the "Lamar" came straight on, snarling, glaring into the eyes of Sisi, the chief. He sensed death in that dread roar, "Lamar! Lamar!" but he came squelching on. And in his clenched hand, the blade hidden up along his wrist, was the knife.

A knife that had taken the lives of men.

Warriors closed round him as Sisi swung his club and leapt to the kill. But the other had leapt a second faster, and his blade plunged down into Sisi's heart. On the dying man's chest he stamped his foot three times as with face and bloody knife to the thunderous skies he shouted, "Wongai! Wongai! Wongai!"

To instant silence he stood thus as if invoking the Thunder God, whose voice at his command growlingly faded away. The rain steadied, ceased as if by magic, sunshine bathed the village—and still not a movement, not a murmur.

Gazing upward thus, his eyes saw the tall sarokag pole fronting the dead chief's hut, a large bamboo pole with short cross-pieces of bamboo high up. From these dangled five skulls, victims of Sisi.

He glanced down, knelt, and, taking the mai of chieftainship from Sisi, placed it around his own neck. Then, seizing the long ringlets of the dead chief, calmly he began to hack off the head, grunting at the job as if he and the dead man were alone in the world. He cut strongly and deep, completely round the neck, then screwed the head round and cut again, as with a wrenching tug he completed the grisly task. Then, calmly walking to the sarokag pole, he placed his arms round it and slowly began to heave, backward and forward, backward and forward, as the pole loosened in the sodden earth.

He brought down the pole, contemptuously threw the skulls aside, then fastened to the very top of the pole the bleeding head of Sisi, once Mamoose of Badu, tied there by its own ringlets.

Then, by what seemed to the breathless onlookers super-human strength, he lifted up the pole, manoeuvring its base to slide back into the hole. With bony feet he stamped tight the earth.

He had never once looked behind, never by one sign shown he took any account at all of all those hundreds of staring, terrified eyes.

He leapt up to the platform, stooped down, entered the house.

The dead chief's three wives crouched there. He kicked them out. Petula, the youngest one, hissed viciously, superstitious terror overwhelming the hate blazing from her eyes. She leapt from the house platform with a scream and ran to Sisi's body and threw herself upon it.

Petula had loved her husband, the chief Sisi. She loved him still.

Hundreds of fear-stricken warriors, brave men all, stared silently up at the dripping head of Sisi, then down at the dark entrance way of the hut.

CHAPTER V

WONGAI, CHIEF OF BADU

He who had taken the dead chief's hut was now for all time named "Wongai". He did not yet know this as he crouched at bay awaiting their next move. But they drew back to the village centre, a huddled mob of superstitious warriors, terrified women and children. Awed, whispering, they gaped towards the hut. But no hostile move.

Why did they not fall upon and club him? He seemed to have played upon some deep superstition of theirs. What was it?

Only the raindrops gave answer.

If he could only grasp the elusive reason, it might save him again. Gripping the dead chief's spear he waited, thinking desperately.

He had landed here, though he did not know it, at the height of the worst drought and during the most violent tropical storm known to the islanders, to whom the Thunder God was a real, a living entity, brother to Sida, God of the Crops, who was brother to Kwoiam, God of War.

And Wongai was Sida's lieutenant. Friend also to Kwoiam, God of War.

This was part of these people's firm belief, their creed of the Life Before, the Life Now, the Life After. But he, crouching in the hut, did not know this. Why was it, he was wondering, that the chief on seeing him had howled that one word "Lamar"?

And they had rushed to kill him—and yet their berserk rage had faltered to fear immediately he shouted, "Wongai!"

He frowned at this critical puzzle, which might mean life or death to him.

The answer was that all Torres Strait islanders firmly believed that any white person was a "Lamar", a spirit in human form, a reincarnation returned to earth life. And as such should be instantly killed so that the spirit would be released to fly back to the world of spirits again. Otherwise disease and death and unutterable disaster would be theirs— which explains why ship-wrecked white people landing on the Torres Strait islands were immediately clubbed to death.

(With very rare exceptions, which occurred only when an islander fancied a resemblance in the castaway to his dead son or daughter, and claimed the castaway as the reincarnation of his lost one. The castaway was then allowed to live. History gives us barely a dozen instances, notably Barbara Thomson saved from the wreck of the cutter *America* because she was believed to be "Gi'Om", reincarnated daughter of Piaquai, chief of the Murralug Islands. And the two boys Will D'Oyley and Jack Ireland, only survivors of the wreck of the *Charles Eaton*. All on the raft were clubbed and beheaded except young Will D'Oyley and Jack Ireland, later claimed by old Duppa and Oby of Mer to be their reincarnated sons; They were eventually rescued by the New South Wales Government rescue schooner *Isabella*.

Another case was of two very young boys, Charles and John, washed ashore in a whaleboat on Aureed Island. The full name of the boys and the wreck were never known. Both "Lamars" were recognized as reincarnations of children who had perished, were claimed by their "parents". Both lived until young manhood on Aureed. Finally a passing schooner took them off, very much against their will, according to old inhabitants amongst the islanders. Charles eventually returned in a boat of his own, loaded with presents for his old friends. Later he was killed by the Turi-Turi men of New Guinea.)

The man from the boat, when he had killed Sisi the chief, had shouted, "Wongai! Wongai! Wongai!" which had seemed to mesmerise these bloodthirsty savages.

Why? Why had their own war-cry stayed their clubs even while he was hacking off the head of their chief?

But it was *not* a war-cry. Wongai to them was the lieutenant of Sida, God of the Crops, responsible to Sida for bringing the rains that make the gardens grow. In the "Long Time Ago" it was Sida, God of the Crops, who had come to the Islands and brought the people their fruit and vegetables, taught them how to make gardens. A "long time after", he had made Wongai his lieutenant, to work with the Thunder God in bringing the yearly rains without which the gardens would perish and the people be left entirely dependent on fish for food. It was Wongai himself who had brought to earth the treasured plum of the Coral Sea, that season so fondly named the "Wongai season". "He who eats of the wongai," they say to this day in the Strait, "will surely return."

And now, to the islanders' very eyes, their superstitious minds, their frightened hearts, Wongai had returned to them as a Lamar—had been reincarnated by the might of the Thunder God just when they needed him most—when the islands were perishing in the longest succession of dry seasons ever known, even in their legends. He had come as a Lamar, a spirit man, in the flash of lightning with the beloved rain, the roar of thunder. And shouted his name, "Wongai!"

Thus he slew the chief, his arm strong with the might of Sida's brother Kwoiam, God of War.

But he in the hut knew nothing of this, that for all time now he was Wongai, beloved lieutenant of Sida, God of the Crops, friend of Kwoiam, God of War.

As he crouched on the dead chief's mat the islanders had crowded into the larger huts, sopping faces of men, women and children in hysterical delight as they held up their arms and began a chant to the hissing rain. To them it meant life again, the coming of the wet season they had feared had vanished for ever, the rains sent them by Sida through his lieutenant, Wongai.

He who had dreamed of becoming an island chief was already now a chief in fact. He was Wongai, Mamoose of Badu.

Not yet of the large island of Badu, but of the main village, Badu. As he listened alone, alert for attack, how he would have gloated had he known the facts! And known that even now excited runners, their great news urging them on against the fear of the ghostly "mari", the "mad ub" swinging its bull-roarer, the hideous "dogai", and other dreaded spirits of the night. Speeding through silent bush at uttermost speed they ran, praying that the "markai", the friendly spirits, would keep evil from their lonely path. For were they not running with news of the reincarnation of Wongai, friend of Sida the Ad Giz, greatest spirit benefactor of all time? Messengers racing to all the scattered tribes throughout the island, bringing news from the powerful Beizam, Tapimal, Kodal, and Dangal clans that Wongai, brought by the Thunder God, had been reincarnated to them as chief in the form of a Lamar.

How amazed the desperate convict would have been had he known, and had he understood that now the excited people listening to heavily falling rain were swiftly building desire on thankfulness. Eyes questioningly gleaming, a warrior here and there hissing, "Kwoiam! Kwoiam!"

Kwoiam, God of War, brother to Sida, God of the Crops. Wongai, beloved of the Thunder God, beloved of Sida.

Would not Wongai, friend of Kwoiam, help them in war?

The war against the clans of Moa was turning disastrously against discouraged Badu. Defeat after defeat had set their allies of Mabuiag to a sullen grumbling, a barely disguised sneering at a once great Badu come dangerously close to defeat.

Now that the rains were pouring down the war would stop until the close of the wet season. But afterwards!

The man in the hut, now wishing they would come and end this uncertainty, could not dream he had landed so propitiously into the climax of a bitter island struggle.

Should Mabuiag withdraw alliance from Badu, then the moral effect alone would be disastrous. For Mabuiag was Kwoiam's island.[1]

And there in Augudulkula, the Sacred Cave by the Great Kwod reposed the Kutibu and Sar, the War Augud, sacred trophies of Kwoiam, in full possession of the men of Mabuiag.

Without these trophies carried into battle ahead of the warriors, Badu believed defeat practically certain. Should Mabuiag withhold the War Gud, then—

But now that Wongai had come, the people of Mabuiag would never dream of withholding the War Gud from the service of Wongai, friend of Kwoiam, God of War.

Wongai, who had killed Sisi, and taken his place as chief of Badu.

Far into the dawn in village after village as the messengers arrived, warriors discussed what might happen now. But later in the Zogo-houses shrewd old men sat in shadow under the ghostly green flame from the sacred skulls, thinking on this rumour so avidly seized upon by the people, wondering in truth what this Lamar now acclaimed as Wongai really was, wondering whether best to wait, or whether he should die suddenly, or secretly.

But he in the Mamoose's hut knew not of this as yet. Hungrily he ate of the wretched food to hand. Though they were the food of a chief, the withered relics spoke eloquently to him, a lover of plant food, of disastrous drought. He realized he was foolish to have kicked out the chief's wives—they would have cooked for him, helped him in other ways. He determined to repossess them in the morning. Later, if he lived, then when he felt upon his feet he would marry the daughter of a chief.

As the moments, the hours, dragged by and he still lived, firmer grew his exultant belief that he would continue to live.

He kept the fire in the hut gently smouldering, but allowed no flame lest it bring an arrow from the rain-drenched dark outside. He would not close an eye tonight. On the morrow he determined to take over the village as chief.

He was astonished at the ease with which he did it.

---

[1] Kwoiam, God of War, now a legendary figure, had actually lived and fought on Mabuiag Island. The greatest warrior known in the legends of that particular island group, he had been deified into the God of War since his fighting death.

CHAPTER VI

THE GHOST OF SISI

But then, he did not realize that he was already chief. As cold dawn exposed the shape of the palms outside he sprang erect, spear menacing the doorway as a moan arose into a blood chilling wail. It died away, only to be answered from away down in the village. It arose again outside the hut, poignant, heart-rending. He shivered.

But they did not come.

He stepped out on to the house platform.

Down there, kneeling in the muddy earth, Petula was wailing by the sodden, stiffened body of Sisi. She raised a tear-stained face to the palm tops and the death wail moaned out again.

Not only the distraught face of the young widow but some deep tone in that death wail told she was wailing in earnest. Not so the other two wives Mek and Naina, now emerging from a distant hut. Grotesquely, on hands and knees, crawling over the mud to come and take their place beside the body and wail, as was the custom.

No one else in sight.

Frowning, he re-entered the hut. Something forbade him to interfere. Later, to whispering outside, he peered from the entrance way. By the palm-fringed shore many people were whispering, pointing. Others hurrying towards them.

Right at the shore edge opposite the dead chief's hut a large shark was slowly cruising backward—forward—backward—forward. The awed people knew what it was.

It was the mari, the ghost of Sisi.

Not the shark. But *in* the shark now dwelt the spirit of Sisi.

For Sisi had been of the proud Beizam, the Shark clan. And all men knew that very often indeed the spirit of a man recently dead appeared to them in the body of his totem animal, bird, fish, or reptile. For there is a strong mystic affinity between members of a clan and their totem.

And the shark was the totem fish of the Beizam clan. And here was the spirit of Sisi in this great shark, come to show himself to his friends in his totem shark cruising so slowly forward—backward—forward—backward—while high on the sarokag pole his head glared down.

The mari, the ghost of Sisi, might stay in his totem shark quite a time, perhaps even two months, before the spirit messenger came to take it away far up in the sky to the Isle of Kibu. There it would live some time and be taught, slowly developing into markai, a Le la mar—a man's spirit. Then, when his markai, his spirit, was fully developed, he would be a perfect spirit man and would fly away through the skies to Boigu, Isle of the Blest.

But now—he was but mari, his ghost slowly cruising in his totem shark—showing himself to the silent people.

Petula, the distraught young widow, gazed wildly, then with a moaning wail rushed to the shore and would have jumped in and thrown her arms round the shark, but that the men held her back.

Quietly they carried her, wailing, back to the village. Only frightened children remained to gaze at Sisi's totem shark.

Wongai watched a long time, frowned at it all but then—he did not understand. Turning into the hut he bedecked himself in the gayest of the dead chief's regalia, examining each barbarous article lest he put it on wrongly, or appear a fool. The broad-banded headdress, scarlet with berries, gleaming with chips of mother-of-pearl, with a dense plume of cassowary feathers rising like an enormous busby above the forehead band, cascading like purple-black hair upon his shoulders. A short skirt of black plumes with the long bone dagger at the waist. He fitted armlets of boar's tusks round his big arms, the crescent mai of chieftainship round his neck. On the walls were other ornaments of tortoiseshell and feathers and plumes, shells and vividly coloured berries. He hesitated, and rightly so. Otherwise this new "king" may have gone out to receive his people's plaudits with a love charm adorning his neck.

Around the walls, too, were long, heavy, carved spears of varying patterns. A bow that only a strong man could handle. Sheafs of arrows. A broad wooden sword edged with shark's teeth, a disk-shaped club, a "pineapple"-headed club, a star-headed club. He took the star, and did right again.

The rain eased off and he stepped out on the house platform, threatening eyes scanning the brown, thatched roofs under the dripping palms, the cold water like a broad river between Badu and the wooded beaches and mist-clothed hills of Moa. Like magic from each house appeared the ringleted head of a warrior, then his strong brown chest as he stepped outside or on a house platform. And beside him the frizzy heads of his wife and children. Hundreds of eyes staring at the savage figure on the chief's platform.

Wongai, the chief, leapt down from the platform and stood there arrogantly, gripping the club as if he owned the place. There came forward to meet him a fine-looking man, unarmed, smiling. Pleasant of face, deep-brown eyes from which shone respect and admiration. He stood a moment before Wongai, bowed slightly, muttered something in low voice. Then, smiling, stepped forward and with outstretched arm lightly touched the mai of chieftainship around Wongai's neck.

The gesture of allegiance. Wongai thrilled to the obvious fact, his grim face smiled.

This man was Kosabad, who rightly should be chief. But he did not dream it was so. To him this man was Wongai, their chief reincarnated from the skies.

Heads of clans now came forward in order of precedence, the Beizam clan, the Kodal, the Dangal, and Tabu (the Snake) —these the most powerful clans. Humbly yet proudly their chiefs made obeisance.

And he who but recently had been a killer, a man-eater, a brutalized convict, acknowledged their oath as to the manner born.

To think that only a few hours earlier this outcast in rain and thunder had leapt ashore to kill or be killed! But so it happened.

Perfect understanding accomplished, the new chief calmly made the rounds of the village. Worthy warriors were these for an ambitious chief to work upon. Savage but intelligent, strong brown men with the deep chests that in coming years were to make the Torres Strait islanders famous as divers.

Athletic, shrewd, laughing-eyed women. Tinkling shells of vivid colours in their lovely mops of hair, no flowers or butterflies now because of the drought. Lively children, even though so young arrogantly proud of their clanship. Everywhere he noted friendly faces alight with curiosity, though with a timidity tinged by fear.

He made the rounds of the village then strolled through the outskirts inland, stepping out from among the palms to the gardens, from which he could see a watery sun glinting on the grass-clad slopes and dales towards the island interior.

It surely was Fate again that of the many things he could have done that morning he should do the very right thing—walk straight to the Wongai shrine!

And the people following, all eyes, expecting him to do this very thing. Along the shaded path past the quaint carving of the Tomog Zogo, revered oracle that could only be consulted by warriors of the Shark clan. He strolled past, straight to the Wongai shrine.

In a wooded dale the white of giant clam-shells caught his eye, symbolic were these of a reservoir, overflowing now with precious "sky" water. Containing pebbles signifying seeds springing from the fecundity of the earth. A latticed arch of painted bamboo roofed the shrine. The arch represented the rainbow and from this "rainbow" hung a screen of native string, representing falling rain. From strings stretched from tree to tree were suspended bull-roarers. The wind at night whirled these round and to the moan and whine of the bull-roarers danced the fairy spirit of the shrine supplicating the Thunder God for rain, for Sida to make a plentiful crop of fruit and cause the seeds of the earth to spring up and grow. By day this fairy keeper of the shrine vanished to sleep in the earth. Enclosing and radiating out from the shrine were rows of large Fusus and other shells and carved figures with quaint charms hanging from tree branches, all with deep symbolical meaning that the shaggy outcast regarding them sensed he must quickly learn. He stared at the central figure of the shrine, a stone carving squatting like a Buddha. The rough hewn face wore a good-humoured, quizzical expression, the nose grotesquely large, the mouth hiding a smile. The white chief wondered as he stared at this benign figure that so nonchalantly seemed to be regarding him. This savage brute and quaint image were the very opposite in expression, yet weirdly seemed to hold a fleeting likeness. To the savage people regarding both there was no doubt. He who stood there was Wongai, the figure in the shrine symbolized Wongai—Wongai who in the Ancient of Days had from Sida brought the wongai plum-trees to earth.

From the hell of Norfolk Island straight to the Wongai shrine on far distant Badu. And there were so many other paths, so many other shrines that his questing footsteps could have found. What strange fortune had guarded this man through sea distances and the elements and ignorance, safely past the superstitions and bloodthirsty passions of wild men to this?

He strolled on and took another path and presently, instinctively, he stopped.

The path entered a gloomy scrub. Suspended from a pole slowly swung a human jawbone tied to a mop of hair and dyed streamers of grass. A sufficient taboo sign, even to the uninitiated.

He walked on alone.

In a clearing in the scrub stood a dome-shaped hut enclosed by totem-poles from which dangled painted charms. Beside the door crouched a hideously carved figure of a spirit-devil, splashed across face and animal body with bars of coloured ochres. Eyes of nautilus shell glared menacingly in the shaded gloom. But Wongai crouched down and crawled into the opening of the hut.

In the gloom, coals glowed upon a clay fire-pan. Suspended to a string tied to a rafter dangled a painted divination skull, eye-sockets and teeth livid with phosphorus. Below it squatted Enoko the zogo-man, chief sorcerer of Badu. A red painted bowl before him was a portion of a skull from which rose a wisp of incense—a live coal upon dried, scented leaves.

Wongai stared down into the cruel, unflinching eyes of the sorcerer. Upon his head was coiled a black, scarlet-throated snake like a massive skull-cap, its squat head above the sorcerer's forehead, its beady eyes staring up. Wongai wondered at the two little holes in the tip of the sorcerer's nose, he had noticed similar among some of the warriors. Such men were of the Tabu clan, whose totem was the snake. The little holes bored through the tip of the nose represented the nostrils of a snake. Silently these two cunning men measured one another while the phosphorescent skull slowly, very slowly spun between them, came to a stop, facing Wongai.

Gradually, queer things touched his consciousness, as if with ghostly fingers. He felt within him that here around him were live things or rather, live *feelings* not seen that peered at him just as intensely as he was staring into the eyes of the sorcerer and the snake.

Something warned him that it was better not to interfere—not now. He glanced round the hut at the grotesque charms, the smoke-dried lizards and frogs and remnants of birds, stared uncomprehendingly at other more frightening, withered, smoke-dried wisps of men and women, glanced at the drying bulbs and roots and berries that were poisons, at other yet more queer things he did not understand—as yet.

And then—

The skull came to life! He could almost have sworn it.

The phosphorescent eye-sockets gleamed tremulous in eerie green, seemed to quiver in ripples of greenish light. Again and again. He could have sworn that green was tremulously urgent—*demanding* attention. Slowly then the skull turned round, facing the sorcerer. It trembled there awhile, then spun round while the eye-sockets blazed at Wongai, the teeth shone in greenish glow with hideous menace.

"Begone!"

With a last glance round, taking his time, Wongai turned to the door entrance, crept out, then walked back down the path.

He was glad to be gone.

CHAPTER VII

THE KILLERS ARE COMING

Wongai had left the sorcerer unhappily confounded. For hours past Enoko had been musing as to whether it would be best to stir up the people to kill this Lamar who had upset the village. The Zogo-man had been in telepathic communication with the priesthood headquarters of Augudulkula on Pulu, sacred isle of Mabuiag, informing the chief Zogos of the cult all about this Lamar from the spirit world, this "Wongai" who had taken Badu village and all its clans by storm, inquiring if this Lamar really was the reincarnation of Wongai. And if not, advising that he should be quickly killed.

It was while Wongai was staring at him that the eye-sockets of the divining skull had grown luminous—warning that a message was coming through. An important message, as the agitation foretold. But disquiet had disturbed the sorcerer's mind immediately Wongai entered the hut, an uneasiness that increased while the Lamar stayed there, becoming agitation when the eyes of the skull shone its message.

At last the accursed spirit man had gone.

But so also had the placid, receptive state of the Zogo-man's mind. Impossible for Enoko now to receive the message.

What delicate vibrations, and what command of them, in the hidden recesses of the human mind are necessary for the receiving and sending of telepathic messages we do not know. Many folk deny that it is possible. The Torres Strait islanders were positive that trained men among the priesthood of the Zogo-le communicated thus regularly. And the power was developed in a few among the people, too.

This particular message, according to greybeards of Pulu, of Mabuiag, and of Badu, speaking long after the influence of white people had destroyed their native culture, was a vitally important one. It was to the effect that a strong band of Mabuiag warriors, smarting under defeats at the hands of Moa, had landed the night before on Badu and were even now hurrying across the island to attack Badu village, convinced that the clans of Badu Island had purposely let them down. Their men, fighting under the War Gud of Kwoiam, were always successful. But their far more numerous allies of Badu again and again gave way, bringing defeat after defeat upon all. Mabuiag was now seeking revenge—and heads. This punitive expedition might well bring Mabuiag and Moa together in a war of extermination against Badu.

The crisis now was this news that Wongai, beloved of Kwoiam the War God, had landed in reincarnated form at Badu village. And hurrying to attack the village were men of Mabuiag, carrying the sacred War Gud of Kwoiam. If this Lamar was really Wongai then disaster must happen should he clash with the warriors of Mabuiag. The message ordered Enoko to intercept the raiding party and order them back. At all costs he must stop them.

But, concentrate as he would, the sorcerer could not receive the message in its entirety. The more he tried, the harder it became to withdraw his mind "within itself" to receptivity. The more he received of the jumbled message the harder he tried and the more he defeated himself. And time went racing by.

When Wongai left the Zogo-man's house he walked back down the path and into open sunlight again, where all the people awaited him. Turning into a side path he walked to the gardens, just as if he had known it would lead there. He examined the gardens with close attention. It was natural he should do so, for was he not Wongai, who brought the rains for Sida, God of the Crops?

Kosabad, with the headmen of the clans grouped eagerly round him, pointing out their gardens and the havoc wrought by the long drought. And to his attentive interest voices broke out on all sides explaining things to him and he listened and nodded as if he understood every word—which he was trying hard to do.

The gardens of banana, taro, yams, manioc, sugar-cane, of komalo the sweet potato, were the islanders' second source of food supply. The first came from the sea. But there were times when fishing was impossible. Also there were occasional "droughts" in seasonal fish. If the gardens failed and the sea yielded but poorly then these vigorous islanders went hungry. Against them, too, was that these western islands were not of the luxurious volcanic soil of the Eastern Group, where the gardens were a picture and the envy of the Coral Sea. Here on this big island of Badu, as across the waterway on the still larger island of Moa, good gardening soil was only in small patches here and there.

Almost all that day Wongai strolled amongst the gardens and very soon not only the headmen but the warriors and women and children were pointing out things to him, chattering as if he had lived amongst them from birth, chattering as if he understood every word. And presently Kosabad brought to him Bagari, chief of Upai village, of the Tapimul clan, and Sagigi, chief of Wabait, of the Dangal clan. Hurrying to join them were half a dozen other chiefs from distant villages, each with his bodyguard of warriors, all eyeing Wongai, chief of Badu, envious of the magical fortune that had befallen the people of Badu village. Wongai glowed as he noted that far as he could see among the palms and along the waterway chattering people were hurrying to join the now dense crowd in Badu village, all wildly excited to see with their own eyes the reincarnated Wongai, lieutenant of Sida, God of the Crops, friend of Kwoiam, God of War.

Wongai's interest in the gardens was genuine. Though a fighter, because nearly all his short life he had had to fight, above all he was a man of the land with an abiding passion in the soil. How often, during those terrible times in the black horror of the solitary cell, in the slave labour of the chain gang and the breakwater, he had saved his reason by fiercely dreaming he had a farm of his own, he was tilling the soil, he was making things grow, he was making tools to till more soil and make yet other things grow. His dream gardens...

And now—!

Happy day! Confident now that he had all these people with him, he planned to consolidate his position, then overcome tribe after tribe until he had this island united under him—Wongai. His very own island. And here now was the land, his dreams again come true; there were years of work here in teaching these people how to develop these scraggy gardens, how to make the good earth yield many times more than it was doing now. As they talked and explained he noted so much that could be done. And his plans were destined to bear fruit within a very short time.

Long after the whites overran the Strait the elder islanders told of the great Wongai, of how he made the gardens of Badu increase and bear fruit and prosper far beyond the wildest dreams of their grandfathers.

But on this wonder day, unbelievable though it was, there were two humans who, despite the great events taking place, were not a bit interested, except to delightedly take advantage of those startling events to steal as far away from the madding crowd as possible.

Lu-esa and Kartoy.

Lu-esa, beloved daughter of Kosabad, chief clansman of the Crocodile clan, warriors all.

Kartoy, a lad of the Stingray clan—alas, a peaceful clan, born mainly but for work. No man not of a warrior clan dared love the daughter of a chief.

Kartoy dared—and Lu-esa loved him. Unhappily so.

If they were found out it would mean death to Kartoy, deep disgrace. Death, too, to Lu-esa, for she knew she would throw herself into the channel of the sharks, where Kartoy would be thrown.

Casting aside despair, they were walking in silent adoration along the broad path leading across the island, leading right across to the shore opposite their uneasy allies—the men of Mabuiag. The path meandered between low hills splashed with sunlight, across shady flats soon to be emerald green with the coming of rains. They waded little creeks now gurgling so prettily after the long parched drought; sweet indeed was the kiss of the water upon their bare feet that for so long had felt only the blistering, sun-baked earth.

Already they had walked a long way inland from the village, forgetting time and distance, for they were so close—so blissfully close—to one another. No jealous eyes to see. Just the trilling of birds joyous that the rains had come. Just the swish of her little grass skirt, the tremulous rustle as it kissed his as they walked side by side.

Brown girl, brown boy. She with a single flower in her lovely hair. He with a song in his heart. Just that, and the call of the birds, and the listening silence, that silence in which they talked so much but said no word.

By a quiet dell fragrant with bushes they stopped, brown eyes gazing deep into brown. Noiselessly they entered the dell. Sat down, grass skirt by skirt, his face buried in her mop of frizzy hair. They could see, but not be seen. Through the bushes, see the path. No one would come along that path, they knew, but they were dallying with death—if but a shadow came along that path they must see it—he might have to kill.

The sun drifted on, his face sometimes covered by clouds that threw deep shadows upon path and bush. Then he would shine out again, like the love-light in Lu-esa's eyes. Then, alas, the shadows—like the shadows upon their hearts.

Oh, to hold her always like this! To have her for ever and ever! But he never might—for to win her he must be a member of a warrior clan. He was not. For a man not born into those proud clans he must do something great to gain initiation—something great indeed. But seldom could such a thing be. If only he could gain initiation in such a clan then easily he would become a warrior—he would take the head of a man—he would implore Kwoiam to aid him in the very next raid upon Moa. Ah, but what great deed could he do to bring him into clanship with the clan of the Shark—the clan of the Snake—the clan of the Cassowary—with any warrior clan!

Deeply he sighed. And the cloud stealing over the face of the sun was not near so deep as the shadow upon Kartoy's heart. And Lu-esa felt it—she held him close.

Lengthening shadows warned that they must return unless at last their absence be noticed. It was Lu-esa who sat up first—if anything should happen to her Kartoy! To the fear in her eyes he sat up with a sigh. She entwined her arm round his shoulders.

Presently she gazed at him in a questioning way, feeling his body slowly tauten, seeing his eyes big and staring—his face—intense and listening—intense concentration.

Breathlessly she gazed. There was not the faintest sound.

Effortlessly he stood up, warning in his eyes as he put finger to his lips. Then she was gazing at his back as noiselessly he parted the bushes and stepped towards the path. And now lithe as the panther was the figure she loved, leashed strength thrilling with the danger instinct of the primitive. He stepped to the path edge, peering inland along it.

A second and he was beside her, eyes blazing, fingers convulsively clenched.

"Lie still and hardly breathe till they have passed by, Lu-esa," he hissed. "They come! Raiders from Mabuiag, the scarlet band upon their brow. Lie still for your head, Lu-esa!" and he was gone—racing as he had never raced before-racing to warn Badu village.

MASKED DANCERS

CHAPTER VIII

THE AMBUSH

Near sundown all hands were still loitering in the gardens, though the women should have been cooking the evening meal. From the inland bush Kartoy came panting to throw himself before Wongai.

"They come!" he gasped. "The men of Mabuiag. To kill—they carry the War Gud of Kwoiam!" And he pointed back inland.

To hushed silence weapons were gripped, startled eyes upon Wongai. He beckoned the way the lad had come and the boy leapt to his feet, Wongai following, the thud of the warriors' feet like the beating of waves.

The main path leading inland emerged from a patch of scrub to an open forest incline leading up to a divide between two low hills. Up the slope to either side was thick scrub reminiscent of a bullock's horns, the path emerging from back in the "forehead". Up at the top of this divide Kartoy crouched, Wongai peering over his shoulder.

Down there on the other side of the divide, along a stretch of open grassland, two long lines of warriors were coming, quietly, steadily running, their plumes dancing as they ran. Across their foreheads the scarlet band, criss-crossed round their chests creamy bands of palm-leaf. Plumes of the cassowary, long feathers of the sea eagle and white pigeon. Cruelly armed. Wongai gaped awestruck at the oncoming leaders of each column, two gigantic figures, terrifyingly gigantic because of the towering plumes and hideous war-masks that once had been worn by Kwoiam himself.

These the two Augud-men, fierce bearers of the War Gud, the masks and amulets and crescent Gud of turtle-shell that blazed with light at night—a secret paste extracted from the phosphorescence of fish.

Wongai took it all in at a glance. Their pace steadied to a quick, lithe walk as they began to climb the divide. They would come running down it into the main path, their speed increasing to a frenzied but disciplined race ending in the howl of the war-cry as they burst into Badu village.

Wongai turned and spread his arms in the shape of the scrub lining each side of the path, then clashed his arms together.

They understood. instantly. He waved towards the scrub and they vanished into the undergrowth. Only the group of chiefs remained around him. He beckoned and hurried back down the divide and into the dark of the path. Expressively he signed to Kosabad that he, Wongai, would kill one Augud-man. Kosabad must kill the other.

Proudly Kosabad nodded, crouched by Wongai's left side.

Silence in the glen, but for a sun-bird sweetly calling.

But that silence seemed breathing—the ominous breath of Death. Men tensely crouching with the blood working up to that most terrible of all lusts of savage men—the lust for heads. But for the coming of Wongai, how different it would have been! For then the raiders would have surprised a near-dispirited people helpless in their huts, brooding over a famine meal. And the raiders would have carried the invincible War Gud of Kwoiam. But now they were prepared and Wongai himself was with them, Wongai trusted of the Thunder God, Wongai, beloved of Kwoiam, God of War.

Up over the divide appeared waving plumes as two gigantic figures strode up. For an instant the ambushers' blood chilled at sight of the invincible War Augud under which they had so often fought, then each man whispered, "Wongai!" Over the divide, now running down it, appeared the two columns of warriors, swiftly racing now straight down into the jaws of Death—and were there as a ferocious figure leapt out and his knife thrust straight into the chest of an Augud-man as Kosabad was clubbing the other to a roar of "Wongai! Wongai! Wongai!" as from both sides men poured into the flanks of the raiders. Thud of clubs, hoarse grunts, startled groans of stricken men, and the raiders had broken away into the scrub and gone.

Leaving around thirty fallen men, a mass of bestial victors struggling against each other to hack off the head of a man.

Wongai stood taking it all in. So this was the secret of successful native warfare—ambush, and surprise. And this the abiding passion of these savage warriors—the taking of heads. Everything that took place along the broken, struggling line he noted. Here and there warriors passionately quarrelling as to who had killed a disputed foe. Even with the blood-lust blazing in their eyes, yet they showed deference to certain warriors, certain men were referred to even in the furious heat of quarrel. The younger men on the outskirts in staring envy of the successful warriors. Then, all quarrels settled, a silence. And the grisly ceremony as the victors whipped out the upi knife, the ceremonial cutting off of the head, the stringing of it through the jaw in the singai loop, then each head held on high and the triumphant roar and thunder of feet bursting out upon the coming night.

In an instant they had formed into a square with the front-line victors brandishing the heads towards Wongai as they stamped in unison with a roar of song in the victory dance of Kwoiam. Women and children appeared from nowhere and joined in the dance with a howl of savage exultation that startled even Wongai.

Presently Kosabad, standing beside Wongai, held up his arm. Strangely fell the silence.

Kosabad was looking across at a lad clutching an ugly wound as he gazed enviously at those who had won a head. Kartoy had flung himself into the fight and tried very hard. But instead of a head he had received a nasty wound.

Kosabad beckoned. Kartoy limped deferentially yet proudly before Wongai.

"Speak!" ordered Kosabad kindly.

"This morning I wandered far along the path towards Mabuiag," answered Kartoy quietly. "I was hoping by chance I might find a bees' nest. Because of the drought my belly has long hungered for sweet things. It was while resting late in the day that I saw the raiders coming along the path. They did not see me. I raced ahead to give the alarm. I am sorry — very sorry — that I did not win a head."

"Plenty of time for that." Kosabad smiled. "You have saved *us* many heads. You have done far more!" and he glanced down at the fallen War Gud, which no one had dared to touch. "To-day you have brought to us, to our great chief Wongai, the precious War Gud of Kwoiam. You have this day won your right to ask our village of Badu your wish. Name your wish!"

Kartoy gazed at Kosabad, his lips partly open, cast an appealing glance at the great Wongai, then swiftly back at Kosabad. Thrice he tried to speak. When he did so, it was an entreaty.

"I wish to be initiated into the Beizam clan, the clan of the Shark."

Shrewdly Kosabad gazed at the lad, glanced at the War Gud at his feet.

Finally he spoke, addressing Wongai while with a sweep of the arm bringing all the silent people into the audience.

"This lad Kartoy has done a great deed, O my chief! That he has saved the lives of many of our people is nothing — any man would have been proud to have done that. But —" and Kosabad paused impressively — "not only has he saved us from a defeat, but in victory he has brought to us the War Gud of Kwoiam." Kosabad paused again, gazing straight at Wongai. "It is fitting, O my chief," he said impressively, "that on this very day Kwoiam, God of War, should send to the feet of Wongai, his friend, his own War Gud!"

In the appreciative silence, hemmed in by those hundreds of staring eyes, Wongai nodded understandingly.

Kosabad then placed his hand on Kartoy's shoulder and in ringing voice said, "Kartoy has earned his desire, O my chief, and I recommend him his wish—that he be initiated into the Beizam clan. It is for you, the chief of chiefs, to say."

Wongai knew not a word, but he guessed that some favour was being asked. He smiled at the boy's entreating eyes, nodded his head and with arm upraised growled in English, "I agree!"

Kartoy swaying there with a roar of voices in his ears, Kartoy whose head was going round and round, Kartoy who had won his greatest wish—the wish that soon would bring him Lu-esa!

And she, out among the crowd with hand to breast over her thumping heart, how she wished she could now go to him! Lu-esa, who had so nearly, so very nearly lost her own head, Lu-esa who had disobeyed.

For Lu-esa had not lain still as Kartoy had ordered, Lu-esa had risen to her knees and peered out among the bushes. When the last raider had gone by she had slipped out on to the path and—followed.

They had outdistanced her. And presently the sudden roar of war-song had burst out a little ahead of her. She ran on.

Something sprang through the bushes.

Glaring eyes of a maniac, his face a bloody mass as he tried to scream and leapt at her. She had dodged and run for her life, but he was after her—she felt her lungs panting her life out, but she lasted, his life was going in gurgling gasps of blood. He collapsed, she had run on.

Yes, Lu-esa had come very, very near losing her head.

But she was not thinking of it now, she was smiling across at Kartoy—a song within her heart.

And then, just as it grew dark, Enoko, the sorcerer, appeared. Silence greeted him. He stood gazing down at the fallen War Augud of Kwoiam. Glanced at Wongai with hate in his eyes. To some voiceless signal a few queerly marked men stepped from the ranks and Wongai knew again he was witnessing another phase in the intricate cultural life of these people.

These men were of the Tabu clan, a strangely worked picture of a snake coiled round each leg, seemed to be carved into the skin. Each man was a Maidelaig, a sorcerer's assistant, much inferior in class to Enoko. Several of these reverently picked up the War Augud. Enoko turned, and stepped noiselessly back into the path. The two Maidelaig followed him, bearing the War Gud. Wongai felt all the expectant eyes, he followed the Maidelaig, the chiefs and warriors followed him in single file down the path. Enoko branched off toward the Zogo-house. At the taboo sign, Wongai halted. They all waited in silence until the Maidelaig rejoined them—under Enoko's orders they had left the War Gud in the Zogo-house. Then Wongai turned, they made way for him, he strode back down the path to the village, they fell in behind with a roar of the triumph song.

And the rain came down.

It had been a great victory.

No one but Wongai could have achieved it, Wongai who was Kwoiam's friend. Kwoiam himself had fought on their side.

THE EXACT SPOT WHERE KWOIAM FELL

The leaves of the nearby shrubs are spotted with scarlet, which is the blood of the hero—so the warriors say.

CHAPTER IX

THE SKULL OF SISI

Wongai now was unassailably established in this large village of Badu. And Bagari of the Tapimul clan and chief of Upai village came before him and rendered temporal homage, followed by Sagigi of the Dangal clan, chief of Wabait. It only needed some further decisive action to unite these three main villages. After which he might one by one unite all the villages of the island.

This cunning, ruthless outcast eventually did this. And much more. Almost as if gods of the skies really were watching over him.

Meanwhile the rain poured down a fortnight and more. He made good use of this breathing space, holding court in his hut to the chiefs and headmen of the three villages of Badu, Upai, and Wabait. So eager were they to forestall his slightest wish that quickly he knew their chief tribesmen by name, their totem and clan, a few every day customs, and a smattering of the language.

Badu Island was in a fever of excitement over these great events. The coming of Wongai, lieutenant of Sida the defeat of the Mabuiag raiders, and above all the capture of the War Gud.

But on distant Mabuiag the villagers whispered in stunned disbelief. Such disaster surely could not have happened to the War Gud of Kwoiam—to them!

While on the Sacred Isle of Pulu, in the holy of holies, Augudulkula, brooded the Council of the Zogo-le.

Squatting upon a coral dais a little above them frowned old Bauri, chief Zogo of the Zogo-le, scorn in his fellow-priests masking the puzzled indecision in his glittering eyes.

High above Bauri squatted the Great Au-gud, a fantastic image fashioned of plates of polished tortoiseshell, adorned by a necklace of painted skulls. From the sockets of skulls suspended from the roof floated pungent whiffs of a native incense. Like sentinels in the gloom, ranged round in a horseshoe, were crouching mummies of the Chief Zogos of the past, effigies of life and death.[2]

---

[2] Though the main lodges of the Zogo-le of the Torres Strait islanders used to mummify their Chief Zogos and any particularly outstanding hero, their art was not nearly so perfect as that of the ancient Egyptians. Maybe the art had come from scatterings of the Egyptians in migratory upheavals of thousands of years ago. Perhaps from ancient civilizations buried under the seas. But all is surmise.

Step by step, move by move, the problem of Wongai was to develop into a problem indeed for the Zogo-le.

In three weeks the sun shone again on the hills and dales, the valleys and beaches of all the islands and islets of Torres Strait, over all the Coral Sea.

Petula, young widow of Sisi, the slain chief, cared not whether it was wet or dry. But this bright morning brought her a stab of happiness, like sunlight piercing the clouds. Yes, this bright dawn was an omen. For she was to receive the skull of Sisi, her warrior chief.

It was to be *hers*—not that accursed Wongai's. But he would not know that.

For Enoko, the sorcerer, had promised her—under fearful secrecy. The dreaded Zogo-man, working his mysteries in the depths of the Zogo-house, had been preparing the skull for *her,* not for Wongai, the chief. Alas, it could not divine for her. But then—it *never* would divine for Wongai the accursed Lamar, killer of her beloved Sisi.

And Enoko, though again under unbreakable secrecy, had allowed her to refine the beeswax that was to mould the cheeks. Of course, he must melt it again and charm it with mystic rites. How carefully she had strained that wax, making it so clean, so smooth, so pure of colour. It would be the purest wax that had ever been moulded into the cheeks. and nose and face of a divination skull. Only she and Enoko—and the spirit of Sisi—would ever know.

Enoko had whispered to her that Sisi's mari had now come from his totem, the Shark. Sisi was now a "kazi", a spirit person, hovering in the Zogo-house awaiting the preparation of his divination skull. And at propitious times he would enter it. Petula would not be able to see him, for she was not a spirit-seeing person. She would not be able to touch, or to hear him, for she had not the gift of spirit-hearing. But he would be there to watch over her.

Enoko had also secretly given her and allowed her to grind the ochres that were to paint the face. How careful she had been—especially with the scarlet—Sisi's forehead was to wear the scarlet band. For he had been a killer.

How many secret hours she had worked, when she could be alone in the hut. She had worked, too, almost by touch and love alone, in the dead of night when the others slept.

And then—Enoko had given her the hair, Sisi's own hair, to prepare.

She had worked most carefully of all with this, fondling it at night while the others slept. With her own warm hand she had fondled love into it—Sisi soon now, Sisi's spirit would *always* be with her in the hut.

Sisi, in voiceless words, speaking to her alone. Speaking voiceless feelings she would feel in her heart.

So, on this morning, for the first time since Wongai had come, Petula smiled as willingly she prepared breakfast by the bright dawnlight gradually streaming into the hut—silently stealing in like the coming of the spirit of Sisi.

That morning, when all were busy in the gardens she would steal away.

Enoko would be waiting under the hut. He would come up inside. He would allow her, with her own hands, to tie the cord to the rafter. The cord from which would be suspended the skull of Sisi.

Enoko, the sorcerer, working alone in the Zogo-house, had taken very especial care in preparing the skull of Sisi, once chief of Badu village. The baking in the oven, the cleaning. The moulding of the cheeks of wax, the nose. The gleaming eyes of nautilus shell. The painting. The hair, Sisi's own hair. The picturesque coronet of feathers extending from the forehead, circling back over the centre of the skull itself. Wisps of the sacred plant, the "sarik pas", embedded in the forehead wax. The luminous paint of green phosphorus round eye-sockets and teeth. Yes, Enoko had worked as if obsessed. This was the skull of a chief, and was to be a divination skull, rare because there always are but few chiefs. A divination skull, the most precious possession of all to the islanders. Skilfully Enoko was preparing the skull, as was his duty, that it should take its place where it rightfully belonged—to watch over the household of Wongai, chief of Badu.

But the skull of Sisi would never divine for Wongai, would never whisper to him news of happy, nor of grave import, never whisper to him of danger! There, in the gloom of the Zogo-house, alone with the whispering of the spirits of the night, the gnarled old sorcerer worked over Sisi's skull, by the glow of the coals below his own divination skull, watched silently by his living totem, the snake. And the concentration of his brow, his snake-like eyes, his voicelessly whispering lips, his tremulous finger-tips all seemed impressing a "something" into the skull of Sisi. So strangely, too, for hour after hour the grim visage seemed developing some dreadful caricature of the living expression of Sisi, he who had been chief of Badu.

And when the work was near finishing, the pupils of Sisi's eyes, jet-black spots of black bees-wax centres in the gleaming eyeballs, began to glisten like the eyes of the snake coiled upon the sorcerer's head. While the divination skull above suspended motionless upon its string glowed eerily—as if through it Enoko was seeking strength from the Council of the Zogo-le in Augudulkula upon Sacred Pulu.

Truly Enoko the Zogo-man, lost to the world in his work, seemed really trying hard to imbue this divination skull of Sisi with something very weird indeed.

On the evening of that sunlit day Wongai, with the chiefs, came strolling hungrily back from the gardens, very pleased with his day. He entered his house-stood stock still.

Suspended from a rafter—directly above his sleeping mat, the skull—or was it a caricature of the death face of Sisi? —glared malignantly at him: He frowned deeply. His eye somehow caught on Petula's face such a queer, fleeting expression of happy hatred as she bent swiftly over the cooking.

Wongai did not like it at all, frowning again at Sisi. He had killed men, but never had he dreamed of the death's head of a slaughtered one glaring over him as he slept at night. And this one brought a feeling of revulsion—a lightning memory of death bulging the eyes of Sisi when he plunged the knife into his heart.

He scowled, squatted undecidedly upon his mat. It was their blasted custom, he supposed. There was such a skull in the house of Kosabad, and he remembered the other in the Zogo-house that sheltered that swine of a sorcerer, Enoko. He supposed he must put up with their customs.

He scowled upon his three wives as deferentially they laid food before him.

CHAPTER X

MOA CHALLENGES BADU

With the break in the weather the sea was losing its anger in playful waves, no longer a lovely blue, but dirty because of the sediment churned up from the bottom through subterranean turbulence of storms and tides.

Migratory fish had left beforehand for more peaceful feeding grounds. But with the easing of the weather stay-at-home fish that had sheltered amongst the countless reefs ventured hungrily out to eat and be eaten while the going was good.

While on land a bushy-browed, confident outcast, now widely known as Wongai, chief of Badu, found himself the centre of a tiny island world and of a strange, haunting culture involving beliefs of ancient days. He acted his part marvellously well, though groping in the dark.

Peace between Mabuiag and Badu was a foregone conclusion, it being unbelievable that the War Gud of Kwoiam could rest in any place but within Augudulkula, Sacred Cave within Pulu, Sacred Isle of the Western Group. Badu and Mabuiag drew breath again. All was well.

Day by day the drums throbbed, the sombre rhythm rolling on from village to village around both islands. Hoarse blasts from the boo, only to fade at the throb of the drums again. The waterway shore and Badu village crowding with warriors, strange chiefs among them, all intensely curious to study Wongai. Grouped round him were Kosabad, jealously followed by Sagigi of Wabait, and Bagari of Upai. With heads of clans, attended by their picked warriors. This outcast now chief of Badu village had gone a long way in a very short time.

Noisy preparations for a feast, the women arguing as to how far the scanty supplies would go. But now, from across the waterway, away back on the Peak of Moa, a column of smoke rose up. The warriors growled, rattling weapons towards the distant Peak. Came the bellow of a war-boo, another and another. From across the waterway befeathered warriors leapt into canoes and came racing towards Badu village. But midway they halted, the warriors stood erect, waving weapons and shouting insults to the blaring boos.

Wongai's blood tingled. Here was the chance of a lively fight. But he realized that the warriors crowding into Badu village were not out for battle, they wanted to feast and enjoy the ceremonies. Angrily they shook weapons at these enemies who would spoil their fun.

That rolling smoke from Moa Peak was the challenge to Badu to come and battle. It might be answered today from craggy Butai Pad, or not for weeks. It was not to be answered for three months.

Laughter and song in the village now, squad-dancing for which Badu has long been noted. But each night early would come a moaning cry swelling out over the palms to sigh away. And the women and children would quietly arise and creep away into the houses. Again the cry would wail out, again and again. And every here and there men would arise and step silently away. Wongai guessed rightly that the lower in rank of totem or clan were retiring first.

"But why?" he wondered. "What does it all mean?"

It went on until only a group of Mamoose and chiefs were left. Their turn came, each with a grave salutation to Wongai quietly left for the seclusion of a house.

Wongai remained alone in the village centre. He stretched and rose, walked casually through the deathly quiet village to the foreshore and stood gazing across the waterway towards the purple-black shadows of Moa, so close he felt he could stretch cut his arm and touch the hills.

He wondered what might lie deep within that big island. All soft shadows, lovely it looked seen thus across the starlit waterway.

Leisurely, though alert for treachery, he walked back through the village to the house.

And scowled at the skull of Sisi grinning at him from the rafter, its glaring eyes green-rimmed with luminous phosphorus.

Petula, shamming sleep under her sleeping-mat, hated him. For Mek and Naina were sound asleep and she had been alone with the spirit of Sisi.

Again the silence wailed to uncanny sound, a wailing cry in the palms. Then silence, and a feeling as of ghostly figures hovering. Then a moan, and a laughing chuckle near by. Silence—then the swaying of a bush in the breeze—but there was *no* breeze.

Wongai, lying on: his mat with weapons to hand, wondered what devilry the sorcerers were up to now. By the light of the coals he could see the motionless shape of his three wives, huddled together under a sleeping mat. Evidently this was some occasion during which women had best keep quiet indeed.

"Good job, too!" he growled to himself.

He found but scant pleasure in his wives. He would have been surprised had he known what disappointment they found in him.

Not that Petula cared. For the spirit of Sisi already had gazed at her from the skull.

Wongai was to learn that the lives of these apparent savages were strangely complicated. Actually, some of their beliefs stretch back to dim ages, clinging to some vague form of a civilization. Right back to the Ancient of Days, to the First God, the Ad Giz, the Founder, the God of the Very Beginning.

But it would be a long time before he understood these really deep things.

One sunlit morning the chiefs and warriors in ceremonial dress came before Wongai, obviously expecting him to take the lead. He suspected the Zogo-house, so with a nod took the path. He halted a few yards back from the taboo sign, the chiefs and headmen behind him, while away back amongst the shrubbery silently awaited the people. At last, coming proudly down the path two gigantic figures, appointed by the Zogo-le to carry the War Gud of Kwoiam back to Sacred Pulu. The fiercely proud, defiant faces of the broad-chested warriors were framed in the brilliant forehead band of towering black plumes. On one warrior's chest gleamed the Giribu, crescent mai of Kwoiam, of polished mother-of-pearl carved in fretwork design, inlaid with mottled scales of tortoiseshell. His companion warrior wore one also, this one the Kutibu. For Kwoiam in life had worn one on chest and back. These were "Kwoiam's eyes, one before and one behind", the most precious war charms of all the western islands.

Creamy cross-bands of palm-leaf were fastened round these men's chests, each wore a heavy skirt of cassowary plumes, each carried across his left shoulder an amulet of Kwoiam, and a war-bow in the right hand.

Through each of these, and other relics carried, the people believed that the spirit of Kwoiam watched over them and advised them through their Zogo-le from his home in the spirit world.

The bearers of the War Gud marched fearlessly by Wongai and entered the path that led inland. Behind them in line came twenty grotesque figures almost hidden under giant masks in the form of men, animals, reptiles, and fish. Painted in coloured ochres, clothed in skirts of leaves or feathers, they followed silently on in the footsteps of the War Augud.

These were chief sorcerers come from Sacred Pulu to escort back the War Gud. Wongai wondered for how long they had been hidden there in the Zogo-house. From the expressive faces of the chiefs round him he took his cue and followed on.

Out to the forest country and up the wee divide that had witnessed Wongai's ambush and disaster to Mabuiag. Down the divide and on into open bush under bright sunlight with birds singing. And Wongai's intense interest at the hills and dales, the little flats, the scrubby patches, the open bushland and little valleys of this, to be his very own island.

And not even the clink of a chain disturbed memory as he breathed in freedom, as his eyes gazed at the blue vastness of sky, the green and grey of hill and dale.

A different feeling for young Kartoy, who with joy in his feet glanced swiftly aside when passing the glen where he and Lu-esa had made love on that never-to-be-forgotten afternoon. Soon Kartoy would pass his first initiation into the Shark clan. With a beating of the heart he peered away out over the warriors towards the big figure of Wongai striding behind the sorcerers. When, oh, when would the great chief carry on the war with Moa so that Kartoy could win his head? The head that would win him warriorhood and-Lu-esa.

By midday the women and children and numerous men halted, watched the procession out of sight, reluctantly returned to their villages. Through the afternoon more men kept dropping out according to their clans and degree. For not only must the waterway villages be manned against possible attack by Moa, not only was there lack of food for such a big crowd, but this ceremony was exclusively the business of the Zogo-le, and a select few of the more important chiefs and heads of clans.

When they reached the coast only fifty warriors remained with Wongai. But following the War Gud he noted a hundred others, sorcerers of varying degrees.

It took them three days to reach the opposite coast, for ceremonies were held on the way. From a low hill Wongai gazed out over this "back" boundary of his people, towards the land of Badu's important and close ally, the people of Mabuiag.

Only five miles off shore he was gazing at the wooded hills of a small island. Mabuiag, with around it on three sides a chain of tiny islets from one of which, on the western side, rose skyward three unwavering columns of smoke.

To the nor'-east, far as he could see, were dark clouds upon the water that were the trees of low-lying islands. Here and there, lighter green of water betraying shoals. Then something momentarily froze his blood — the distant sails of a ship!

He watched it with a snarl, he hated remembering civilization and ships. She was cautiously threading her lonely way through a maze of reefs. She would hasten to clear this dangerous sea with its islands savage as the sea. With a grim smile he felt himself not only perfectly safe, but master of all.

At the coast were waiting canoes decorated with palm branches. And a group of chiefs among whom was Nomoa, chief of Mabuiag, all intensely curious to meet Wongai. Here, too, awaited other sorcerers, concealed behind masks to receive the precious War Gud. He felt their eyes upon him, hostile eyes, fearful eyes, eyes burning with intense interest as they filed aboard, each in his own place and clan. And thus they sailed for Pulu.

A WARRIOR OF BADU

CHAPTER XI

THE WAR GUD RETURNS TO MABUIAG

Presently the trees, the grass-covered slopes, the sombre grey rocks upon Mabuiag were plainly visible, a little beach opposite Pulu brown with people. Wongai gazed from them to Pulu, but a stone's throw from Mabuiag shores. A mere rocky islet with scrubby, wind-blown trees here and there. Weird-looking place. Pillars of uncut stone reminiscent of Stonehenge, of some old retreat of the Druids, with the sacred smokes arising. The canoes ran up on to the pretty cove in Mumugubut Bay, enclosed by grey rocks seared and fissured as by the axe-blows of giants. Kosabad pointed to a hook-shaped boulder silhouetted above massed rocks.

"Kwoiam's wommera," he said.

Wongai nodded as if he fully understood that this represented the famous lever stick that gave power to Kwoiam's arm in the throwing of his spears. On that spot Kwoiam, in real life, had put his wommera standing in the ground and rested after killing twenty-two raiders from Badu. And now legend ascribed the hook-shaped rock to the wommera.

Just so legend in every race has ascribed some unusual natural feature to the story of its ancient heroes or gods. In this case, however, Kwoiam had actually lived.

Zogo-le in masks an ceremonial dress awaited on the beach. Behind them armed warriors stood silently.

Wongai found himself following the sorcerers as the procession marched between the warriors, heading inland and round the islet.

"That is what gave purchase to Kwoiam's foot when he speared the raiders of Badu." Nomoa pointed reverently towards a flat ledge of rock. "The killers were sleeping after having made the slaughter. Kwoiam's deadly aim killed man after man as they slept."

Further on among the bushes lay a row of black rocks side by side, loose boulders at the ends of them. Nomoa pointed, eager to explain the stories of Kwoiam to Wongai.

"These represent the men killed by Kwoiam after he had cut off their heads. But in earth life you have seen all this many times before."

Wongai nodded as if he fully understood.

They entered a narrow cleft painted with strange signs. Like barbaric sentries stood carved and painted and feathered figures of wood, some with grotesque heads of men, others of fish or reptile or bird. In a recess hung skirts of feathers, others beautifully woven from leaves and silken fibres from sea and land.

"Here dress headmen of the Maidelaig sorcerers," whispered Nomoa, "before they dance in the Kwod before the Zogo-le."

In yet another recess fires smouldered, initiates of the Maidelaig busy round cooking-pots. Under an overhanging ledge were cases made of bamboo and snow-white tea-tree bark, guarded by silent figures whose eyes gleamed through hideous masks.

"The Sacred Gud of Sigai and Maiau," whispered Nomoa, "are hidden in there. None but the Zogo-le, the Maidelaig, and warriors of degree dare enter this cleft. For a woman foolish enough to do so would mean death."

The cleft opened out on to a patch of open ground. Through the trees at one edge a glimpse of the sea with distantly the isles of Aipus and Widul, with much closer Kalalag, a hill on Mabuiag. As the procession filed out on the Kwod grounds Wongai gazed curiously at the huge stone Mangizi'-kula, the "stone that fell from heaven", covered now with ochred paintings of warriors, sorcerers, birds, and reptiles.

More drum-beats now swelled the steady rhythm while blasts from boo shells blared hoarsely across the water. In the centre of the Kwod a monstrous thatched house overshadowed all else. Built on piles ten feet high, it was two hundred feet long and seventy feet wide, the opening at both ends approached by step-ladders. The posts of the massive structure painted with the red badge of Kwoiam; decorated with trophies. Wongai wondered how many years of warfare and raids had gone by in the collection of all those grim relics. He never thought how lucky he was that he had not gone to swell the number. On the war-dance ground warriors awaited opposite the criss-cross kag poles from which were suspended the heads of the slain after a raid. He had a glimpse of giant carvings, of painted rocks and designs of stones arranged in squares and triangles and other symbols, before he found himself marching up the ladder-like steps into the Kwod House.

They marched on deep into the gloom of the great house where barbaric figures of the Zogo-le awaited them. Against the shadowy walls, stood what appeared to be gigantic black bats. They were sorcerers, draped in a bat-like costume of purple-black cassowary plumes. High up, dangling from the rafters, divination skulls slowly swayed, glowing with phosphorus.

For hours Wongai watched weird ceremonies in the welcoming back of the War Gud of Kwoiam to Sacred Pulu. He noted and memorized everything possible — ceremonies, persons, ranks, customs, every incident, every gesture, tried to interpret even the glance of priest and sorcerer. In the late afternoon the ceremonies terminated, to be carried on later throughout the night by the Zogo-le alone. He walked out on the Kwod grounds with Nomoa of Badu, Kosabad, and Bagari. Sagigi pointed to two peculiarly-shaped stones protruding from a patch of white sand enclosed by a chain of Fusus shells.

"That is where Uga, maid of Mabuiag, and her spirit lover Tabepa swore their love. And here, too, they left their presents of bows and arrows and food for Uga's people." Then Nomoa took up the tale and told them the love story of gentle-eyed Uga and her handsome spirit lover, Tabepa, which eventually led to a terrifying war between Mabuiag and the markai, the host of spirits. The spirits eventually triumphed by overwhelming Mabuiag with waterspouts from the sea.

Wongai nodded gravely as if understanding all that was being explained. And Nomoa, Kosabad, Bagari, and Sagigi, secure in their knowledge that Wongai, like all Lamars, must be re-educated after reincarnation, carried on, their eager explanations envied by the lesser chiefs following on behind the great Wongai.

Wongai walked across to five monstrous piles of bones, arranged in the form of an oblong. Skeletons of dugong, shark, cassowary, snake, and crocodile. By each pile a totem-pole carved and painted according to the heap over which it towered.

"The Kai Siboi," explained Nomoa, "and there are the five fire-places of the five chief clans of Sacred Pulu and Mabuiag. The Kodal (Crocodile) clan, the Tabu (Snake), Sam (Cassowary), Dangal (Dugong), Beizam (Shark). From these clans come all the headmen, both of the Zogo-le and the warriors."

Scattered over the grounds were shrines to sky men and they that control weather and seasons, the sea and good fortune. Painted rocks portraying spirits dancing, smaller enclosures crowded with young boys. For the Kwod was not only sacred to the Zogo-le and the many ceremonies, it was the centre of any important meeting of the warriors, and the training ground for boys. Wongai noticed that the boys treated the greybeards especially with deep respect, listening quietly, and that when attending to their wants they would approach with a humble bow, then return to their places walking backward, still bowed. More than ever he determined to familiarize himself with every aspect of the obviously complicated lives and beliefs of this savage culture. These were not merely club-wielding savages, there was something very deep here, he was going to make himself an island king, but he realized now he could not bluff these people merely by ferocity and cunning. If he was to wield all these people into one it would be a long, intricate job. One bad slip and his life would not be worth a moment. He was still striving to understand why he was so popular with all the warriors. He knew it was not so with the Zogo-le and the sorcerers.

Next morning the War Augud was carried in state to Augudulkula in the centre of the little isle, was borne out by the two giant bearers down from the Kwod House and through ranks of silent warriors. Wongai noticed that the escort round the War Gud of Kwoiam had been greatly strengthened by masked priests of the Zogo-le. The procession entered the bush, heading through the centre of the isle. The way grew wilder, the wind-blown scrub with gaunt, crooked arms seemed to be reaching out to gather them in, boulders in fantastic shapes frowned from above the rank grasses by dwarfed trees whose bare roots like serpents were clenched round the rocks. Clan after clan, according to etiquette, dropped regretfully out until only the chiefs of the tribes and the ever-gathering Zogo-le remained.

When approaching the cave of Augudulkula, Wongai uneasily felt that unseen eyes were watching him—watching *all* of them. Such was a fact, this holy of holies was guarded by the Watchers, the oldest yet powerful men of the clans of Pulu and Mabuiag. Hidden men in a circle watched around Augudulkula, no human could approach this cave unseen, even on the darkest night. Any who did so without authority— died. A fitting setting this, to weird figures making obeisance to the gods of the universe in queer rites born in the womb of Time.

And now, only the War Augud bearers, the Zogo-le with sorcerer escort, Wongai and the chiefs of tribes were left to wend their way through bush. A weird chanting from unseen men broke forth, swelling to vibrant triumph as the War Gud of Kwoiam approached Sacred Augudulkula. Under a rock towering above its fellows was the mouth of the cave, painted with strange symbols, guarded by carved figures of crocodile, of cassowary and snake, dugong and shark. Lining the approach to a dais, rows of silent figures, barbaric in masks and feathers—the Watchers. Facing the oncomers, the chief priests, Council of the Zogo-le. And Wongai felt he had come to the heart of the culture and life that ruled in a grip stronger than fetters the destiny of all in these islands.

The masks and dress of the Zogo-le were magnificent in savagery. Carved from mottled tortoiseshell inlaid with mother-of-pearl, huge masks with a demon face of man surmounted by a hawk's head, or gaping jaws of crocodile or shark. Towering purple-black plumes of the cassowary contrasted in vivid beauty with the colourful plumes of bird of paradise. Where portions of the brown body were visible it was splashed with scarlet ochre, blood-red badge of Kwoiam. Symbolic ornaments of tooth and fang, claw or shell, or limbs adorned with flashing stones that brought a deep breath from Wongai, amazement to his eyes.

While above them, in the form of a crescent moon upon rock, skulls painted with the scarlet band of Kwoiam.

With obeisance, the procession came to a halt, Wongai staring at the most barbaric figure of all. There came over him an eerie feeling of power absorbing him from the gleaming black eyes behind the mask. Instinctively he fought back, trying to shield his mind with a blank, he had never experienced such a feeling. The man behind that mask was Bauri, Chief Zogo of the Zogo-le, easily the most powerful man in the Western Group. In the dim recesses of the cave Wongai got glimpses of horrid-looking things, withered mummies of Zogo, and a huge, squatting figure carved of mottled plates of tortoiseshell, this the Great Au-gud. Above it, invisibly suspended, there seemed to be floating five luminous skulls.

Around that massive figure were the baskets containing the sacred skulls, with near by, like boxes of silken linen the long containers that housed the War Gud of Kwoiam.

Throughout the remainder of the day, and throughout the night when the Sacred Cave, the rocks around, the carvings of fantastic animals, birds and fishes glowed with green phosphorus, Wongai watched this scene with a feeling that he was among shadow beings from some nethermost region. It was not until just on sunrise that these ceremonies were concluded. The War Gud of Kwoiam had been received back to Sacred Pulu. Mabuiag again was master of its destiny and controller of the Western Group, the organization of the Zogo-le supreme.

They welcomed the dawn by a phalanx of upraised arms, hidden drums throbbing, hoarse blasts of the boo.

From the distant Kwod drums and boos answered, from across the water at Mabuiag deep voices softly chanting to the rosy rays of the sun.

The War Gud of Kwoiam had returned home.

CHAPTER XII

THE STORY OF KWOIAM

Wongai with the chiefs returned to the Kwod, enthusiastically welcomed by the warriors, Wongai responding like a pleased bull. With song the canoes took them across to Mabuiag, welcomed by noisy crowds. Strange chiefs came crowding round, Wongai among a mass of people, the centre of eyes, eyes—eager smiles.

What a transformation this from the jailers, the guards, the red coats— clink of irons, back-breaking weight of stones, the groans, snarls, curses of the chain gang.

He did not yet clearly understand that to all these excited people he was the actual reincarnation of Wongai, lieutenant of Sida, God of the Crops, beloved of Kwoiam, God of War.

He spent five instructive days on Mabuiag, though he could not have absorbed the symbolism of its complex culture in many months. Soon now, this culture, the last link with a vanished people, was itself to vanish. Wongai, standing there in his strength and confidence, developing dreams, would have laughed such a fancy to scorn, not realizing that the very fact of his standing there was a sign of coming times.

For everywhere that a white man has trod, others have followed.

Especially now did the people delight in showing him those localities associated with the deeds of the great Kwoiam.

For this was Kwoiam's island. And Wongai had been his friend in the spirit world.

They took him to Gumu, where Kwoiam had lived with his old mother.

Proudly Nomoa described the deeds of the strange hero, this wild man who had come to them, Nomoa explained, with his "half-wild heart". Wongai was fast picking up the language but naturally he was constantly puzzled, especially when they spoke of the dead as of still-living persons.

Before the wet season was over he was to become familiar with the story of Kwoiam, to learn the man was not a mythical war god, but that he had actually lived, and not long ago.

They climbed with him to Kwoiam's Ridge (Hill of Kwoiamantra) where are laid two long rows of round stones that represent the number of heads he took in one famous voyage of vengeance. They led him to Kuikuyaza, which is Kwoiam's Spring, ever trickling in a little singing stream. Here Kwoiam, so Nomoa explained, being thirsty, thrust his spear into the rock and water gushed out. They took him to the reddish rock where Kwoiam used to sit and make his spears, they pointed out the grooves in the stone where by friction he used to sharpen the stone and bone spear heads. Near the top of a hill they showed him Kwoiam's house, the walls were still standing, the old mother's cooking pots of shell lay there, and the Boo shell through which, on sighting approaching enemy canoes, Kwoiam would send a warning blast over the island. The heavy dugong harpoon was there, with other tools and weapons he had used in life. They climbed with him then up Kwoiam's Hill, a tor of rocks that had been his look-out. And Wongai's fierce eyes gleamed at the lovely view that threw a "kingdom" of islands at his feet. But they were proudly pointing out to him, away down on the coast, and farther along towards Wagedugam village, and then down towards the heart of the island, localities famous in the fights of Kwoiam, who repelled the invaders so often arriving to attack Mabuiag. They told him the saga of the fights against Badu, when again and again they would have been overwhelmed but for the cunning and ferocious bravery of Kwoiam. At last the warriors had given up the warfare, they had not only suffered far too heavily but came to believe that Kwoiam of Mabuiag was invincible. For Mabuiag, though, there had been little breathing space, because the men of Moa had taken up the fight and the thinned ranks of the Mabuiag warriors began to dwindle away. Finally came the last great attack, Kwoiam's presentiment of his death, and the last fight. Kwoiam, badly wounded, fighting alone, a pile of dead before him. Then his last fighting weapon broke, his wommera. Facing them, he retreated, his arms clutching out for a stick, a stone, a weapon. They rushed him, but he charged with a shout and they broke. Again and again they rushed him, but none dared face his berserk charge. At last he climbed right up here. And here he fell and died.

His enemies had crowded round him, silently gazing down. Then one man bent over to cut off his head—half-heartedly, though, for he was still afraid of the dead hero.

"Leave him alone," the others had whispered. "We have done enough. Were he alive, he would be cutting off *our* heads, not we cutting his."

And they had left him alone.

They pointed to the bushes all round, some of them scarlet, others with reddish leaves.

"The blood gushed out of the cut on Kwoiam's neck," explained Kosabad, "and stained the leaves. And the bushes have grown so to this day."

They showed him Kwoiam's grave, overlooking Sacred Pulu and the isles he had loved so well.

Wongai curiously examined the cairn of rocks under which Kwoiam sleeps, his head facing the rising sun. On that day when the puzzled convict stared down, the cairn was still decorated with symbolic shells, and some of Kwoiam's personal ornaments.

The story of Kwoiam is a remarkable saga in the history of island life. Not only did he save the people of Mabuiag from certain extinction, but his influence brought about the alliance of Badu and Mabuiag against Moa, while the moral and cultural influence arising from his deeds and philosophy made the Mabuiag people believe themselves invincible—to such an extent that they, from being hunted tribes, became overlords of the Western Group.

An extract from the work of Professor A. C. Haddon, of the Cambridge Anthropological Expedition to Torres Straits, throws a sidelight on Kwoiam.

> I cannot do better than close this account of Kwoiam with a sentiment actually expressed to me by Nomoa, the then chief of Mabuiag, when he told me the story of Kwoiam in 1888. I much regret that I did not take down his very words, but I have accurately preserved their sense. "The fame of Kwoiam caused the name of Mabuiag to be feared for many a long day, and although the island was rocky and comparatively infertile, Kwoiam covered it with honour and glory, thus showing how the deeds of a single man can glorify a place in itself of little worth."[3]

But what makes the story of Kwoiam almost unbelievably remarkable is that he was not a Torres Strait Islander at all. He was an Australian aboriginal, a wanderer who set off in his canoe seeking—who knows?— but very probably an "island of his own". And his northern route, strangely enough, was the very one later followed by the escaped convict. But where the storm had driven Wongai into the waterway separating Badu from Moa, Kwoiam had paddled a few miles farther along the Badu coastline, to Mabuiag.

The strange fate that guarded the lone aboriginal past the many critical dangers to the isle of his destiny may have been the same fate that later guarded the escaped convict. It seems both had a temporary job to do in a now vanished phase of island life.

Kwoiam's story must have been strange indeed. Even the islanders of lesser culture looked upon the distant Australian aboriginal as merely a

---

[3] Cambridge Anthropological Expedition to Torres Straits, *Reports*, vol. v, p. 83.

wild animal, fit only to be exterminated.

Kwoiam's voyage in his rude dug-out canoe into the heart of the Coral Sea, his survival amongst these people who despised and detested his race, his leadership of the highly cultured Mabuiag clans, his subsequent history and deification by them is an epic in savage history.

Wongai climbed slowly back and up on to Kwoiam's Lookout. He faced west, gazing across a nearly empty sea. Slowly he turned north, facing New Guinea, slowly towards the east and out over the chain of reefs and islets and cays and islands stretching right across the Coral Sea to lovely Eroob and Mer close by the northern end of the Great Barrier Reef. Midway out there were the big Warrior Reefs, and tiny Warrior Island with the already famous young chief, Kebisu, in active command of his sea-going warriors. Wongai did not know that, but was eventually to learn that it was Kebisu with his canoes who had passed him away south when he was an outcast crouching among the bushes of a barren islet. If he had fallen into Kebisu's hands, how different his fate would have been—short and sharp. He turned slowly facing the "Needle of Naghir" rising from the sea, turned until he was facing Badu with, behind it, Moa. Thoughtfully he sat on Kwoiam's Stone, gazing out exactly as Kwoiam had done many and many a time.

KWOIAM'S HILL

CHAPTER XIII

WONG AI UNDERSTANDS

He was now beginning to realize, this escapee from the Norfolk hell, that these people for some inexplicable reason regarded him as something very close to Kwoiam, obviously their greatest legendary hero. In a brown study, he tried to reason it out.

Just below him, all round the crown of the hill, the people silently waited. It appeared so natural that Wongai, on his first visit to Mabuiag after his reincarnation, should wish to sit and think alone upon Kwoiam's old seat where his friend, the God of War, had sat and planned so often before.

But Wongai was not brooding upon memories of his supposed past, though many of his thoughts were strangely akin to what they believed of him. Had it not been for the invasion of the whites even then beginning, this outcast convict would have grown into the hearts and lives and culture of these people as one far greater even than Kwoiam.

His gaze wandered over the rough hills, then along the wooded coast with here and there a village, an islet off shore.

"Only very small patches of fertile land here," he thought, "difficult to cultivate, but more could be made of what ground there is. An easy enough island to defend, protected by these scrubs and rocks. Though a strong force, if well led, could outmanoeuvre these people into these little hills. Surround them, and fight it out one way or the other." Which was what had happened years ago to the main clan, at the overthrow of Kwoiam.

Wongai's eyes lifted across the water to the long coastline of Badu and Moa with their hills misty from coming weather. Those long, wooded hills told of a wild inland well in from the coast. He could not be hunted there like a mad dog and cornered, as in this tiny island. Should disaster come, he could vanish inland and live, then emerge to fight again.

Sight of that distant sail had awakened bitter memories—fear, too.

Lost in reverie, this ruthless renegade clad in his regalia of savagery, brooding upon a hero's rock on the crest of a crag overlooking a scene of wild beauty. The worshipping people firmly believing he had come to them from another life—so he had, but not the life of those who had passed on. He had come into this life from civilization, almost as different as their imagined spirit life of the dead.

And from this, their life, he determined to make for himself a chieftainship beyond his dreams. He warmed to the certainty of his destiny. Had he landed on almost any other island he would have been clubbed or, at best, existed as leader of a few savages. And then again, had it not been for those raiders from Mabuiag he would still have been sitting at Badu village, knowing nothing of Badu Island except for the few tribes along the waterfront directly facing Moa. He would have been gazing across the waterway towards those enemies on Moa, believing his life was bound up in a few villages and the waterfront of Moa, knowing nothing of Mabuiag, not dreaming of all this that lay "behind". But now from here he saw the island system in a way that expanded his vision geographically, in other ways even more so. This intricate system of warriorhood and clanship and ally, and something more important still— this queer system of priesthood, mysticism, and sorcery. Had he remained at Badu village he always would have been at the mercy of the sorcerers, unaware of the organization and influence woven into the lives of these and how many other islands? It was not the chiefs that really ruled the lives of the tribesmen, it was the controlling, the unseen power over all-the Zogo-le.

His life had depended upon a slender thread indeed.

The Zogo-le behind the scenes might still strike him down and he would never know from whence the blow had come. He determined to treat the Zogo-le and their sorcerers and spies with respect and cunning whilst strengthening his position with the warrior clans. The sooner he was back on Badu the better. There flashed into his mind again a plan to attack Moa village and thus win over the tribes of all the waterfront. Then, as Wongai, chief of the main fighting clans of Badu Island, his position should be greatly strengthened.

A lovely sunset had bathed in beauty islands and sea before he rose and walked down the Hill of Kwoiam, the people falling in behind him. There were to be further ceremonies tonight down below in the Kwod grounds of Mabuiag.

Ten days in all Wongai and the chiefs were absent from Badu. The evening on which they returned rain began falling again, fell for a fortnight, followed by a week of fine weather, and so on for nearly four months of a particularly wet season brought to the islands, as all firmly believed, by the Thunder god through the agency of Wongai, lieutenant of Sida, God of the Crops, and friend of Kwoiam, God of War.

Throughout the Wet Wongai concentrated on learning the language, finding it surprisingly easy with Kosabad, Sagigi, Bagari, the headmen, and all the village eager to teach him. This man was almost to forget his mother tongue—wished to forget it. Before the wet season was over he could speak almost like an islander, understood the intricate degrees of chieftainship and clanship, the complexities of rights of land and fishing grounds, of initiation and family life, of warfare and magic. Of alliances among the island groups, of the system of trade to New Guinea governed by island agreements, carried out only by "traders" of certain clans. There were numerous other matters, ceremonies, customs, and beliefs that were seasonal and that he would only learn and master with the coming and passing of the seasons, and of events. He learnt their intricate totemism, folklore, and legendary stories, of the super-men who from the spirit gods had brought all things to earth. He was amazed to learn that these people believed in spirit life as implicitly as of everyday life. That night and day spirits both good and bad were always round them, that numbers among them could either see, hear, or mentally converse with their departed ones. When he began to understand their deep beliefs in spirit life his interest rapidly intensified as he began to realize that he was "Wongai", reincarnation as a Lamar, a spirit man, returned from spirit life to live again in earth form. Unbelievable it was—a gift from the gods. And to think that it had all hinged on that thunderstorm bringing the rains—and on that one word shouted at the critical moment—"Wongai!"

And he had thought "Wongai!" a war-cry!

With absorbed interest he listened to the stories of the great lover, Sida, God of the Crops, of his lieutenant, Wongai, who had brought the wongai plums to earth, and of Kwoiam, the War God.

Smoking his "zoob", the native pipe of bamboo, in the hut one night, he pored deeply over this astounding information, which now made everything plain to him. With a shiver at the base of his neck he glowered up at Sisi's skull. But for that shout "Wongai!" *his* skull would have been leering there—how devilishly lifelike the blasted thing looked—just enough movement at the end of the cord to create tremulous luminosity in those phosphoric eyes. Scowlingly he wished the preparation would die out—surely it could not last for ever!

As if Petula would ever allow the light in Sisi's eyes to die out! For rather would she have dimmed the light under Wongai's shaggy brows.

Scowling he glanced away. Somehow he did not like staring at Sisi's skull—the blasted thing gave him the creeps.

Yes, what luck! Almost as if he really *had* received help from some other world—some other life. For a long time he could not really believe such luck. Then he began to develop a confidence made overwhelming by a superstitious belief that his own destiny must have brought this million-to-one chance about.

Eagerly he learnt all he could of the mysterious Zogo-le. He pondered on the advisability of killing Enoko, the sorcerer, who, he suspected, was spying on him. But he must work craftily indeed.

As impatiently as the islanders he awaited the coming of the lovely star Kaek which would signify the ceasing of the rains, the coming of the south-east season when fruits would bloom in the earth and fish, dugong, and turtle teem in the sea.

But just before the active sea work that he knew now would soon take place he determined to unite Gud, Tulu and Wadauibad villages with Badu, Wabait, and Upai under his close chieftainship by inflicting a crushing defeat on the dreaded Moans. By swift surprise attack Moa village and wipe it out.

A BOWMAN OF BADU

CHAPTER XIV

THE PIPE OF DEATH

The village slept in a deathlike quietness—no sound even of raindrips from the leaves. Black clouds hid stars and blanketed sea and earth. But Wongai did not sleep. And his suspicious eyes were long used to darkness. Eyes that had glared into the eyes of rats in the dungeon, that knew the glint of starlight on a tumbling wave, eyes that had seen on the darkest sea. Deeply thinking now, though apparently asleep on his mat. His three wives slumbering near by. His thoughts flashed to Miria of the laughing eyes, favourite daughter of Wypali, chief of Tulu village—an important village. Miria was a handsome wench, gay of heart, but Wongai thought not so much of that as of her sturdy body—she should toil well in the gardens. He already knew that women could be an infernal nuisance, not always to be kept under by the strong arm—but they had their uses. He had had no chance of anything at all to do with women during his hunted life. He was discovering now that he had much to learn about them.

Wypali, Miria's father, was a proud chief who could put a hundred and fifty club- and bow-men into a fight. Wongai had decided to marry Miria and through her to bring Wypali and Tulu villages under his chieftainship. That, and very much more, would come to him could he only wipe out Moa village. Deeply he planned.

The coals upon the fire-place had burnt down to a dull red. Though dark night was flooding in the open doorway it still contained light, and the apparent sleeper's eyes concentrated on it, as they could absorb light from those dull coals. Which was why he gradually became aware of a "something", fairly high up. Only because it slowly "glided" did he become aware of it.

It hovered, a wispy, reed-like thing it might be, though it seemed but a shadow moonbeam.

As he concentrated upon it it seemed to withdraw backward into the hut wall—vanished.

Breathing as if in sleep, he lay there trying to solve the problem of this shadow wisp, which must have some material origin. Before he had become aware of it it was already there, hovering over his tobacco leaf— he stared at those leaves hanging from a string stretched across the hut. They were only vague shadow now, but in daylight they would be long, yellow-brown leaves of cured tobacco. Ready for his pleasure to smoke in his zoob. And—the wisp thing had hovered over the leaf he next would smoke. He had. already smoked half of it, naturally he would take his next smoke from that leaf.

Why had that long, reed-like, wisp-shadow thing hovered over the leaf he next would smoke?

And what was it?

It seemed to have melted back into the wall of the hut. Therefore, it must have *come* through the wall, and have been *pushed* through.

Someone outside had noiselessly cut a slit in the matting. And pushed that long, reed thing right through until the end of it hovered over the tobacco leaf!

What for? And—what *was* it?

For long he lay there, then in a flash remembered having seen a long reed standing up in a corner of Enoko's house during that first day when he had wandered through the village, then along the taboo path to the sorcerer's hut. While in there, with the sorcerer glaring at him under that agitated divination skull, among other weird things he had noticed the long, slender reed in a corner. It must have been nine feet long, he had wondered even then what it could be for.

Enoko had pushed that reed through the wall of Wongai's house and gently touched the tobacco leaf with it.

A reed is hollow.

Instantly he was on his feet with his hands gently touching the tobacco leaf. He was disappointed. It was not wet. Enoko could not have blown a liquid through the reed.

He lay down again, frowning, gazing up at the leaf, thinking deeply. Suddenly he sat bolt upright.

What if Enoko had blown a puff of *powder* through that reed tube?

He could do nothing now, but he believed he had solved the problem. Stealthily he crept from the house and washed his hands—such instinctive cunning was destined to save his life again and again.

In the morning, after breakfast, when the women went to the gardens, he cleaned thoroughly a broad shell shaped like a dish and used as such. Its inner side was white as the whitest enamel. Carefully he took down the tobacco leaf, placed it in the shell and put it on the warm ashes. Slowly the leaf dried. He shook the leaf in the shell. And snarled as a film of yellowish green powder settled on the white shell. He shook it again and again. Then collected the powder together—a quarter-spoonful of fine, almost vapoury yellowish-green powder.

He collected it in one of the tiny bamboos the islanders fashion into bottles and boxes. Then hung a tobacco leaf in place of the poisoned leaf, breaking off half. Hid the treated leaf and washed out the dish. Just in time, hearing the voices of Kosabad and the headman coming to yarn.

He knew that if he were to be watched it would be at night by one of the lesser village sorcerers. By day he would be in sight of all. So that when at midday he saw Enoko the sorcerer walking through the village he acted, walked amongst the houses, casually greeting friends, in the direction of the gardens. Slipped aside into the bush, then into the taboo path and swiftly to the Zogo-house. Entered and glared around.

Only Enoko's snake was there. He slipped the little box from his shirt and dusted the powder on the tobacco leaf hanging from the roof—on the leaf that Enoko would smoke next. Then swiftly ran down the taboo patch, then through the bush, and was chatting with folk in the gardens.

That afternoon Wongai called Kosabad and the head clansmen of Badu. Sent for Bagi, Chief of Upai, and for Sagigi, Chief of Wabait.

He proposed a bold stroke—the warriors of the three villages to combine and attack the main village of Moa, headquarters of the dreaded chief Kabara, chief of all the Italagas. He proposed also to send word to Sacred Pulu as was the custom, asking the Zogo-le to invite their Mabuiag allies to co-operate, all to fight under the War Gud of Kwoiam.

Eagerly they listened, joyfully accepted, a runner was despatched with the message to Pulu. Throughout the afternoon they listened to Wongai's plan, discussed it, agreed upon the number of men and canoes each village and clan could muster.

That evening crowds of excited warriors, women, and children clustered round Wongai's house, discussing the coming attack. Inside, Wongai sat preparing his zoob for the evening smoke. Kosabad, Sagigi, and Bagari later on all remarked how the chief Wongai had appeared to enjoy that smoke. When smilingly they remarked to him the tobacco must be very good indeed he threw back his head with deep-throated laugh, his fierce eyes flashing delight.

"Thus we will smoke out Moa village!" he roared, and blew a cloud that filled the house.

Away back in the gloom of the Zogo-house Enoko the sorcerer, squatting on his mat, his snake coiled upon his head, was also preparing his zoob. A two-foot section of polished bamboo, beautifully carved in totem designs of the snake, for the sorcerer was of the Snake clan. The "mouthpiece" was a neat hole near one end of the bamboo, the "bowl" a larger hole towards the other. Enoko was thoughtfully poking the tobacco leaf into the bowl, his skinny claws kneading the leaf deep into place. He frowned as he worked, and the deeper he thought the more the wrinkles of his skinny old visage hardened into the tattooing on a devil imp's face. Enoko was a sorcerer with a grudge—a double grudge now. Long ago, he considered, he had earned his reward—he should have been one of Them, one of the Council of the Zogo-le, helping in the directing of all human affairs in the holy of holies, Augudulkula upon Sacred Pulu. And at long last, just as he was about to be called to headquarters despite the intrigues of his hated rival Barza, had come this accursed Wongai to spoil everything and trouble all. Hastily the Zogo-le had cancelled their order, ordering him now to remain at Badu until this vexed question of Wongai the Lamar was settled for good and all.

Enoko, very troubled himself, wished this accursed Wongai into the nethermost depths of the island hell. Fear dulled his curses, for he was not certain whether this Lamar really was or was not the reincarnation of Wongai, lieutenant of Sida. Woe for Enoko should it really prove so, for in such case Sida would set aside a special hell for him when his turn came to enter the spirit land. But whether or no, the Council of the Zogo-le had at last taken the greatly dreaded step. Whether this Lamar was or was not Wongai, he was to be sent back to spirit land again.

And Enoko had obeyed the order. Grimly now he knew his troubles on earth at least would soon be over, for at this very time the chief Wongai also would be filling his zoob-filling it for his last smoke.

With a touch of the finger Enoko flipped aside a small, live coal to the fire-place edge. Then completed the filling of the pipe. He had believed that Wongai would have smoked his particular pipe alone. But the deepest laid plans can go awry. The chiefs were with Wongai, all the people would be outside his house listening to the planning of this attack on Moa. Enoko grinned evilly, certain that that attack would never come. The Zogo-le did not wish it, and what the Council wished not—was not.

Enoko leaned over, grasped the coal and deftly placed it on the pipe bowl. Lifting the bamboo he put puckered lips to the mouthpiece and drew long and steadily. Then laid the pipe across his knees, his thumb pressed on the mouthpiece.

He had not inhaled that smoke, for such is not the custom. The art is to first get the tobacco leaf well alight, then draw upon it until the hollow bamboo is densely full of smoke. Not until then is the smoke inhaled.

Squatting motionless, Enoko frowned at the coals. Yes, he wished Wongai had smoked alone. Now the people would be there—it would not be so good as if he had smoked his last pipe alone. However, even the Zogo-le could not foresee *everything*.

The snake hissed warningly. Enoko listened. But all he heard was the whispering voices of the night—there was no one there.

Enoko took another long, steady pull at the pipe. Plugged the mouthpiece with his thumb, laid the bamboo across his knees again, sank into deep meditation.

Again the snake hissed, its squat head uneasy above the centre of the sorcerer's forehead. Enoko was very fond of his living skull-cap; his totem the snake. It had been his skull-cap many years now. Had warned him in the deep silences of danger, when with creepy warmth it tautened upon his skull. It tautened now.

Sometimes Enoko's small, wrinkled, evil face seemed to absorb the expression of the snake. Certainly their cold, jet-black little eyes gleamed with the same malevolence when they were angry. And now the snake seemed uneasy, though comfortably feeling the warmth of the man.

Enoko fondled his zoob, engrossed in thought.

Yes, through him, Enoko, the Zogo-le, had acted only just in time. This was a clever plan of Wongai the Lamar—the attack on Moa was only a blind. Through it he would unite Badu, Upai, and Wabait villages under him, probably Wypali and Tulu also. And cement for all time the alliance between Mabuiag and Badu. Enoko knew how delightedly the warriors of Mabuiag would greet that runner, bearing Wongai's invitation to march with the War Gud of Kwoiam and help in the annihilation of Moa village. It would bring the fighting clans of Mabuiag on his side, wiping out the last traces of that humiliating defeat.

Enoko took another long, steady pull at the pipe.

He had plenty of time; the runner would not have arrived yet. As soon as his sorcerer, his Maidelaig assistant, came creeping to tell him of Wongai's death, he would call up the Zogo-le telepathically. They would be awaiting that runner of Wongai's, would see that he delivered no message to excite the warrior clans of Mabuiag. But the Zogo-le must hear of Wongai's death first.

Enoko took another pull at the pipe, ears alert for his Maidelaig sorcerer who would appear at any moment with news of Wongai. Enoko wondered a little that the Maidelaig had not already arrived.

The snake hissed urgently, tautening upon the sorcerer's skull. Enoko wondered why, for the Maidelaig did not come.

When Enoko had filled the bamboo dense with smoke he put his lips to the mouthpiece and inhaled deep and long. He filled his lungs to the depth with smoke and held it there. Such an inhalation would have smothered a white man, but that was the way the islanders trained themselves from boyhood to smoke.

He laid the pipe across his knee, absorbing the smoke deep into his lungs, thinking deeply.

And thus he smoked, in a silence deep as the silence of death.

Presently, his eyes quivered slightly, widened in puzzled alarm. Suddenly he dropped the pipe and jerked up his head and exhaled in a wheezing gust that brought volumes of smoke pouring out of mouth and nostrils. In frantic alarm he struggled to expel every gasp of air from deep in his body. His chest, his arms stiffened as his head stretched back with his eyes staring from their sockets, his face now convulsively monkey-like, lungs stiffened with cramp—his stomach felt about to burst, he tried to stagger up but his nerves were paralysed, he could not gasp for breath, while the snake hissed agitatedly from swaying head, beady eyes open in alarm, its forked tongue hissed out, while Enoko could neither breathe nor expel air, nor move his bulging muscles nor tautened sinews, he could only stretch slowly back, his face a devil's mask as he smothered with nerves and muscles paralysed.

Agitatedly the snake unwound from the dying sorcerer's head and slithered hissing away.

CHAPTER XV

THE ANNIHILATION OF MOA VILLAGE

Four days later Badu village was thronged with fighting men. Wongai led them well back behind the village and explained they must camp and prepare there, out of sight and sound of the watchers across the waterway.

When Nomoa arrived, leading the warriors of Mabuiag with the War Gud of Kwoiam, enthusiasm was unbounded. Wongai energetically set about teaching them discipline and tactics altogether new to native warfare. They hung on his every word and rehearsed their parts with a tense eagerness that augured well for their grim purpose. For Wongai was spirit friend to their War God, Kwoiam. Who better than he to teach them the arts of war?

He organized them into four forces, the Mabuiag men under Nomoa, the Badu men under Kosabad, the Wabait men under Sagigi, the Upai warriors under Bagari. Wongai explained to each chief how to appoint their heads of clans as "officers" and "non-coms", according to order of precedence. He took joy in the task, as they did to learn. But a grim memory made him sneer. If the redcoats could only see him now! What glum astonishment! They would not be so ready to give a clump in the teeth with a musket butt! A poke in the behind with a bayonet! A smash of musket butt on tired, sore feet! How he wished he had some of the blood-letting swine here now! He clenched his teeth in a snarling rage of memories.

But there came the noisy chatter of birds squabbling in a thicket. Plaintive call of sea-birds from away back on the waterway. And the breath of freedom, sweetly scented with wild bush flowers bursting to the sunlight of the new-born sou'-east. He wiped memory from his mind, grinned at Kosabad embarrassed in a tangle he had just made in the training of his men.

Thus the renegade built the groundwork of his first four "regiments". A groundwork which, developed by the years, was ultimately to wipe out the tribes of Moa.

According to how he had judged its size and position from his scouting canoe on the waterway, he set them to building a skeleton village of Moa. Then gave the chiefs their orders and from four directions again and again "attacked Moa village" until all were letter perfect.

Wongai knew now that Moa village was doomed. And still more happened, to his satisfaction. For among the crowd daily looking on was

Wypali, cautious chief of Tulu. Presently, infected by the enthusiasm, he eagerly accepted Wongai's invitation to join in with a representative squad of fighting men. An example quickly followed by three lesser chiefs from the interior, to Wongai's immense satisfaction.

Meanwhile, on distant Pulu the Zogo-le were worried and puzzled. The Maidelaig assistant to Enoko had hurriedly sent them news of the sorcerer's death. The Zogo-le had ordered it to be kept quiet. Sorcerers had buried the body secretly by night.

A mistake had been made—somewhere. And the Zogo-le would not actively move until that mistake had been solved and atoned for, lest the failure recoil upon them.

Increasingly the Council was worried about this Wongai. Had he only come to the Zogo-le as the reincarnation of Wongai, then all would have been well. He would have strengthened not only his own hand, but theirs also. But he had come to the warriors and the people. And his increase of influence was alarming. Bitterly they resented his return to earth to upset the balance of power between them and the warrior clans and through them of the people.

So they had passed secret judgment-the zoob, the pipe of death.

But it had been Enoko who had smoked the pipe. And the Zogo-le were confounded.

Across the waterway, the tribes of Moa Island had lost caution, were eagerly looking forward to the sou'-east season with its good weather bringing food of sea and earth. For all in the Coral Sea had hungered more during the great drought than any remembered before. Men, women, and children were busy building fishing traps, looking forward to eating and eating. After which would be time to think again of the war against Badu.

It was the last dark night of the nor'-west season. Strangely, numerous creamy bands, like broad ribbons gliding from the shore of Badu.

These bands were the creamy inner leaf of the coconut palm worn across head and chest by many warriors to distinguish friend from foe at night. Thus Wongai's fleet took to the waterway, the soundlessly moving canoes merging into the water blackness. And the War Gud of Kwoiam was in the leading canoe, the canoe of Wongai.

They landed noiselessly in their allotted distances apart, then. under their chiefs mustered into columns and without a whisper stepped cat-like towards Moa village.

The tall stockade was a huge, circular wall above which showed a few dark roofs. Shadows merged into the blackness vanishing round each side of the stockade towards the big gate leading inland, and the gate facing the waterway.

The watchers by both gates were sound asleep. Each woke to a terrifying pressure—each was noiselessly strangled. Shadows then drifted in through both gates and melted among the huts.

And still not a sound.

A red star gleamed low down on the black earth, it licked a red tongue up the thatched wall of a hut. Other stars gleamed out—many stars—tongues like fiery snakes licked up into devouring fire.

Came a startled shout—a thud—a shriek. Bewildered cries drowned in a roar of war-song and hell had broken loose.

As the unfortunates leapt out of the blazing houses they were met by club and spear and arrow. In the blood-curdling terror of shrieks and war-cries the village panicked in the roar of fire. Survivors dashed instinctively towards the inland gate—it was ablaze. Wheeling frantically they dodged past maddened figures towards the waterway gate—it was not on fire. They dashed through to safety—were met by arrows, a wall of spears.

Moa village was annihilated.

From away down the waterway war-boo after boo in hoarse blasts warned other sleeping villages, while high up on the Peak of Moa a bonfire blazed to warn the inland tribes. But what cared the victors, that blood-crazed mass of warriors driven back from the blaze of the stockade walls? Some among them were now racing to the waterfront to seize what canoes they could as spoil in this great victory.

When Wongai's canoes returned in roar of song to Badu people from all villages came hurrying in to witness the triumph—the greatest complete victory ever attained against Moa by men of Badu and Mabuiag. Wongai had planned it—Wongai had led it.

Badu never again would go in fear of Moa.

During the week of wild ceremonies that followed the victory, the chief Wypali followed by chiefs of inland villages, came anxiously to give full allegiance to Wongai.

Striking while the iron was hot, Wongai claimed Miria, daughter of Wypali, as bride. And in the enthusiasms of victory and marriage was proclaimed by all Wongai the Mamoose, chief of chiefs of all Badu.

A remarkable triumph for him whose back would ever carry the scars seared deep by the cat o'-nine-tails—to be proclaimed chief of chiefs of every tribe in this large island in such a short time.

It was written in the courses of the stars. Otherwise his head long ago would have dripped upon Sisi's sarokag pole.

CHAPTER XVI

ENOKO'S TOTEM SNAKE

So thought Barza, squatting on his mat in the sorcerer's house, thoughtfully smoking his zoob. Barza, appointed by the Zogo-le to take Enoko's place.

To the grim satisfaction of Barza the Silent, one big step closer to a seat in the Council of the Zogo-le now that happily his old enemy, Enoko, was dead.

But he must be very, very careful on this his last big job before he was called to Sacred Pulu.

Enoko had been known to be more than careful, had been credited with "the cunning of the snake". But he must have made a mistake—one fatal mistake.

Brooding over his zoob, Barza determined *he* would make no mistake.

The night silence was deep within the hut. The coals glowed brightly against the chill of the outside air. A gecko clinging to the roof chirped like a lively baby bird. Came a rustling of the bushes outside, only a vagrant breeze sighing away.

Then—Barza saw the snake. Enoko's snake, come gliding into the hut, looking for Enoko. It stopped, its ugly squat head, its beads of eyes glaring up at him.

It wanted Enoko. But Barza sat on Enoko's mat.

For a long, long time man and snake glared one at the other. The man felt the snake resented, distrusted him. Barza hated the snake.

For a snake had killed his father years ago. Barza had not forgotten. But *this* snake, with its shining, jet-black head and body, its blood-red throat…

He longed to kill this snake but he dared not—yet. For he knew instantly it was Enoko glaring so hatefully at him from the snake's eyes— for the Snake was Enoko's totem. Barza's was the Cassowary.

The spirit of Enoko in his totem snake had returned to his hut to find Barza sitting on his mat. Barza, his enemy, at long last now chief sorcerer of Badu village.

How long, Barza wondered, would it be before he dared kill the snake. For even a sorcerer took a very grave risk in killing a totem thing when the spirit of a fellow sorcerer was believed to be inside.

A mari, a ghost, might hover over, or inhabit its totem but a few days or weeks. But a markai, a spirit, for some definite purpose could remain for months.

For how long would the spirit of Enoko inhabit its familiar, the snake?

Barza glared down at the snake, thinking back over the intrigues he had indulged in to curry favour against Enoko with the Council of the Zogo-le.

The snake glared back. Its tongue shot out—it hissed sibilantly.

Barza felt the spirit of Enoko might inhabit this accursed snake for quite a long time. And he sensed its determination to stay with him in the hut—once Enoko's hut and home. The meanings of the shadowy things within the hut, the musty taint of smoke-dried things once living, of herb and fungus, incense and poison glands, the heavy atmosphere still seemed to breathe of the thoughts and crafty schemes hatched here by Enoko during years past.

Silently Barza smoked on. He dared not seize a club and smash the thing. But, in certain circumstances it was permissible to kill in other ways…

A glitter in Barza's eyes, his mouth a twisted grin. Could he *poison* the snake?

He knew a lot about poisons—had used them efficiently. But he had never had reason to poison a venomous snake before.

Could such a snake be poisoned?

The more he pondered over it, the more intriguing the question.

Poison a poisonous snake—how?

The snake hissed.

It seemed to Petula, weaving a new grass skirt for Miria's wedding as she sat facing Sisi's skull, that the wax face of Sisi seemed sad. She wondered if it were for Enoko, the sorcerer, whose clever fingers had modelled his cheeks, had arranged his hair, fitted his eyes, charmed divination into him as became the skull of a chief. Uneasily Petula wondered just what had happened to Enoko. He had vanished—people believed called to the Council of the Zogo-le on Sacred Pulu. But she, Petula, knew more than the people—she and Enoko had been very close—where Sisi's skull was concerned.

She sighed deeply. She had loved Sisi.

Ah well, she had much time now to be with him, for work in the gardens was forgotten during the victory ceremonies and preparations for the chief's marriage feast. She was not jealous of Miria as were this accursed Lamar's other wives, Mek and Naina, ah no! How she hated him! She hoped his new wife, Miria, would prove a thorn in his sleeping-mat. She blessed the outdoor excitement of all in the village, for while it lasted she could stay with Sisi and silently comfort him.

Deftly her clever fingers worked over the long silken strands, strands cleverly produced from the shredded roots of the banyan-tree, fibres, too, from shredded banana leaves. Prettily dyed. And the waist would be ornamented with scarlet berries hard as stone, with little stars and crescents, moons and suns of brilliantly coloured shells. Yes, when finished it would be a pretty wedding petticoat indeed. And Petula well knew how Miria's shapely limbs would show it off. Petula smiled sourly; she doubted whether the big chief would even notice. But still Miria was not to know that. With a sigh, Petula glanced up at Sisi's skull— remembering Sisi's eager smile on seeing her in *her* wedding petticoat.

But out in the village Miria was in love with life, not death. Miria, her buxom young body shining under massage of coconut oil, flowers and tinkling shell and living butterflies pulsing scarlet and orange, green and gold from the fuzzy mop of her beautifully kept hair. Miria with the saucy brown eyes ablaze with curiosity, Miria the envy of all the women, Miria who was so alive and so eager and so proud to become the youngest wife of the great chief, reincarnation of Wongai.

And the glances, whisperings of the other women, so avidly curious to know what life with a Lamar husband would be like. For all knew he had not taken to Sisi's wives, Mek, Naina, and Petula. After all, it should be only the best for a Lamar chief. In stories they knew of marriages between spirit men and human women, but never before had they known of human marriage with a spirit man in reincarnated form.

And Miria, pouting, kept their curiosity at boiling-point. She did not know yet, she was not sure whether she would tell them when she *did* know. But this fascinating problem she surely was going to solve.

Which was not Wongai's way of looking at it at all. By marrying the daughter of the proud chief he had cemented Wypali and the important village of Tulu to him for all time. As to the rest, the girl, a hefty wench, should make a good enough wife. And he would see she earned her keep in the gardens.

Miria had other views.

The surly Wongai was presently to learn that the joys of harem are not all they are made out to be.

Especially with a Petula and a Miria to stir up trouble for their lord, even though he be the reincarnation of a cultural hero and friend of the great War God.

CHAPTER XVII

DOMESTIC BLISS WAS NEVER LIKE THIS

With the coming of the sou'-east season the storms died away, sunlight bathed blue again the Coral Sea. Eagerly the people of all the islands thronged the coasts and reefs seeking the fish coming in ever-increasing numbers, while the women and lesser clansmen tilled the gardens.

Wongai gave almost all his attention to the gardens. The men would joy in the fishing, Wongai would joy in the gardening—to immeasurably strengthen his hold on these people, for he would teach them how to develop a much-needed source of food.

The warriors saw nothing demeaning in the big chief working in the gardens. It was natural for him to do so, for he was Wongai, lieutenant of Sida, God of the Crops. When sterner business called, he again would become Wongai, friend of Kwoiam, God of War. Meanwhile they took to the canoes and combed the reefs with fish-spear, line, net, and trap, eagerly anticipating the coming of the turtle and dugong seasons.

Wongai had long since planned.

And one plan was to bring considerably more man labour into developing gardens. He did this easily by ordering all the men of the almost despised Shovel-nosed Skate clan to garden work. And the clan liked it. For it presently gave them a standing in the community they had never enjoyed before.

A hard taskmaster, he worked not only to enlarge but to bring new gardens under cultivation, to increase the crops of banana and yam, of komala, the sweet potato, of manioc and sour-sap.

His workers proved very willing, their interest rapidly quickening.

Soon, in the canoes fishing at sea, in the villages at night, all were eagerly discussing the rejuvenation of the gardens, the new lands being brought under cultivation, the strange new methods Wongai was teaching. And for this news all had to listen to the women, whose conversation had never been so popular before, and who made the most of it. And to the despised men of the Shovel-nosed Skate clan, who never had been popular at all, which was probably the reason why this peaceable clan was noted for saying very little. Later, odd men of the Dog clan began drifting to the gardens, Wongai immediately finding jobs for all. The gardens responded noticeably. What a great boon it was going to be that Wongai had been reincarnated by Sida to teach them the secrets of Mother Earth. Already the bee-eaters in swift flocks were flying north.

The glorious star Kaek had appeared, the Waur, the sou'-east wind had come, soon the eagerly awaited fruits would ripen. Enthusiastically they discussed what crops of yams the Usiam and Taigai stars would bring — never had the people taken such an interest, a growing pride in their gardens. But then, they had never before had Wongai to teach them.

For some months now no war-boo had bellowed its challenge from Moa. The people chuckled when they glanced across the waterway at the charred posts, the burnt-out patch where Moa village had once stood.

There was only one regret from that victory. The chief Kabara had not been killed. That very morning he with the pick of his fighting men had left Moa to take part in a ceremony held by an inland village.

All Badu laughed, though, at the report of the thunderstruck visage of the noted chief when he returned and gazed upon the wreck of what once had been his pride, and the largest village on Moa.

Thinking deeply on revenge, Kabara collected his outlying Italagas together and energetically set them to. rebuilding the village of Moa. And warned his villages of Totolai, Dabu, A-dam, Dualud, Waira, and Zurzur to look to their defences.

One of the few who had escaped the massacre happened to be one of the watchers of the gates. When Kabara caught him he used him for shark-bait — alive!

On Pulu, where the smoke of the Sacred Fires ever coiled slowly skyward, the matter of the gardens was being discussed in Council, every move of Wongai faithfully retailed by the sorcerer Barza, he who had taken the place of Enoko.

Uneasily, the Zogo-le puzzled over the matter. More and more it appeared as if this Lamar really was the reincarnation of Wongai, lieutenant of Sida, God of the Crops, beloved of Kwoiam, God of War. Now certainly beloved of the peoples of Badu and Mabuiag.

From whence this escaped convict, cast up by the sea, had won his love of gardening, his knowledge of tools and timber work, time has left us no record. Perhaps he had been son to an English yeoman on an English farm. Perhaps transported for poaching. As to tools and timber and rock-building, he would learn that the hard way in the convict gangs. But certain it is that he had a deep love and knowledge of the earth.

But his ambitions had to be greatly curtailed, to his frowning disgust. Lack of tools.

What simple tools they had were of wood, bone, stone, or shell. And for gardening these were merely a digging stick, a shell as a scoop, their hands, and a basket.

The simplest gardening operation was not only inefficient and laborious, but ate up something very precious—time!

Well into the night now he kept the tribe at work, teaching them how to make hoes, picks, shovels, rakes of wood and bone and shell, making blades of the big strong shells so plentiful on the coral reefs.

Even this essential work ate up—time.

Each evening people from adjoining villages came and watched.

And Wongai impressed upon these that they, too, must start the good work in their own villages.

But it would be a long time before each village had made its own "modern" implements. How much time must pass before he had every village trained to agriculture, every village ground under real cultivation!

As time passed, the impatient Wongai realized what time could mean.

There had been a time when day by day dragged by, each a never-ending step down the long road to hell. But now—the days were *flying* by!

As the sunny months sped by, bringing their seasonal shoals of fish to fill the bellies of the people, still more of the lesser clansmen came to work in the growing gardens, now the boast of village after village. Even so, it was nothing like the labour Wongai was so anxious to throw into tool-making and cultivation. But he could do nothing about it. These people had to live, and to live must be constantly active at the fishing.

Though there was abundance of fish in the seas all had to be caught, speared, netted, or trapped. So in other work only a few men in the clans were proficient, while most considered such work beneath their dignity. Beside which, time must be found for rigid ceremonial life. Not only the mysticism of the Zogo-le but the happy ceremonies and dances ushering in the yam season, the sardine season, the kingfish season, the turtle season, the dugong season, the wongai season of the wild plums—time taken up in eagerly preparing for the many dances symbolizing magic and mourning, war, cultural heroes, largesse of sea and earth. And the very important initiation ceremonies.

And Wongai grudgingly realized that he must not interfere with mystic, and ceremonial, and "play" life. In fact, he was expected to take part.

Meanwhile, his seldom pleasant temper was further exasperated by discord in his domestic circle.

For Miria was disappointed. Angrily so. And when a high-spirited girl like Miria, daughter of a chief, becomes angry, then someone must suffer. And Miria saw to it that the chief sufferer was Wongai, though not caring a gnat who else got hurt in the process. A cunning process. Irritating woman's guile, and wiles, smiles and "don't care" and "I won't" and sulks, even to downright insubordination. That is, to the point where

Wongai was about to grab her by the scruff of the neck and kick her out of her hut. She did not want that of course, because that was just what the other women wanted.

This powerful lump of a savage-tempered brute had not turned out to be in the least what her dreams whispered—the great chief, the reincarnation-of-a-spirit husband, should be. Not even. an ordinary sort of lover. While instead of her queening it over all the other women in the village, he expected her to do her share of the housework, and slave in the gardens as well. She, Miria, daughter of a chief, wife to Wongai, chief of chiefs of all Badu! Bah! And Miria spat in disgust.

A nice girl, Miria, when a good girl. Pretty, with laughing brown eyes and bewitching smile, a girl made to be loved and made much of, not made into a garden slave.

Miria was not going to have her shapely shoulders hardened into callouses through carrying heavy burdens, develop a kink in her athletic back through bending over a wooden hoe. Her shapely hands and fingers made for combing her lovely hair and plaiting love charms round seductive limbs were not going to be turned into stubby talons through clawing holes in hard earth so that a seed might grow—oh, no! Not on your life! Not even for a bad-tempered reincarnated son of a sour-tempered bull dugong—and one hated by the Zogo-le, too!

A smart girl, Miria. Dangerously smart—dangerous to herself, had she only cared. She was to care—too late.

For a while she had played ball. There was no more willing worker in the gardens. Hers the merry laugh, the joyous repartee that kept all within hearing in laughter and chatter that had so much lightened the labour. And the big chief had been pleased, had even praised her and growled a joke with her now and then.

But Miria soon learnt that he was not pleased with her because of her charms, he was only pleased because she set such a good example to others—she was a decoy to urge others to work. All *he* did was prowl from garden to garden, supervising the labours.

So Miria took to reclining under a shady tree, combing her hair and entwining bright flowers in it. And Wongai promptly ordered her back to labour, frowning at the bad example she was setting others.

Miria, one morning, had pouted and refused. Deliberately, Wongai had pulled up a stake. She saw by his face he would have thrashed her in front of all those onlookers. She would have fought him with tooth and claw had they been alone in the hut. But she, a chief's daughter, could not stand the indignity of being thrashed before others.

She worked now only when she had to. And as she worked she

schemed. While in their domestic life, in a way that women have, she made all the trouble she could. And that was some—with four women and a bad-tempered man to work upon in the same hut.

At times Wongai was driven to the verge of violence at the bickerings of the women. "Miria would not do this!" "Would not do her share of that!" "All she thought about was titivating herself, the stuck up —!"

To which Miria would reply with a self-satisfied shrug of disdain. Until Wongai would roar that he wanted just one more word—!

Mek and Naina would cower, silently creep under their sleeping-mat. Miria would hum a song, titivating herself unconcernedly. Petula would remain silent, always the silent one—with her eyes of hate.

The women loved it—such fearful joy, goading a tiger. And Mek and Naina would so love to see that stuck-up Miria taken down a peg—there must come big trouble some time. They had nothing against the great chief—they were far too much in awe of him—never ceased to wonder at their luck in being the wives of such a mighty man. Though loving the constant domestic intrigues, they took humble delight in ministering to his every want. As all good wives should.

As to Petula—no one quite knew what Petula thought, except that she hated her husband, the chief Wongai. Just because he had killed her husband, Sisi the chief.

Which seemed an absurd point of view to his wives Mek and Naina—and Miria.

Yes, though Wongai had eaten men, though he could command a thousand fighting men who would exult in following him anywhere, he was glad at times to depart in growling anger from his own home.

CHAPTER XVIII

THE ABANDONED SHIP

As the calmer, warmer weather brought the turtle and dugong and Wongai season the people grew lively and fat, with more time on their hands. Wongai heard eager murmurs among the warriors to carry on the war against Moa. Then came an embassy of chiefs beseeching him to lead them and the men of Mabuiag against A-dam village on Moa.

He frowned, played for time. He assured the chiefs the time was not ripe, ordering them to tell the people he was planning a blow that would cripple Moa.

Back in the hut, in the thoughtful hours, night after night he brooded. He must wield Badu and Mabuiag firmly under his hand—ever careful how he intrigued against the jealously watchful Zogo-le. He dearly wished to bring all land capable of cultivation upon Badu to bearing, to train the people in the working of timber, to teach them to build the big war-canoes into almost ships, to train them to fight on sea as well as on land. While against him were their infernal dances and cere- monies, their laughter-loving disposition.

What a task!

Time!

To war against Moa would eat up yet more time, besides delaying his cultivation plans. He was not afraid of Moa any more, despite Kabara and the population. He had numerous trained men now; with their discipline they were more than a match for Moa. But his warrior clans had realized the fact, too. Night after night the war-drums throbbed, the dancing warriors crazy to try their new-won skill again against Moa. Whereas he planned. to subdue Moa in his own good time.

Time!

Staring at the coals upon the clay fire-pan he frowned. And Sisi's hideously-faced skull leered above him, as slowly, so very slowly, it spun at the end of its string.

Time!

Iron! If only he had iron, iron tools, iron with which to *make* tools.

How valuable was time.

How valuable was iron.

He had never given thought to these everyday things before. He had hated iron, for it had chained his ankles, and hated time, for it seemed never-ending. And now one was slipping away while the other was unprocurable.

Iron. Apart from heads, the most eagerly sought thing in all the Coral Sea. Iron could only come from the wreck of a "Lamar canoe", a "spirit ship". And it was the war-canoes of Kebisu that seized almost all the wrecks.

Wongai frowned. Kebisu! That sea-warrior cropping up again and again to thwart his plans.

To defeat Time he must possess iron, iron for weapons, iron to make tools to till gardens and make ships.

Iron only came from wrecks. Wrecks were only found in the sea. And Kebisu's sea rovers *commanded* the sea!

He soon had startling proof.

One starlit evening, under the village palms he was holding court when all hearkened to the distant blast of a boo.

It came again, a hoarse, long-drawn-out bellow.

A war-boo!

Again its warning, then another joined in, another—another—another.

From seaward, back towards Mabuiag—an attack?

Like the lifting of grass in the wind every soul arose, hushed and listening.

There could be only one meaning—an attack by Moa on Mabuiag.

Wongai shouted an order and Karmala the broad-chested filled his lungs with air, then lifted a war-boo to thick, pouted lips. And out upon the night sped the deep hoarse boom, at such close quarters like the challenge of a bull.

Answered by village after village along the shores of Badu.

The call to arms!

Defiantly answered from village after village upon Moa until the long narrow waterway reverberated with challenge and counter-challenge

But neither side attacked. Each stood by to see what the other would do—was doing

Several hours later a light canoe came racing down the waterway. The messenger leapt out and rushed to Wongai, gasping, "The men of Mabuiag have captured a great Lamar canoe—the men of Kebisu are taking it from us—come quickly!"

A ship! A captured ship! Wongai's eyes grew wide.

"There are but three war-canoes of Kebisu," gasped the messenger, "and Kebisu himself is not with them. But they drove us off our ship! They are looting her now, smashing everything up and loading their canoes!"

Only three war-canoes of Kebisu's feared men! All hands rushed to the canoes.

They raced down the waterway, canoes from village after village joining in. While the people of Moa gazed bewildered, that mass of canoes were racing not towards them, but straight down the waterway towards the open sea.

And just off the coast they saw the ship, tall masts a maze of rigging, idly flapping sails beautifully silhouetted against a clear, starlit sky.

A roar of frenzied delight from the crews as they surged forward like hounds already feeling their fangs in the prey.

To Wongai's amazed though puzzled delight he soon saw the ship was not a wreck. With all sails set, she obviously was unharmed.

With the breeze dying down, she had struck the cap of a reef, gently sliding up on it. The crew had panicked, had taken to the boats. At high tide the ship had floated off, the tide and wisp of a breeze had carried her down here. An unharmed ship, she was Wongai's for the taking, a prize beyond his wildest dreams.

He stood up and roared at his canoes, trying to get some order out of this hysterical mob, urging the war-canoes to the front.

But all surged on, the big canoes scattered among a medley of fishing and light canoes packed with shrieking fools ignorant of discipline at sea, every man passionately anxious to reach the prize first.

Dark figures were now visible scurrying upon the deck and soon came a roar of contemptuous defiance. As one man Wongai saw the right arm of every man aboard raised high with clenched fist, heard thrice repeated the solid stamp of feet. Then the figures broke up, busily throwing spoil down into canoes.

Thus, for the first time, Wongai heard the defiance of Kebisu's men, and recognized discipline. Again he shouted and beckoned, urging his vessels into fighting order for the mob of little canoes masked all chance of manoeuvre of his large armed canoes. Though there were but three of Kebisu's vessels, Wongai wished to take them with as little loss as possible for the sake of prestige. He had no doubt of the ultimate result, for this mass of canoes would swamp them. What a chance! To take three of Kebisu's war-canoes—he might never get such a chance again. And then he would have the ship and firearms and all in her, all and more than he had been dreaming of these months past.

And now they were quite close to the ship, could see the dark figures sliding down her sides.

Wongai roared to cut them off and his leading canoes swerved with a howl to intercept this apparently easy prey.

It was only when the three canoes shot out from beside the ship that

Wongai realized their size and efficiency. Each two-masted, with huge matting sails, the fighting platforms spread well out over the water above the paddlers below.

The canoes had been forest giants hollowed out by the canoe builders of New Guinea, the depth added to by planks loop-holed for arrow fire. Men could stand upright down there and fight and not even their heads be visible. The sails were tautening under the light breeze but the canoes forged ahead under paddles, pulling with perfect rhythm. Upon the fighting-platform stood befeathered warriors, long bows to hand, armed too with lance, club, and cassowary-bone dagger. A tough nut to crack, these three, and now Wongai keenly admired their fighting formation.

In the form of a triangle, each canoe nearly within bowshot of the others. No matter which canoe was attacked, both others with the easiest movement could bring arrow fire upon the attacker. In perfect formation, moving at exactly the same speed, and they were not actually running away. Keeping straight on their course, the paddlers were conserving their strength. They would carry straight on, simply fighting their way if necessary—but they would carry straight on.

Wongai dimly began to realize how Kebisu on his tiny, barren islet, with a fleet of canoes such as these and manned by such disciplined seamen-warriors, could and actually did command the entire Coral Sea.

Fiercely he desired these three great canoes and the spoil in them, exultantly he seized this fine chance of striking a blow at the sea chief. These three canoes could not escape, the breeze was too light, they were too heavily laden with loot. His canoes were empty except of men, they could encircle these canoes then overwhelm them by flood of numbers. There would be a savage fight, but his men were howling for fight.

He shouted at his scattered war-canoes, roared them to follow him, to paddle fast and get ahead of Kebisu's canoes. He raised his voice above a shrieking bedlam to the fishing canoes ordering them to fall back then come up astern and crowd the flanks of the enemy, but not attack until his war-canoes outdistanced the enemy, then came about and rushed down to the attack.

In a yell of war-song, his paddlers strained to take the lead.

CHAPTER XIX

THE CUTLASSES

Wongai, urging his war-canoes ahead, did not notice in the confusion that his smaller canoes were racing to attack. Only when the deep-throated war song of Kebisu's men rose above the din did he glance astern—too late. A hundred bowstrings twanged and death flicked straight down into packed humanity. Howls of pierced men, crash of colliding canoes, men leaping overboard to dodge a following flight of arrows. A roar of laughter from Kebisu's men while their big canoes forged steadily on.

Wongai went berserk, only to make confusion worse confounded. The smaller canoes fell away, their men sheltering in the water, madly resentful that their war-canoes had not helped them. While the war-canoes now drifted undecided, to contemptuous jibes from Kebisu's men. The infuriated Wongai again by gesture and voice urged his war-canoes forward, still determined to get well ahead then turn about and bear down upon the enemy.

His men commenced to obey but Wongai felt the vim had gone out of them. Good fighters on land, good at sea if against their own quality, Kebisu's disciplined men had them beaten. Had Kebisu been aboard he certainly would now have turned upon and routed them.

After strenuous paddling Wongai had almost gained position to attack when a piercing yell drew their attention astern. To see a dull flame creeping skyward. An exultant roar from Kebisu's men—they had fired the ship before leaving!

A blaze shot up. Trickles of flame licked up the rigging, lurid grew the blaze below now belching up and out of the hold—a sail caught alight—then another.

Swiftly the blaze illumined the sea, creeping out—as now to them came a growing hum of fire. And an agonized howl from the canoes as they saw black dots leaping overboard down to many canoes. The men of Moa! While Wongai was chasing Kebisu's men, the Moans had sailed out to exultantly loot the ship.

To a howl of thwarted fury Wongai's men commenced paddling back to the vessel to destroy the accursed Moans looting *their* ship! To derisive laughter from the Kebisu canoes.

Wongai knew the fight was over. He roared his men back to the ship to save what they could.

Before they got there the ship was an inferno. The Moans, retiring, howling triumph and laughter.

Away out from the heat, Wongai's men watched the blazing vessel rivalling the rising sun as it burned to the water's edge. Wongai helplessly watching what could have saved him from Time plunging to the bottom in a cloud of steam and smoke. His dull fury aggravated as they paddled dolefully away to chant of the death wail—mournful dirge to welcome a home-coming.

The small canoes had lost forty men, others would die of wounds.

Wongai, through no fault of his own, had suffered his first defeat.

He ground his teeth, sensing the Zogo-le would turn it to account against him.

The people, though, would be difficult to stir. For though Wongai was friend to Kwoiam, their War God was a god of war upon earth, not upon the sea.

He had barely landed at Badu village when he learnt for the first time that the men of Mabuiag had saved many great "Lamar knives", precious "toorook" (iron) from the ship.

He ordered his bodyguard straight back to his own war-canoe, unappreciative of the lovely morn as they sailed round the coast to Mabuiag.

The little island was in a fever of excitement. The Mabuiag men had taken thirty-two cutlasses from the ship. It was while gleefully playing with these that Kebisu's three canoes had stolen upon them, boarded the ship and driven them away.

Wongai savagely wished to commandeer those cutlasses so proudly exhibited; what could he not do with that steel!

But he realized he dare not seize this precious treasure. Three men already lay dead, cleft through the skull in dispute over ownership. These weapons of steel were of far more value to the owners than their weight in gold would have been to us. There were only two things that might buy, possibly, a cutlass; one was a large canoe, the other a head. And it must be a warrior's head—of supreme value to the man who had not a head— apart from his own.

After solemn conclave, the thirty-two lucky ones presented the chief Wongai with a cutlass as a token of appreciation to his friend, their War God, Kwoiam.

Wongai accepted the gift, made at a great sacrifice.

He remained at Mabuiag for the triumph dance and feast, then sailed back to Badu to take his part in the mourning ceremonies for the dead.

And at night squatted in his hut, the cutlass across his knees, dreaming dreams.

Iron dreams.

As a weapon the cutlass was greatly to be desired. And as such certainly would add to his prestige. But its only use was for killing men. And he had an armoury of savage yet efficient weapons for doing that!

No. This long, heavy blade cut up into short lengths could make so many knives, so many chisels. With them he could commence the building of things, timber work for larger canoes particularly. Again and again he measured the blade, estimating what lengths he could cut from it to make the most tools with least waste. He had no doubt that he would. find a method of cutting the blade into lengths.

He fell into a brown study. With those other cutlasses he could fashion sufficient tools to set Badu village at work with tools of steel. To control other islands than Badu he had bitterly learned he must possess larger canoes. He had seen what great use of planking was made by Kebisu in enlarging his giant canoes. Kebisu got his planking from wrecks, because he controlled the sea.

Wongai must have tools to hew his planks from the timber of Badu.

There were no forest giants on Badu, these must still be traded for from New Guinea. But by enlarging his canoes he could trade himself. He now fully realized how dependent Badu was for many things by trade along slow and tortuous channels. And Badu could only buy the "left-overs" from Kebisu's great trading venture every year.

He lapsed again into a brown study. Those thirty cutlasses. There were only two things that could buy any one of them. A large canoe, or a warrior's head.

Thirty canoes! Impossible. Thirty heads?

For long he pondered. But he always came back to those thirty heads.

Then—he smiled grimly, fingering the edge of the cutlass. Men of Moa would supply the heads!

CHAPTER XX

THE HEADS

But, while Wongai planned, the possessors of the cutlasses were the proudest, the most envied of the warriors of Mabuiag. Thirty great knives of the Lamars! Spirit weapons! Invincible!

Day and night the owners fondled their weapons, whirling them through the air at imaginary foes, feeling the thrill in the grip of the hilt while the men, women, and children gazed on, goggle-eyed.

Ah, but to handle a dangerous weapon develops the hunger to use it!

It was the Council of the Zogo-le who did the actual planning, seized the opportunity to counteract a little the influence of that accursed Wongai.

Upon Moa Island, upon its northern shore, nestled the small village of Obernud. And the men of Mabuiag, by virtue of reciprocal fishing rights just off its shores, had always enjoyed more or less amicable relations with this small sub-tribe.

That village only comprised forty heads. That is, warriors' heads.

Mabuiag sent the chief a message of peace to come with his people to celebrate a great feast in honour of Mabuiag "taking the Lamar ship". In view of their long friendship, the chiefs of Mabuiag wished on this festal occasion to commemorate their friendship by a gift to the people of Obernud—a precious gift of toorook, Lamar iron. As a gesture of their regard, they begged the chief to accept a token.

A cutlass!

Breathlessly the timid people of Obernud examined this priceless gift. For some days their qualms held caution in the balance. But the sight of that steel set their hearts beating—who but knew that the gift of toorook promised at the feast might mean more wonder weapons such as this!

"If only you will come," promised the envoy impressively, "we will give you plenty of iron—*plenty!*"

They accepted. Dressed in their simple best, a bath of coconut oil and a grass skirt. Manned their little canoes and sailed.

They were greeted at Mabuiag by welcoming blasts of the boo, and lavishly entertained. The girls of Mabuiag wore their brightest smiles, prettiest flowers in their hair.

In the friendliest fashion the first day went by, piles of foods were carried to the cooking fires. The first night of dancing was enjoyed by all. Came the day of the great feast. That night, after the squad dances, the wonderful, the mysterious present was to be given these honoured guests from Obernud. They saw, examined, envied the cutlasses laid out in state on the house platform of the chief of chiefs of Mabuiag. Every man among them hoped, longed, that one of these wonderful cutlasses would be for *him*.

And the men of Mabuiag strongly hinted that such would be a certainty.

Upon adjoining Pulu rose smoke from the Sacred Fires, drums throbbed in honour of the occasion.

Came starlight night, dancing, sweet chant of girlish voices, a dense circle of people squatting down singing and feasting, applauding the squads of dancers.

And an indefinable "something" surging through all that crowd, hundreds of gleaming eyes, flash of smiling teeth, a feverish thrill of a big "something" that was to mark the finale of the feast, a finale, some whispered to the guests, a finale in which their honoured guests would take the star part.

Eagerly they, guests and all, awaited the grand finale.

In the centre of the circle sat the people of Obernud, full-bellied, laughing, happy, their minds at ease.

And now amongst them, jokingly bearing steaming piles of foodstuffs came the thirty heroes, they who had taken the cutlasses from the Lamar ship. As a gesture of supreme honour, they themselves would serve Mabuiag's guests of Obernud.

No sign of weapon upon them of course—for each man's cutlass was hidden under his grass skirt.

As their guests held up their hands for the food came the blast of a boo—the food fell upon upturned faces, thirty cutlasses flashed in the flame light and to shocking thuds the massacre commenced. To screams and shouts it was over in moments. Every man of Obernud lost his head.

Their chief lost more—his prized cutlass as well.

When a messenger came running to Wongai, gasping of the "triumph" of the Mabuiag men Wongai was shocked. Not at the treacherous massacre, but at the fact that every owner of a cutlass now possessed a head-a warrior's head!

How infinitely more valuable those cutlasses were now! So quickly had they proved invincible—those spirit weapons of the Lamars.

Wongai ground his teeth in impotent anger. He could not think of anything he could now offer that would buy those weapons for tools.

He had not struck in time.

Only when through Kosabad, through the channels of intrigue, he learnt of the quiet satisfaction of the Zogo-le at the affair, only when he witnessed their efficient methods of boosting across all Badu Island the prowess of the Mabuiag fighters who in a night had taken forty heads to recompense for the forty heads their beloved allies had lost in the "chief Wongai's sea battle", did he grimly ponder.

From then on, cautiously but with the concentrated energy and cunning that was much of his strength, he delved deeply into intrigue, and the secrets of native poisons.

He might need both.

Another man, too, was thinking of poisons—Barza, in the sorcerer's hut.

Barza was a good poisoner, almost as good as Enoko had been. But. Barza was disturbed. He had tried to poison the snake, Enoko's totem snake.

He had failed.

Squatting in the gloom of his hut Barza pondered on the: snake. The thing was there, glaring at him from across the clay fire-pan, its, crimson throat all fiery from reflected glow. The thing came, and was gone, when he least expected it. It appeared at startling moments, it vanished instantly—as if knowing the moment when an act of harm was meant against it. It had abandoned its hole in the hut floor—after Barza came. Barza had craftily watched, but failed to see it go to its hole outside, could find no hiding-place among the roots of the trees.

He had tempted it with bait of a live rat cleverly poisoned inside. A live frog, a poisoned bird. The devilish thing had ignored the baits, even though he had tied the terrified rat where it would be right under the brute's ugly nose.

He had tied a rat, bird, and frog outside the hut. By morning each bait would have died of slow poisoning. By night the snake would be glaring across at him.

He had tempted it with warm, poisoned milk. Had tempted it in all the cunning ways his cunning mind could devise.

It had ignored every bait.

Barza was keenly disappointed. Not only because he had failed to poison the snake, but because of the experiment. He never had had cause to poison a poisonous snake before, had never known it done. It would be interesting to see a poisonous snake writhing under the effects of poison. Particularly *this* snake—Enoko's totem snake. To sit smoking the zoob and watch as Enoko's spirit fought to hold life within the snake, to watch the snake die hard while Enoko's spirit was unwillingly forced from its temporary home before its time—yes, Barza would love to watch Enoko's spirit struggling thus.

How helplessly furious Enoko's spirit would be, forced to leave before it had done its job—whatever that job might be.

Smoking his zoob, yet again Barza wondered why Enoko still remained within his totem snake—what *was* the reason?

He could find no reason.

Drawing deeply at the zoob mouthpiece, his mind wandered back again to how to poison this snake!

Of course he would do it, Barza the Silent never failed.

The snake's head swayed slightly, its. tongue slithered out, hissed.

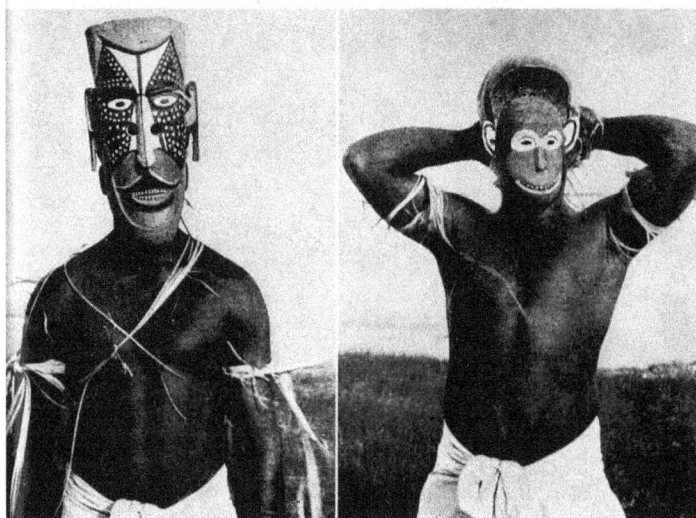

A BAY OF MABUIAG
MASKED MEN OF BADU

CHAPTER XXI

THE GIANT

As a new sou'-east season advanced, bringing its rotation of the crops, Wongai's gardens yielded more and more, carrying his mana ever higher. He slaved, not sparing others. While in the evenings, under the palms reflecting the light of the fires, he was studying-geography.

His geography.

A large circle had been cleared upon the ground. In the centre a stone, representing Badu. Opposite, a larger stone, Moa, nor'-west of Badu a very much smaller stone, Mabuiag. Around it its satellites, islets in the form of pebbles—Kulka, Pulu, Aipus, Kuongan, Marte, and other islets of the Zogo-le.

And then again, in correct geographical position off shore from Badu and Moa, pebbles representing the islets of Portlock, Tobin, Duncan, and others.

South of Moa, running west to Duncan Island, a long, crescent-shaped stick representing Long Reef. From the Mabuiag islets, running near north to Turnagain Island, long, curved sticks represented the big Orman's Reefs, smaller sticks the numerous smaller reefs.

The native map-makers chose each stone and stick in proportion to the island, islet, reefs, and sandbanks, each in geographical position, each at a correct distance apart. And told names of villages upon each inhabited island, the chiefs and people and manner of living.

Wongai, asking a question now and then, learning "his" island was but one of a group closely intermingled, with their warring people, peaceable people, their distinct fishing grounds, their trade rights, their culture from the naked savage to the Zogo-le.

Several nights later the map-makers again got to work, and thus Wongai learnt that his island group was but one of three, comprising possibly one hundred islands, stretching for a hundred miles between Cape York Peninsula and New Guinea. Eastward, the map was bounded by a long line of sticks running north and south, representing the Great Barrier Reef. At a point representing a hundred and twenty miles east of Badu, another group of stones was placed-Mer, Eroob, Ugar, with their smaller islands comprising the Eastern Group.

Kosabad assured Wongai that those people were very cultured, the islands of Mer and Eroob very lovely, with splendid gardens, for the soil was richer far than that of Badu and Moa. And on Mer dwelt the great

Zogo C'Zarcke, chief priest of a very powerful Zogo-le. While the grim little islets near by—Waiar and Dauar—were the headquarters of the dreaded sect of Waiat. These people owned large war-canoes, bought in trade through Kebisu from New Guinea. Each year they did a big trade with New Guinea, their vessels sailing with Kebisu's fleet.

Forty miles south of Moa, the map-makers placed another group of stones, representing Murralug, (Prince of Wales Island) largest island in the Strait, Horn Island, Hammond, Thursday, Friday, Entrance, Goode, Possession, and others of this group.

Piaquai was the chief of chiefs of the numerous Kowraregas of the Murralug Islands, explained Kosabad, but these islands were poor, neither coconut palms nor gardens grew there.

"Their people are but little above the savages of the Great South Land," broke in Sagigi contemptuously. "They have many canoes but few large war-canoes. For they can only depend by trade for canoes through the traders of Moa, who barter for them from the New Guinea canoe builders."

"They have even more difficulties and delays in trading than we have," added Bagari, "but they are only savages, anyway."

"So they are friends with Moa?" inquired Wongai.

"More, they are allies—but not of much importance."

"So. Have they ever attacked us?"

"But seldom," answered Sagigi. "We often wished they would," he added boastfully. "We would have hung their heads upon our sarokag poles. But a few picked men among them have helped the men of Moa at times."

Fifty miles east of Moa, Kosabad marked the long line of the Dungeness and adjoining reefs, running north to the great Warrior Reefs that spread away north almost to the shore of New Guinea. And on the southern end of the Warrior Reefs the map-makers placed a ridiculously small pebble.

"Tutu," explained Kosabad proudly, "Warrior Island."

For the Badu men were enviously proud, though they were enemies, of the Warrior men who ruled the sea. The little sea that washed their shores, the only sea in the world to them.

Wongai stared at this pebble that represented tiny, barren Warrior Island, headquarters of the redoubtable Kebisu. Kosabad assured him the island, but a few feet above high water, was so barren that there was practically no fresh water. Many shells of the giant clam were laid out below the scraggly pandanus palms. A bamboo cut as a trough was laid against the trunk and into each shell. Thus, when it rained, the rain trickled along the pandanus branches and down the trunk into the bamboo trough which led the water into its shell basin.

According to his custom, Wongai listened while Kosabad explained Yam Island in detail. Revered in island lore for its stories of the gods, Segar and Kulka, Bomai and Malu, and the Waliserser Shrine, Kebisu treasured it particularly for its spring of water, for it had no strategical advantage to the seaman chief. A few little hills, about three hundred feet in height, with huge grey boulders scattered here and there across the island, some poised one upon the other.

"The Giant's Marbles," broke in Bagari, "the first Giant threw them there like that when he was playing."

To Wongai's puzzled expression, Kosabad nodded gravely and explained, "That is so, or it is our story. It happened long, long ago, when the men from the skies, Abob and Kos, built the Great Sai. The Great Sai is a wall of rock built in the sea enclosing much of the coast of Eroob. That wall has openings into a maze of smaller walls. And into these stone-wall pits, every tide brings fish of the sea, and leaves them there. Even turtle, and sometimes a dugong. All that the people of Eroob need to do for their fish is to walk down to the Sai and get them. That stone wall built in the sea has stood against the storms ever since. When Abob and Kos finished it they built other works upon other islands, then, with the great Segar, returned to the skies again. But one giant remained, he was only the most lowly labourer of all their labourers. But he loved earth life, he asked permission to remain and live again as an earth-man. He was the Father of the Giants, the ancestor of the Giant today."

Sensing by Wongai's silence that he looked upon this merely as some childish folk legend Kosabad shook his head in solemn denial.

"It is a true story," he insisted. "A Giant lives today on Giant Island. Truly, he is 'father' of only sixty people, poor fishers. And he is not the Giant of old. He is very small compared to them. And he could not even move one of the Giant's Marbles, let alone lift them up one upon another. But he is a Giant, all the same."

Wongai nodded gravely, though passing over this story merely as legend. As the map took shape he began gradually to realize in what a strategic position was Warrior Island, how utterly dependent for life were its people upon the sea, and how necessary for existence that a line of fierce chiefs should build their warrior people into a compact sea force that could hold in check their big neighbours merely by commanding the right way of sea and land trade in this little sea.

Just to the north of the Warrior Reefs the map-makers drew a long boundary that they called "Dowdee", New Guinea. And that was the end of their world to the north. A land of mystery, as at that day it was to all white sailormen also.

From the top of the map, the north, they now worked away down to the bottom, the south. And here jutted a cape.

"The Great South Land," explained Kosabad.

And Wongai recognized Cape York Peninsula, northernmost tip of the Australian coast. It was up along there that he had sailed—it seemed now a long time ago.

Deeply, Wongai studied this map, the islanders' world-now *his* world. Hemmed in eastward by the Great Barrier Reef, on the north by New Guinea, the west by the Arafura, the south by the "Great South Land".

Only Wongai knew, *thought* he knew, what lay far away down to the south. He frowned, his mind clouded by "the terror of Civilization", where Bishop Ullathorne had said "the cruelties practised here make demons of men". How were Kosabad and Sagigi and Bagari to know in their puzzled silence that behind the big chief's frowning face was the sweat and searing hopelessness of men building their own gallows, gaunt, fierce human beasts quarrying walls of stone that shut them in? To the renegade's haunted mind the "Great South Land" faded to the Norfolk hell.

As the days and nights dreamed by the map-makers, absorbed in their job, added other islands and reefs, right across the Coral Sea to New Guinea.

Albany Island, the Two Brothers, Dugong, Naghir, the Three Sisters, Giant—

"Giant?" inquired Wongai.

"Yes."

"Why?"

"Because the Giant *lives* there," answered Kosabad simply. "There is no other man like him," he added with an expressive gesture. "He is bigger than the three biggest men in all the islands. His club is so huge a strong man can hardly lift it, it is the butt of a tree that he pulled to earth with his own hands. When he swings that great club the strongest warrior trembles. When he roars down upon his enemies there is nothing left to do but to run—or stay and be smashed to pulp."

Story after story they poured out about this giant and his mighty deeds. Wongai listened more carefully, growing convinced that at least a "giant" of sorts must exist, some huge and powerful man. He was thinking of what such a man would look like as a bearer of the War Gud of Kwoiam. Such a man would appear a giant indeed in the towering and bizarre regalia of the War Gud. With a real giant to one side of him, the other bearer to his left, the giant swinging that great club and roaring, Wongai could charge down upon his enemies with his picked men howling behind him. No natives, he felt sure, would stand up to the terror of such a charge. The terror of Wongai, friend of the War God, Kwoiam, the giant and his club, and the War Gud—why, the fear of such an association alone might make the bravest enemies panic. He resolved to try to bribe this "giant" to come and live at Badu under the chieftainship of Wongai.

"And yet he is quiet and peaceful," broke in Sagigi eagerly. "It is only when they goad him up to fight that he grows so terrible. And he hasn't much brains. He just likes to lie in the shade and yawn, and eat and sleep and yarn, he is like a boy, he loves being told stories, loves to lie in the shade and laugh, loves to have his toes tickled. Of course, he never works. They bring all his food to him, the women quarrel for their turn to cook it, he eats as much as any six men. When he eats and sleeps in the shade on the beach the fishermen joke about his snores away out in their canoes, for he snores as loudly as a bull dugong."

This "giant" was obviously an island hero, admired far and wide, looked up to with terrified awe.

"And yet," explained Bagari, "he is not even a chief, he is too lazy. His people keep him as the most prized possession in the world. And so he was to them, for in the terror of his name they found safety. They were only a very small sub-tribe, and would have been mercilessly hunted had it not been for the Giant and his terrible club. With such a protector, they could go about their fishing and ceremonial life with bodies and minds at ease-except those who now and then were caught napping by raiders.

Author's Note: Years ago, when I was cruising about the Coral Sea collecting material, part of which has gone into this book, Dr Vernon of Thursday Island assured me that the Giant must have been well over eight feet tall. That wonderful old man, "the Doc", beloved of all in the Strait and of late years by the boy of the Kokoda Track, had examined some of the bones forwarded him by, I understand, an enthusiastic young schoolteacher of native children, young Hudson, stationed then by the Queensland Education Department on Moa Island. Unfortunately the skipper of the lugger sent to collect the bones only took a few to Thursday Island. Sufficient, though, for the "old Doc" to pronounce that the "Giant" had been a giant indeed, well over eight feet tall. The bones had lain there for many years, superstitiously regarded by the Islanders, on the spot where the Giant at last fell, cut to pieces, pierced by arrows, clubbed and clubbed again in his last great fight.

CHAPTER XXII

THE CASTAWAYS

The knowledge that his island was but one of a barely-known though tiny island "world" stirred strange ambitions in the outcast. In his convict days and throughout his escape he had dreamed of fleeing away to some far distant "South Sea" island, and there making himself a chief amongst a few savages. But how different was this!

Savages, yes. But intelligent. A compact society ruled by stringent laws. "Individual" tribes, but combining together when the safety of the Island was concerned. And again, of the main islands each was one of a group, with war and trade alliances. *He* was chief of something very different indeed to a mere mob of savages.

He might win more than *one* island.

Quieten Moa first. Then trounce that buccaneering chief, Kebisu. Which would open this sea, and possibly every island, to the canoes of Wongai of Badu.

But a shock was coming.

A great Lamar "war-canoe" was anchored off Mer!

Making friends with the Miriam people, giving them precious gifts of iron.

He was deeply disturbed.

What was a man-o'-war doing in these waters? Uneasily he wondered. She was still a hundred miles away—much too close. A week later, and news came that the war vessel was anchored off Eroob. And again its men were making friends with the people.

He became increasingly uneasy.

But when word came that she was cruising off Warrior Island but sixty miles nor'-east, he grew seriously alarmed.

Was it possible the man-o'-war was seeking him? Surely not. He had not been seen by a white soul since he had killed the Weasel.

Suddenly he remembered the burning whaler—they had fired at him!

But then—they had seen only his tiny vessel by the blaze of the ship— even if any had escaped they could never guess the shadowy outcast a thousand miles from civilization, was an escaped convict.

Ah, but the Zogo-le! And their telepathy from island to island! Might some native have given news to a passing ship?

Racked by seething fears, the chief Wongai became a terror to the islanders. Only his most trusted chiefs dared approach him.

And one morning-he saw the ship! From craggy Butai Pad. She was just visible, away out towards the Warrior Reefs, but much nearer Badu.

For hours he gazed towards her. She seemed to be just hovering about. Word was brought him that with her travelled too much smaller fighting ships that cruised away from her sometimes for days at a time. Just cruising among the reefs and islands.

He grew convinced that these were pinnaces or cutters seeking—him.

He called the chiefs of all villages together and harangued them, towering on his house platform, threatening with his war-club, savagely impressing upon them the deadly peril in which they stood. For Sida from the skies by spirit talk had warned him to expect a visit from the Lamars, Kwoiam had urged him prepare the people to kill any Lamar who set foot upon the sacred soil of Badu lest terrible woes befall them.

Well he understood now what fertile soil he had to work upon. For these people had ever dreaded the Lamars, those white-skinned spirits from the dead. Craftily he added new terrors. The Lamars would come upon them with the thunder-sticks that were irresistible, they would kill all the men, fire all the villages, take all the women, spread terrible diseases.

These people had never before needed urging to kill white castaways when opportunity offered. But now—

That night, squatting in his hut, taking snarling pleasure in the sleepless fear of his wives, he knew that even the resources of a man-o'-war would be strained to seize him. Every village from Badu, Mabuiag, across on Moa; too, would be alert, fearing attack from the dreaded Lamars.

These "Lamars" would never drag him back to the ankle chains—to the yard-arm.

He had done his work exceedingly well.

The islanders of Badu and Mabuiag and Moa, already greatly feared, were soon to be regarded with especial horror by occasional passing ships.

A week after Wongai had addressed the tribes, the man-o'-war sailed leisurely north, seemed to vanish.

He breathed freely again. She had missed him.

Yes, more unfortunate castaways would inevitably be killed.

And yet there was such a lot of "niceness" among those very men and women—Lu-esa, for instance.

Dreaming dreams.

Young Kartoy was away on Sacred Pulu training very hard for his First Degree. He had been there almost the complete round of the seasons now, with other initiates a close prisoner in the training Kwod under the watchful eyes of the Zogo-le.

Lu-esa sighed sometimes; she knew the training was terribly severe,, knew, too, that there were particular tests, very cruel, that the lads must pass through—things that women must never know.

But it would soon be over now, that is, the first trials that would prove him a worthy initiate of the Beizam, the Shark clan.

Soon Kartoy would pass his First Degree. Then he would be at liberty to return to Badu village, not yet a warrior, of course, but a member of the proud Beizam clan.

And then…

A member of the Beizam clan could make love, even to the daughter of a chief. And Lu-esa was daughter to Kosabad, chief under the chief of chiefs, Wongai, beloved of Sida.

Kartoy would soon return—how eagerly. Kartoy would make love to Lu-esa. How sweetly the sun-bird was calling!

Lu-esa, her eyes alight, gazed up at the two lovely little birds busy with their dainty nest high up in the flowering vine draping the big old palm-tree.

Lu-esa was dreaming dreams.

Several weeks later a whaleboat loaded with seventeen castaways perishing for water, landed near Tulu village on Badu. The villagers attacked like wolves and clubbed them to death. And sent a runner to the chief Wongai to come and see the seventeen Lamar heads dripping from their sarokag poles.

Grimly he received the news. There would be very little chance of any future castaways escaping the Badu natives to spread news of a strange white chief ruling these headhunters. But his satisfaction turned to dismay next day. For tracks upon the beach proved that two castaways had hidden in undergrowth, remained there all day within sight of the festivities round the sarokag poles. In dead of night they had crept to the beach, launched a canoe, and got clean away.

Wongai was dismayed. Had they seen him? They must have—when he and the Badu villagers had hurried to see the heads.

It was through these two lucky escapees that name of Wani (Wongai) the "Wild White Man of Badu", was first to become slowly known to shipping that sailed across the Strait, until eventually he was to become a hunted man again, to be shot on sight if possible.

Yes, the Great Chief Wongai had his worries. Lesser men had theirs, too. Barza the sorcerer was worried about the snake.

It left no tracks!

Barza had planned to track it to its home. But—it left no tracks.

For the last fortnight, though it had come night after night to the hut as if to taunt the man, it left no tracks, either coming or going.

Neither on the soft, moist loam round the hut, nor on the carpet of leaves was there ever sign of a track.

Even a totem snake must leave a track, should conditions be favourable. For the snake is still a snake, it is only that the spirit of a man for the time being breathes within the snake.

Barza went to all the trouble of carrying fine white sand and laying it in a circle completely round the hut.

But in the morning—there was no track. Nor on *any* morning.

Yet night after night the snake appeared, spying over the rim of the clay. fire-pan.

It began to get on Barza's nerves. That snake *must* leave a track.

Some time later, at sundown, Barza was returning to the hut, his mind obsessed by the snake that did not leave a track.

By the hut entrance he happened to glance up.

The snake was staring down at him-from a branch just over-hanging the roof.

For a startled moment the sorcerer stood, then cursed the snake long and vindictively.

CHAPTER XXIII

FEAR BRINGS THE CAT-O'-NINE-TAILS

A week after that massacre and the man-o'-war reappeared. Wongai prepared to take to the hills, certain she must have picked up those escapees and was now seeking him.

But she vanished in the direction of Ugar and Eroob and Mer, where she anchored again.

Finally she weighed anchor for Endeavour Strait by Cape York Peninsula. And anchored again by the Great South Land. She was combing the seas for him, Wongai felt certain. He longed for the approaching cyclone season that had brought him here. That season would take *her* away.

Petula watched him covertly, fearfully curious to discover the reason of his anxiety. If only she could discover what worried the great chief so she would add to his troubles with pleasure. How she wished she had been born one of the spirit-hearing people! But Sisi could not tell her, though his face, his luminous eyes seemed sardonically wise as he hung above the worried chief. Petula from her sleeping-mat watched Wongai as night after night he stared moodily at the coals upon the clay fire-pan. Ever and anon, too, he would lift an anxious head to listen.

And fear then was in his eyes.

Petula could not know that what haunted him was the faint clink of chains. For Petula, had she heard it, would have known it was but the clinking of coral pebbles rolled upon the shore by the playful tide.

But the man-o'-war was not seeking this escaped convict, now Wongai, chief of chiefs of all Badu and war-lord of Mabuiag. Those on board at that time were not even aware of his existence. She was H.M.S. *Fly*, Captain F. P. Blackwood, R.N., continuing ticklish survey work in this most treacherous of seas. Finally the *Fly* vanished into the Arafura, probably to the China Station, Wongai hoped in unspeakable relief. She had missed him. Her captain would report that he had combed the Coral Sea with no sign of an escaped convict amongst savages. He was safe for all time.

He could not read the courses of the stars—nor what time would bring.

For aboard the *Fly* was J. Beete Jukes, the naturalist, even now engaged in writing the *Narrative of the Surveying Voyage of* H.M.S. *Fly*, recommending the formation of a base on Cape York Peninsula.

"The mention of these circumstances [the wrecks of the *Hyderabad* and *Coringa Packet*] leads me naturally to enter on a subject which I believe an important one, namely, the propriety of establishing a post in Torres Strait, somewhat similar to that which has been formed at Port Essington. The reader, perhaps, will hardly be able fully to perceive the bearings of the case until he has read the two following chapters; but I will here briefly give my reasons for proposing such an establishment. Any one who casts his eye over the chart attached to this work will perceive that all vessels passing through Torres Strait will be compelled to come within sight of Cape York. Most vessels come up along shore from the southward, and go either through Endeavour Strait or the Wednesday Island passage, when they must, of course, pass within a mile or two of the Cape. Even, however, if they enter Torres Strait by Bligh's Entrance, between Anchor Key and Bramble Key, the widespread mass of reefs that stretch off the south coast of New Guinea will compel them to keep to the southward, either to Wednesday Island or the entrance of Endeavour Strait. Since the survey of these latter straits they have been shown to be by far the best exit from Torres Strait to the westward, and the only one to be recommended to large vessels. If, therefore, a post were established either at Cape York, or near the entrance of Endeavour Strait, a communication might be had with all shipping passing through, without causing them any detention, or deflecting them from their route a single yard. Now, as the entire trade of the South Pacific, with the whole of the Indian Ocean, must pass through Torres Strait, as the shortest and most practicable route, this facility of communication alone would be an immense advantage to that great and increasing commerce.

"However complete and accurate may be the survey of Torres Strait and the Coral Sea (that lying off the north-east coast of Australia), it must always remain a dangerous navigation. Slight accidents, such as hazy weather, mistakes in the reckoning, unknown errors in the chronometer or sextant, or want of completeness or soundness in the rigging or finding of the vessel (to say nothing of carelessness and incapacity in the navigator) will always cause a pretty high average of wrecks in the vessels passing through Torres Strait. In the greatest number of these cases, if not all, the vessel will merely be stuck upon a coral reef, with ample time to save the lives of the crew and passengers in the boats. These circumstances are of annual occurrence. At the present time the nearest points of refuge are Port Essington, 600 miles beyond Cape York, or Coupang in Timor, 500 or 600 miles still further to the westward. The land about Port Essington is so low and difficult to make out, that it may easily be missed or passed in the night, and when once passed cannot be regained against the wind, in a crowded and perhaps crazy boat. Many poor fellows, after undergoing great hardships, have thus been compelled to throw themselves on the hospitality of the small Dutch settlement at Coupang. Now a post at Cape York, or the neighbourhood, would not only render these long and perilous passages needless for a crew thus situated, but in many cases it would be able to send assistance to the wreck, if the boats could not contain all on board, or would be able to save some of the more valuable part of the cargo or ship's stores. Neither would the wrecked crews or passengers suffer much detention, as in a few days they might be forwarded by a passing vessel to some port in the East Indies, such as Singapore, for instance.

"To these two great advantages, facility of intercommunication and speedy and effectual aid in case of shipwreck, many minor ones might be added, such as the supplying of stores, provisions, gear or tackling, and above all, of *water* to the vessels passing by.

"In a military point of view such a post would be most valuable, and its importance is daily increasing with the augmentation of the commerce passing by this route. If a war were suddenly to break out, a small vessel belonging to an enemy would, by occupying the sea near Cape York, command the whole of our commerce between the South Pacific and the Indian Oceans. By stationing a look-out post on Mount Adolphus, she might be advertised by signals of the approach of all vessels, and of their number and character, and by making herself thoroughly acquainted with the neighbouring reefs and shoals, might easily pick out tortuous and dangerous channels, which would afford her refuge and means of escape from a force superior in strength to herself."

The period written of by Jukes was 1842-6, still in the time of the sailing ships, so dependent on the regular trade winds. With the advent of the steamship it was, of course, unnecessary for a steamship from the south coast of Australia to sail round the eastern coast to enter the Indian Ocean.

Jukes's suggestion bore fruit in 1863, when a semi-military naval post was established at Somerset, Cape York Peninsula, opposite Albany Island. Brave but unavailing attempts were made to build it into "another Singapore". However, under Jardine it fulfilled a very necessary service as Jukes had foreseen, The Residency, under Chester, was transferred to Thursday Island, opposite Prince of Wales Island (Murralug), in 1887, when the great pearlshell rushes were in full swing. As Jukes had foreseen, forts were built there, and in time a coaling station for warships.

To enliven Wongai's worries, Miria seized this critical time to play up with a vengeance, set the other wives at each other's throats, turned the hut into a brawling cat-fight when the big chief was absent, into a sneering, sulky hotbed of barely subdued animosity when he was present. Then placidly sat back to enjoy results.

Poor Miria. She was not to enjoy results for long. She was to *feel* them.

The infuriated Wongai, while prowling round the canoes laid up on the beach for repair, scowlingly watched old Guz-man squatting under a palm, calmly plaiting thongs into a rope for a dugong harpoon. The thongs had been, cut from dugong hide, worked by the deft fingers of old Guz-man into beautifully proportioned long, slim, tough thongs which when plaited together would make an unbreakable rope.

Dugong hide. Tough, pliable as the rhinoceros hide from which the old Boers made the sjambok, that cruel whip with which they sometimes flogged the Kaffirs.

Wongai was not thinking of a whip as he gazed at those long, rounded thongs of pliable hide. That is, not until he suddenly thought of—the cat-o'-nine-tails.

What a cruelly efficient cat-o'-nine-tails such thongs would make! *He* should know. The cat had come very close to taming *him!*

Frowning thoughtfully he squatted down beside old Guz-man, watching those deft fingers so unerringly fashioning a thong, so beautifully rounded where its weight would fall, tapering its length—tapering its length…

Slowly a grin of grim satisfaction spread upon Wongai's broad, harsh face, he licked ot lips as a cat would at some warm anticipation of feline delight.

With expressive visage he rose and strode away. Found himself a ball of native string, picked a nice little cane as a handle. Then mooned away and squatted under a shady tree. Just himself. Laughter from away back in the village. Hum of insects, sweet call of a bird. Lap of the tide on the beach by his feet.

With head bent over the string he became warmly interested in his job. There must have been humour in it, for every now and then his face expanded into one big chuckle, chest rumbled with subdued laughter.

When he had finished, he held up his handiwork to his own admiring eyes.

He had fashioned a perfect little model of a cat-o'-nine-tails.

Hiding it under his arm he took it back to old Guz-man. Squatted down beside the wrinkled old craftsman, carefully explained what he wanted done.

He wanted a cat-o'-nine-tails, a little one. Just a cruelly delicate little thing. Made out of dugong hide, just like this model. Guz-man thoughtfully handled the model, a frown of puzzled interest upon his wrinkled brow. He had never seen such a queer thing before, though it reminded him somewhat of the searching, twining, flexible feelers of a baby octopus. He wondered what the great chief wanted this for? What was its use? What work had it to do?

But his was not to question, his job was but to slowly, perfectly understand just what was required of him. Finally he nodded his grizzled old head.

Wongai rose up satisfied and walked serenely back to his hut, more peacefully calm than he had been for many a long day.

Miria, who had been playing the merry imp among the wives during his absence, glanced up with an innocent smile as her lord strode in through the open entranceway.

Miria wondered what had made the great hulking brute so pleased with himself. Ah, well! He would not be pleased for long! Not when he became embroiled in. the devil's brew of women's passions she had cooked for him here.

Old Guz-man spent a happy week on his intriguing task. And, like all craftsmen who love their work, turned out a perfect job. His reward was in gazing up at the big chief's face. As Wongai slowly handled that beautifully proportioned little whip his grim face gradually smiled, laughter gleamed in his fierce, wary eyes. Oh, what a lovely little Cat! How Miria would love it!

As caressingly he ran the thongs between his fingers he tingled to the feel of the cool, sleek, cruel hide. Ah, yes! Miria would tingle—warmly. She too would feel-the kiss in the sting of these thongs! The tiger-cat! She, and this Cat—they would understand one another—come so warmly close to one another.

"A good job, Guz-man!" he nodded down at the old man. "You have done a good job. You wonder what it is for! You, and all Badu, will soon know. Wise old man-keep a quiet mouth until then—for then a mouth will open to tell you and all Badu *all* about it."

With one hand gripping the sleek little handle, he slowly drew all the thongs together within his other hand. Smiling grimly he hid the whip under his skirt and, with a nod to Guz-man, walked slowly away towards the village.

His harsh face serenely calm, worries had vanished, aye, devilish humour in the piercing eyes, the close-shut mouth under, the big hooked nose. Slowly he walked, slower still as he neared his house, slower it seemed, as if to prolong the coming of a moment of supreme enjoyment.

For this week in particular the women, constantly goaded on by Miria, had given him particular hell. While that very morning—

His teeth gritted with suppressed rage. He knew that if he had not been waiting for the Cat that morning he would have torn that she-devil limb from limb—she had goaded him into madness, he had stormed out from the house lest he lose control and thus lose the joy of the Cat. But now! Ah! The Cat, nestling so sleekly against his legs!

He stepped up into the house platform, surprised at the voice of Miria singing a native melody.

Miria, squatting on the mat with a half-finished dress across her bare, shapely legs, smiled up at her lord, holding up in offering a cool drink of fresh coconut milk. Mek was cooking the evening meal—and it smelt good. Naina was industriously plaiting a new, comfortable sleeping-mat for her chief and master. Petula, softly singing, was busy stringing out a fresh row of tobacco leaves from the rafters.

A scene of perfect domestic felicity. All busy at useful household tasks, all for the comfort of their lord, all happily awaiting the arrival of their lord.

Wongai stood a long, disappointed moment. Painfully, his queer expression changed into thwarted exasperation. Mechanically he accepted the coconut milk from the smiling Miria, sat down heavily, raised the coconut to his lips to drown the raging fires within.

Thereafter followed a week of halcyon peace in the domestic life of Wongai the Mamoose, chief of chiefs of all Badu, war-lord of Mabuiag, lieutenant of Sida, God of the Crops, friend of Kwoiam, God of War.

CHAPTER XXIV

IN WHICH MIRIA FEELS THE CAT

Finally Wongai decided that he had seen the last of that accursed man-o'-war. His wolfish temper, calmed as his fears eased, he concentrated attention upon the ceaseless native intrigues around him, upon the binding of the warrior clans yet more closely together and to him, to the checkmating of the whispering sorcerers of the Zogo-le and to the ceaseless work of the gardens.

His time and thoughts were fully occupied. But not for long upon his pet subjects. Miria saw to that.

For a surprising time she had been an angel. The great chief's household was all he could wish it to be. Uneasily he wondered what was happening. Miria, with her little touching ways, let him slip deeply into his fool's paradise, then brought him back with a jerk. If he would not think of her in one way, the way she desired, she, a chief's daughter and good to look upon, then she would make him think of her another way. Certainly she would give him something to think about—herself.

So, one evening Wongai came back from the gardens to find the wives at one another's throats. The place was again a hot-bed of sneers, innuendos, cat-calls. His evening meal burning to a cinder.

The great chief suffered it for a week. He knew it would simmer and bubble right up to the inevitable bursting point. Grimly he watched the innocent Miria as subtly, by the cutest of womanly wiles, she just now and then fed oil to the bubbling fires, setting Mek against Naina, Petula against both of them, the big chief against all of them. Miria, the devilishly shrewd little wildcat, blissfully unaware that her chief victim carried the Cat under his skirt. It felt so very comforting, it felt it would for once and all end all his home worries—when the boiling-point came. As day followed sultry day and night bitter night, with the tension rapidly growing the more satisfied he felt, visualizing that firm young body, the warmly rounded curves, the nicely plump figure of Miria—while the Cat warmed at his leg.

Then, one evening, he sprang erect in a fury—Miria had overstepped the mark. Sitting cross-legged on the floor in pleasantly sly humour she gazed up in startled fear as he leapt to rush her—her mouth suddenly tremulous. He towered above her, madness in his face, chest panting, clawed hands convulsively twitching—it was the touch of the Cat upon his thigh that stopped him seizing that full brown throat and squeezing and squeezing the life out of it. He stood there glaring with arms upraised, deeply panting as slowly the madness eased from his face. A slow, cold grin brought a chill to Miria's spine. He glared down, she stared up. His teeth gleamed like the snarl of a wolf—never in her wildest nightmares had Miria imagined such a snarl before. Silly little fool! This was a man who had *eaten* men. Slowly, affectionately, his hand reached up under his skirt, appeared again, gripping the handle of the Cat.

Ominously he flicked it and the long, sleek tails unfolded.

Miria stared fascinated at the queer thing. Mek and Naina and Petula cowered in a fearful apprehension, none had ever seen such a queer thing as this. In the tense silence Wongai "felt" their thoughts, they were groping at some horrified belief that this must be a spirit thing, some tormentor of women that the chief had brought from the spirit world. With devilish grin he held out the little whip, the tails dangled down past Miria's nose, she hardly breathed.

Wongai stepped forward. His left hand reached out, quietly fastened upon Miria's neck—she could not move. She felt her head pressed slowly forward, then gradually down, then hard down; she felt her neck gripped terribly between Wongai's legs—slowly she was pressed down, down, her neck gripped below his knees; convulsively she bit at his ankles, strain as she might she felt her head pressed down, down; she was gripped down near the ankles, she could not fasten her teeth in his legs, could not move her own legs for they were under her, her nose now pressed into the floor.

Then Wongai reached over and lifted up her short grass skirt. The other wives gazed fascinated, there was utter silence save for the gasps of Miria and Wongai's throaty chuckles.

With a gentle flick of the wrist, casually and quite gently, he brought the Cat down over Miria's tensely rounded buttocks. With a startled, convulsive squawk she seemed to shiver into life. Wongai chuckled delightedly.

Slowly he swung the little Cat, a trifle faster as his wrist quickened upon the handle, a nasty gleam in his eye. Then—the Cat hissed sibilantly—viciously as he brought it down.

A shriek plunged the village into shocked silence—that village had heard many a shriek—but there was something *different* in this one—

Another shriek! And out there among the palms, in every hut the listeners' blood ran cold.

Another shriek, another and another quicker and quicker in agonized, shrieking crescendo.

Wongai thrashed until some instinct in his maddened fury urged him stop before he cut her to pieces. He eased the vice of his legs and Miria seemed to fly back from him; she back-somersaulted over the house platform and her feet were running as she hit the ground; she ran and ran in urgent, hopping leaps; she ran and ran all the way to Tulu village and threw herself into her father's hut.

And all the way in that race of terror never once did she bother about the spirits of the night.

CHAPTER XXV

UNBELIEVABLE NEWS

Some time later the Chief Sagigi brought a lone fisher to Wongai with amazing news.

A Lamar girl had been captured by the Kowraregas of Murralug. Boroto, young chief of Entrance Island, had saved her from a wrecked ship. She had been recognized by Piaquai, chief of chiefs of Murralug, and by his wife Nakobad as the spirit of Gi'Om, their daughter, who had been drowned some time before.

Boroto had fallen in love with her and was eager to buy her as wife from the chief Piaquai. But Piaquai had asked the ridiculously high price of a canoe. And Boroto had refused and was in the sulks, as any self-respecting warrior would be. A canoe for a wife! And a despised Lamar wife at that! Why, Piaquai the chief must have lost his senses!

For quite a time Wongai doubted this astounding news. A white girl rescued by such savages—and not killed! At this very moment alive on an island barely forty miles away! A white girl living among savages in this very Coral Sea!

But it was true. The girl was Barbara Thomson, girl-wife of the owner of the cutter *America*. The little vessel had been wrecked upon the shores of Entrance Island. The crew had died under tragic circumstances; the girl was taken off the wreck by the young chief Boroto, to be immediately recognized and claimed by the Murralug chieftain Piaquai and his wife Nakobad as Gi'Om, spirit of their drowned daughter. Thus, her life had been spared.

The night that Wongai was absorbing this startling news he sank into a brown study, smoking his zoob in the gloom of the hut. Just the glowing coals, the painted face, the greenish phosphorescence round the eye-sockets of "Sisi" as slowly he moved round, then back, paused, moved round again, suspended by the string from the rafter above. Just that, and the breathing of his wives under their sleeping-mats, and his thoughts.

Unaware that eyes strained with hate were staring at him from the darkness of a sleeping-mat.

For Petula was not asleep.

But Wongai was absorbed in thoughts.

In all this wilderness of ocean and islets and savages. Just he—and a white girl!

And there was born to him a great, a breath-taking dream. He would take the girl and marry her. She would bear him sons as kings to command an island kingdom!

Not only one island, not only one group of islands, but all the islands in this Coral Sea!

He laid the zoob across his knees as if in a trance.

He and the girl—just he and the girl.

Conquer first this Western Group, then the Central. Combine them both against Kebisu. After which, that distant Eastern Group must fall his way.

That would be his island kingdom, every island in the Coral Sea from the tip of Australia to New Guinea.

Every wreck would then be his. And how he could utilize everything within a wreck! All those precious things that these savages in their ignorance spilled overboard before they put a firestick to the still-precious wreck. He could also lay traps and catch vessels in narrow waterways— the treacherous passageways between the reefs. Easily he could cause the wreck of ship after ship. With their cargoes he could do wonderful things, with their timbers and tools he could build vessels, with their weapons he could train his men to attack ships until no vessel dare enter this treacherous, reef-strewn sea. Never then could the clank of irons, the hiss of the lash make hideous his island kingdom. He would be left alone to work out his destiny and his sons' destiny.

With the white girl—and his white sons.

He had accomplished wonders in a very short time while battling only for life and self. But now, with the girl—a white girl—he could form this wonderful island kingdom in less than a lifetime, by the time his elder boys were approaching manhood. A line of white kings to lead brown warriors by sea and land. A sea-girt kingdom in which the horrors of white civilization would never be known.

The only civilization he knew was seared deep into mind and body by the lash, and nightmare memories. Hour after hour he dreamed.

Came the cackle of the wildfowl, heralding a softly breaking dawn. He was still dreaming, not noticing the strengthening light bringing into shape the palm trunks outside the open doorway. And then the huge ground map in the village centre. And he awakened, glanced across the brightening waterway at the black bulk of Moa.

Moa! Why, he was dreaming of an island kingdom and he had not yet subdued Moa!

CHAPTER XXVI

KABARA SIGNS HIS DEATH WARRANT

The realization brought Wongai to his senses.

"Time," he muttered, "it will all eat up time. But I'll go and get that girl. She can be breeding me sons while I take the islands for them."

He frowned towards Moa, realizing he dare not leave Badu while those untamed fighters just across the waterway thirsted for revenge. Even while he gazed, the defiant blast of a boo came harshly over the water. Koted village on Moa was challenging Upai village on Badu to come across and fight.

But while Wongai, engrossed far more than he realized by his great dream was planning to subdue Moa Island, Kabara had already planned and was acting on a desperate attempt to annihilate Badu.

Kabara, chief of chiefs of the Italagas, most powerful tribes on Moa. A fine type of man Kabara, working hard to do for Moa what Wongai had for Badu—to combine the dispirited, scattered tribes of Moa. Then launch a sudden, overpowering attack on Badu village. And now in his two largest war-canoes, with picked warriors in impressive regalia he was sailing to Murralug to try to induce the numerous Kowraregas to join him. They were awaiting him. For the Kowraregas on all the Murralug Islands were intensely interested by the great events happening on Badu. The coming of Wongai, friend of Kwoiam the War God, descending to earth again in the form of a Lamar. Defeating warriors of Mabuiag, capturing the War Gud of Kwoiam, reuniting Mabuiag and Badu, defeating Moa village.

And now he had made himself chief of Badu Island. Where would this reincarnated Wongai stop?

The question that was agitating the minds of the Zogo-le! Where would Wongai stop?

For what ambitions had he been reincarnated?

These startling questions were keenly debated among the Kowraregas! By sea or land, and round the communal fires at night.

The sorcerer spies in each tribe listened while watching, reporting all to the Council of the Zogo-le on distant Pulu.

The Zogo-le must hear, must see, *all* things.

The Murralug Islands were loosely allied to Moa, mainly for trade purposes, particularly for canoes, depending mostly for their living from the sea. They would be in a bad way if, through any falling out with Moa, their canoes dwindled down through loss and wastage.

People think hard and glumly no matter what colour, no matter whether "savage" or civilized, when their main food supply is threatened.

Understandable then, the concern of the Kowraregas at the disquieting news filtering in of the breath-taking happenings on Badu.

A big crowd awaited the arrival of Kabara. The Kowraregas, under the chief of chiefs, Piaquai. And the chiefs Manu and Baki, also the young chief Boroto of Entrance Island, a fine type of young islander, crazily in love with the shipwrecked girl. Barbara Thomson was present at this meeting, in company with her "mother", Nakobad, her "brother", Bazi, and her "sisters".

With due ceremony the visitors were escorted to the Council House. The conference lasted three days, Kabara calling upon the assembled chiefs to combine with Moa to annihilate Badu and Wongai the Lamar before he wiped out Moa, and the Kowraregas, too.

"For he will never stop!" Kabara assured them impressively. "If he conquers Moa then your turn too will surely come."

In deep voice, in measured tones, he described his plan. The Kowraregas and their allies were to mass secretly on Moa. To surprise Wongai and his principal men of Badu and Mabuiag when next they attacked Moa. To wipe them right out—especially making certain of that accursed Lamar, Wongai. Then canoe straight across the waterway and wipe out Badu village. The rest would be easy.

Silence at the Council. At last old Piaquai spoke.

"To transport so many men, far more canoes would be needed than are owned by all the Kowraregas."

"We have planned for that," answered Kabara gravely. "Quietly mass your own canoes at hidden points on the eastern coasts of Murralug. At vantage points, too, let the men of Waiben Island, of Keriri, of Gialug, of all your islands, quietly mass their canoes. Then, very lightly manned, *we* shall come with every canoe possible from Moa. The men you cannot carry in your own canoes will pile into ours. We shall all sail for Moa. Land your men, then return, until all your men are landed."

"Such a great sailing of canoes would be seen and signalled," suggested Manu.

"We will move only at night," replied Kabara.

"Such an increase of warriors swarming the village of Moa would surely be noticed across at Badu," suggested Baki.

"Not until too late," answered Kabara grimly. "We will land the men on the 'back' coast of Moa, until they are all landed. Then, by night, march them across Moa to the coast fronting Badu. There we separate, each tribe and clan marching to its appointed village. Then, by day, camp quietly in the hills behind that village. By night, each clan quietly steals back into its appointed village. If nothing happens, then at dawn all steal back into the hills."

"Ah!" exclaimed Boroto. "And if anything—happens?"

"When Wongai attacks," answered Kabara and leaned forward with flashing eyes, "then in *any* village he attacks he finds just twice the number he expected. Armed men, waiting for *him!* If he attacks six villages simultaneously, it will be all the same—a surprise that will cost him his head. We shall wipe out the attackers, then swarm across the waterway to Badu, load after load, coming and going, racing across. We shall wipe out Badu and the frontal villages, then swarm inland. Wipe them *all* out. Then—" and his teeth gritted—"we shall take Mabuiag!"

It was a master plan—in silence they realized it. "The War Gud of Kwoiam?" murmured Piaquai.

"Will be unavailing," answered Kabara earnestly, "beaten beforehand by the overwhelming surprise awaiting Wongai when he attacks—we kill him and capture—the War Gud of Kwoiam!"

He paused—mesmeric eyes concentrating on the chiefs in this attempt to avert what his far-seeing mind realized could be the end of his people of Moa.

"We shall bring to Wongai," he resumed softly, "far greater disaster than *he* brought to the raiders of Badu. Surprise, annihilation—capture of the War Gud. Then, with the War Gud at *our* head, swarm across and annihilate *all* the villages of Badu. Then face Mabuiag!"

"And then—?" asked Baki softly.

"We shall wipe out Mabuiag," replied Kabara confidently, "it is only a small island. We shall surround it with canoes, wipe out every man. Then," he added softly, "we shall wipe out accursed Pulu."

The one thing he should have left unsaid. He had done such good work. But-the Zogo-le heard all things. There was silence awhile, each startled chief in his mind's eye seeing the working out of this grand plan. None could fault it. And all could see loot unbelievable. But—that last thing—the Zogo-le! Each man doubted whether he had heard aright.

"One thing," said Bazum, chief of Wy-ben, doubtfully, "for all the time of the massing, and the waiting inland in Moa, and in the villages until Wongai attacks, we shall need food for so great—a gathering of warriors."

"We have prepared it," answered Kabara. "We are eating nothing from our gardens, we are storing it all for you. And already each village has sun-dried abundant fish. And when you *do* come, then every man, woman and child of Moa will be fishing the seas for food. There will be food for all."

For three days the conference debated. Apparently all was going well; the pact, it seemed, would surely be made; then some faint, indefinable shade of doubt, of hesitation, seemed to be creeping in. Mostly, it was in silence, or the fleeting expression on a face. Nothing tangible but—it *was* there.

No one spoke openly of the Zogo-le-or of their silent workers. But a whispering campaign of doubt swept among the people, followed by the cold dread of fear.

That Wongai and Badu should be wiped out—yes, that was pleasantly desirable. Mabuiag should be weakened, but *not* wiped out—yes, that was sound policy and pleasant to contemplate. But to suggest wiping out Sacred Pulu—ah, *that* was unbelievable!

Frightened glances, even at the whisper of it. No man had ever before imagined such a terrible suggestion.

Augudulkula, holy of holies of the Zogo-le! Sacred Pulu. Men covertly glanced at one another, not daring to whisper.

Finally, the men of Moa were escorted to their canoes. They hauled up the big mat sails, with uneasy brows sailed away.

The chiefs of the Kowraregas would give no decisive answer. Among themselves, they had agreed they were in a "spot".

And the sorcerers, instructed by the Zogo-le on distant Pulu, kept them ever more so.

Kabara, by one slip, was now a marked man by the implacable Zogo-le.

Courteously, with bold front, he sailed from Murralug. But his heart was heavy with premonition.

CHAPTER XXVII

WONGAI SEEKS HIS WHITE QUEEN

Starlight still reigned when Kabara's men gazed lovingly at the black bulk of Moa looming over the bows. Ears turned questioningly to the breeze as there came the faint blast of a boo, then another—war-boos! Uneasily they listened. The water gurgle at the cleaving bows, slow creaking of the big mat sails and—again those ominous boos. Then, away ahead in the darkness, right on their shore fronting Badu, a torch shone—blazed up—that "torch" a palm-thatched hut on fire!

Another, then another torch lit up, to be engulfed in the lurid fire of fierce, spreading blaze.

Yet another village of Moa was in flames.

In despair Kabara shouted, and the paddles flashed out. But they were too far away, the breeze too light, they could not be in time.

In the growing dawn Kabara's canoes slipped into the waterway to echoing volumes of sound—the boos of Badu. On the Moa shore Zurzur village was still smoking, while the rearguard of Wongai's canoes were landing at Badu to triumphant blasts of the boo, throb of drums, laughter and shouting from crowds of hysterical people.

Wongai had attacked while Kabara was away. And Kabara had thought that the secret would be so well kept. In a flash he cursed his tongue that had whispered against the Zogo-le. This defeat would undo much that he had accomplished to combine the dispirited tribes of Moa.

Wongai had attacked immediately it was whispered Kabara and his main chiefs were away, attacked because of the opportunity, and because he was now crazily anxious to seize the white girl castaway. By striking one violent blow at Moa he believed he could safely leave Badu for a few days. And return with the girl before the Moans could rally, before they would learn of his absence.

He scowled savagely. The Zogo-le!

The Zogo-le knew all things.

Through their Zogo of Moa, would they dare betray him to the Moans? Possibly lay some deep trap for him?

There was nothing he could do about it.

The uncertainty was maddening.

If at that time he could have been listening to the Inner Council of the Zogo-le on Sacred Pulu he would have been both worried and surprised. They dreaded this Wongai more than ever, still could not determine what to do about him. But as to Kabara!

Kabara, the beloved chief of all the Italagas. Kabara the *thinker*.

Ah, but now the Zogo-le knew his *hidden* thoughts! Good! It was all turning out very well—for the Zogo-le.

Wongai was determined to conquer Moa. Kabara was determined to conquer Badu. In murmurous whispers, with sly smiles, the Council of the Zogo-le decided to let them fight it out. It must take a long, long time, one way or the other. Both would be kept busy—which would leave the Zogo-le unhampered to carry on with their own business. Haply, both Wongai and Kabara would be killed before the business was over. If not, and if Wongai should triumph, the Zogo-le would have ample time to plan that he should win but a barren victory.

But—should Kabara win! Then the Zogo-le would have it arranged that the death of Wongai would be the signal for the death of Kabara.

And the Council of the Zogo-le, squatting before the Great Au-gud, leered knowingly at the silent mummies of past Zogos. Had Wongai then known of this confirmed policy of the Zogo-le he would have snarled, "So the dogs would let me stew in my own juice!"

But he did not know, and worried himself trying to see into the mind of the Zogo-le.

But he now had a straight-out worry that maddened him more the less he saw he could do about it. He had planned to sail for Murralug immediately after the attack on Moa. Impossible. His warriors were exultant, the tribesmen from Mabuiag pouring into Badu village enthusiastic at the tidings, drums throbbing, the blast of the boo over all.

War-lust madness in Badu village with roar of voices, stamp of rhythmic feet as the victorious warriors danced the war-dance round the trophies—the pile of heads. And the girls crazy with excitement, whirling in the dance in their prettiest grass skirts, hair gaily decorated with the scarlet wada bean, goa-nut rattles on their shapely, prancing limbs.

Badu and Mabuiag would give themselves over to celebrations for several weeks at least. The heads to be marched in state across the island, there to be embarked in the Sacred Canoe for Pulu, to be taken over by the Zogo-le and prepared for the cleaning ovens. Every available hand to the tiniest toddler would be busy in the gardens or canoes, seeking food for the feasts. Great would be the acclamations to the wonderful Wongai, friend of Sida, God of the Crops, that he had come back from the skies to teach them how to make real gardens, with Kwoiam's blessing how to make *real* war.

Yes, the great chief Wongai would be the hero of heroes at the dances and feasts, hero of gardens, hero of war.

He realized that to order his men to the canoes would have bewildered them. He could have bullied them and they would have obeyed—but at what loss of prestige to him. He ground his teeth and thought of how the Zogo-le would chuckle. He saw that though every man, woman, and child on all Badu—except adherents of the Zogo-le— would obey his slightest wish either proudly or in fear, still he must now often be as enslaved as they by their rigid customs and ceremonies.

In a helpless rage he saw that he would be lucky if he sailed within a fortnight.

Which he did. In his three largest war-canoes, gaily bedecked. With, at the masthead, the palm branch, emblem of peace. The canoes heavily manned with picked warriors, picturesque in their barbaric regalia. With the great chief Wongai most impressive of all. This determined renegade had instinctively realized the value of display in native life. Escaped convict, yes but how far away that day seemed as now, high upon the fighting platform his fierce eyes swept the lazily rolling sea, his three great canoes loaded with husky brown warriors who looked up to him as a god, implicitly believed he was a reincarnated god.

His story was so extraordinary, his success so miraculous, he was in danger of wondering if their belief might really be fact. The largest crowd ever known to congregate upon the Murralug Group awaited the arrival of Wongai. The hills brown with people as they gazed away out over the blue waters at the three giant canoes skimming towards them among those closely packed islands. Wongai, the reincarnated chief of chiefs of all Badu, defeater of Moa, beloved of Sida, friend of Kwoiam the War God.

And among this excited crowd the girl castaway, Barbara Thomson, with beating heart awaiting the arrival of this white man, a white man who surely would help her to escape. Poor Barbara! A white girl alone in this unknown desolation of islands and savagery. This blessed white man, this great chief Wongai whom the islanders looked up to as a god, would help her at last to escape!

The lonely girl stared out from the crowd as the huge canoes glided up on the beach. And a barbaric giant leapt ashore followed by arrogant warriors. The girl gazed fearfully at this figure who strode so tempestuously towards the group of chiefs who waited to greet him. This man was more savage even than any of the savages she now lived amongst. Clad in a towering headdress of bird of paradise plumes, a short purple-black skirt of cassowary plumes, circlets of boars' tusks round his massive arms that carried club and shark's tooth sword. A broad, hook-nosed, savage face above a big black beard. Scowling mouth, fierce eyes that glared contemptuously at Piaquai and the assembled chiefs. Surely, *this* could not be the white rescuer she had imagined, had waited for so longingly!

"Who is he?" she whispered to Magena.

"Why, Wongai, of course," whispered back her friend excitedly, "the great chief Wongai of Badu. Wah! *What* a man!"

The girl's heart sank.

Instinctively she feared this brown savage more than any savage around her.

That evening by the feast fires she was taken before him. But what happened has been described in *Isles of Despair*. He called her a "sawn-off runt of a thing", growled that she might be "the makings of a woman". Told her he would take her back to Badu on the morrow. At Badu he would "feed her up" so that she would be worthy of breeding him sons. As to her timid plea that he help her to reach a passing ship, he laughed the idea to scorn.

Barbara Thomson crept away and with her friends Magena and Laola fled to the hills.

It was just on dawn when Wongai learned of this. He leapt up, mad with rage. Threatened Piaquai himself, and all the chiefs. Seized Nakobad, Piaquai's wife, by the throat and nearly strangled her. Utterly fearless, though his handful of warriors were now hemmed in by hundreds of enraged savages only waiting the signal to attack. And the young chief Boroto with his men hidden by the canoes to cut off his escape.

He did grievous wrong when he laid hands upon the wife of the chief of chiefs. But he did not care. Shouting threats of vengeance he marched straight through them down to his canoes, his bodyguard. compact around him. Manned his canoes and sailed, shaking his fist at them while roaring he would return for the girl and woe betide any who tried stop him.

Thus he sailed, past Wai-Weer, then through the reef-strewn channel between Goode and Kereri islands. From the dark wooded hills of Kereri the Kereri men stared down upon them, sub-tribesmen these of the Murralug men. Even in his fury he saw how strategically strong this group of islands was with its numerous tribes and countless look-out points to watch any channel. They could trap and cut off an invader in fifty places, could trap Wongai even now if they wished.

"If they had the guts!" he snarled. Then the canoes were in Torres Strait, heading north for Badu. And his crews of picked fighting men breathed relievedly, knowing it had been touch and go.

After a while Wongai's fury calmed, his harsh face relaxed, fierce eyes grew dreamy. Upon the fighting platform he sat down in island fashion, staring straight ahead.

He had been a fool, he saw it now, he deserved to have his head baking within the skull-cleaning ovens of Murralug. And serve him flaming well right!

With all he now knew and understood of deeply ingrained native custom he had gone and deliberately flouted the deepest of all. Treated the chiefs with contempt, tried to seize a girl without the slightest regard to etiquette.

He could have had Gi'Om for the price of an ordinary fishing canoe. Piaquai and his brother chiefs would have fawned upon him in gratitude and relief. And not only that, but he might have, without a fight, without trouble, without loss of time, have won all the Murralug Islands to an alliance.

What a fool he had been! His temper had defeated his own interests.

He stared up at the blue sky. Never, unless instant action demanded it, would he act without calm thought again.

The canoes sped swiftly to the slap of the waves, the strain of the big mat sails was a sigh. But otherwise silence except for the screech of a gull for the crews spoke seldom and in low tones because of the anger of Wongai, chief of chiefs.

CHAPTER XXVIII

KABARA ATTACKS BADU

It was in the chilly hours that the dark bulk of Moa loomed up over the bows. Eagerly they gazed, straining for first sight of their beloved Badu. It was at peep of dawn that Wongai's canoes turned into the mouth of the silvered waterway.

And then, straight ahead, in the middle of the waterway it seemed, a flame shot up. Another and another and another. Screams, roar of war-cry, startled blast of a boo, flames that illuminated berserk men smashing into houses, struggling figures in death fights, women and children running screaming for the bush.

Kabara, with his picked Italagas, was attacking Badu village itself.

With an oath Wongai roared, "Out paddles!" and the canoes skimmed towards the spreading inferno. Half Badu village was crackling under fire, the palms brilliantly illuminated, the enemy canoes all drawn up fronting the village, the waterway dancing with light.

Wongai's hut had been the first to go up, but it was Petula who had saved the wives, really saved the village from annihilation. For these heaven-sent days when Wongai was absent, Petula at night had happily communed with the spirit of Sisi. She knew he was there, in his skull with the painted cheeks of beeswax. For the phosphorus around the gleaming eyes glowed so very gently, she could win a smile from the grisly cheeks. But this night, the dead of night with the village bathed in dreams, Sisi warned her, tried for a long time, tried very hard as she gazed into his face. Breathlessly the villagers listened to her next day as she told them how Sisi's eyes seemed boring into her, a shiver of warning rippled across his face as his skull quivered agitatedly though no faintest breath of air was there to move the suspension cord.

For a long time Sisi tried to warn her of a "something". She implored the good spirits of the night to help her understand. At last, in awful uncertainty she stepped out on the house platform and listened with the ears of fear, staring out into the night. And heard no faintest sound—only old Bomba snoring beside Wadwa in their hut way down in the village.

At last came the cackling of the waterfowl. Then, when the Sun God pierced the night with his first faint breath she thought she saw spirits. Just now and then flitting amongst the palms. Then a vagrant star beam gleamed upon a something—the polished pearlshell mai upon Kabara's chest. And Petula screamed piercingly—again and again and again! Then she sprang back into the hut and snatching Sisi's skull to her breast leapt from the hut and ran back into the bush—screaming!

With Mek and Naina and Miria after her, and behind them the growling curses of the cheated Italagas.

It was Petula's screams that startled the village and gave most of them that moment of chance to wake and snatch weapons in a desperate, running fight for life.

Some had been taken completely by surprise. Families had been annihilated on their sleeping-mats, their heads hacked off before the first flames licked their houses. Mostly they had seized weapons on awakening to Petula's screams and leapt out and run for the bush inland. Others had been cut off and were being hacked to death, fighting to the last for their heads.

As Wongai's canoes sped up on the beach he roared to men to push the enemy canoes adrift, others to remain and take his three canoes outstream. Then leapt ashore with his blood-maddened warriors.

They formed up behind him as they raced with a roar of "Wongai! Wongai! Wongai!" They fell upon the astonished Italagas in a fury of cut and stab and club. It was all over in swift moments even as from the bush came howls of joy with yells of "Wongai! Wongai! Wongai!" as the Baduites came howling back to the village. The Italagas panicked and raced back for their canoes despite Kabara's efforts to rally them. Seizing Badu canoes if their own were missing they pushed off and were fleeing back across the waterway with Wongai's men following until up to their necks in water.

Wongai had arrived back only just in time.

As it was, seventy men, women, and children of Badu had lost their heads. The big village ablaze, already half burnt down.

Wongai vowed fiendish revenge with clenched fists to the skies, a demon amongst the roaring flames that now illuminated the waterway right across to Moa. But there was nothing he could do about it—yet. He had learnt that, once started, *two* can play at war.

To wipe out the men of Moa was going to take a long, long time. Kabara was going to strike in turn.

Wongai scowled, not altogether at the thought of the aggressive chief of the Moans. He had been feeling a bit off colour lately, did not seem able to shake it off. With an irritable gesture he began to think again—did not seem to think so clearly as usual—somehow or other. And he suffered hellish dreams at times—not those of the lash and the gallows that he was long used to, but some devilish thing of Barza the sorcerer and a snake all mixed up together with Wongai caught in the coils.

Strangely enough, at that very time Barza was not only thinking of a snake, but was concentrating upon it with grim malice. For he had laid a clever, such a simple trap. He was going to give it the Smothering Death.

Fool that he was, not to have thought of the obvious long ago—when he had failed by other means.

The Smothering Death was a fiery powder that choked the lungs. A mixture of dried poison glands of toads, poison glands of certain poisonous fish, and several vegetable-fungus poisons.

It was blown through the long poison reed directed at the nostrils of the victim.

And now, with the mouthpiece handy to the sorcerer's hand, the long reed lay innocently across the clay fire-pan, the end of it just where the snake's head night after night—if the man had not planted a trap before it—stared at him from above the rim of the fire-pan.

A few inches of the hollow end of the reed, the snake's end, was stuffed with the powder. One puff from Barza's lips at the mouthpiece and the snake's head would be enveloped in finest powder of a choking death.

Barza did not know whether the powder would kill a snake as it would a man who inhaled it, but he believed so, and was very curious, really anxious to find out. He would take grim delight in watching Enoko's spirit fight that powder through the tight little nostrils of the snake.

Lately, he found himself at times talking to the snake, talking to the spirit of Enoko through the snake. He had quite a lot of pleasure at night when certain no Shadow might appear, in baiting Enoko through the snake. He was certain Enoko's spirit heard and understood when the snake hissed at him at times so malevolently, Enoko's spirit so furious that it could not answer back.

But he would not speak to it tonight lest the spirit of Enoko wake to the trap—Enoko, who in human life had mixed that same powder, had used it himself.

Barza was certain this snake was not as other snakes, this snake saw things, heard things, understood things through the spirit of Enoko within it. Patiently he waited for the snake to come.

As he browsed over his zoob the snake's head appeared above the rim of the clay fire-pan; he was startled despite himself, for a moment before it was not there. It often appeared so, and he was startled. He sneered at the snub nose, the beady little eyes fixed so unwaveringly upon him. He hated its scarlet throat.

For quite a time he quietly smoked, gazing across at the snake, his mind all grim pleasure at thought of the surprise he had in store for it. Then his hand groped down for the mouthpiece of the reed and—the snake glided away.

But not all in Badu village were thinking of wars or snakes or sorcerers. Lu-esa was thinking of Kartoy.

Kartoy had returned proudly from the Kwod, a full fledged member of the Shark clan. Not yet a warrior, of course. But he soon would be one.

Lu-esa smiled tenderly, her little brown fingers deftly working at silken strands.

For Lu-esa was making her wedding petticoat.

Kartoy had returned from the Kwod to make love so urgently, Lu-esa smiled at memory of his imploring eyes, his tremulous entreaties whispered under the palms at night.

Lu-esa was making her wedding petticoat.

The two little sun-birds had reared their families-had flown away.

Lu-esa was dreaming.

A week later, while they were rebuilding Badu village word came to Wongai that Kebisu, with men of Mer and Eroob, had completely wiped out the people of the Two Brothers Islands, some seventy miles to the south.

The news was true. One of the complete massacres that occasionally darkened the history of native warfare in the Coral Sea. The people of the Two Brothers had refused Kebisu tribute. He collected his own men. Sailed for Ugar, Eroob, and Mer, then, heavily reinforced by his allies, attacked the Two Brothers Islands in the night and wiped out every man, woman, and child. But that awful massacre has been described in *Drums of Mer*.

Wongai thought ruefully of Kebisu's success. If only he could subdue Moa, though not annihilate its fighting men. But then, Kebisu held the sea, was a chief supremely consolidated, and commanded allies on large islands. The Two Brothers Islands were very small and had held only a few hundred people, easy to surround and surprise. While Moa was one of the largest islands in the Coral Sea, peopled by numerous tribes. Against Wongai also was working this silent, unseen, accursed hand of the Zogo-le.

The Zogo-le! He felt almost certain the Zogo-le had let Kabara know when *he* had departed for Murralug.

Through that accursed Barza, the sorcerer, no doubt. He would send his Maidelaig by night across the waterway with the news to the chief sorcerer of Moa.

He had kept it so very quiet. And the chiefs and clansmen remaining behind would see to it that the people would breathe never a word.

But Barza, the village sorcerer, would know. And thus the Zogo-le on Pulu, who would order word be sent the sorcerer of Moa village, who would whisper it to Kabara.

He lapsed into deep thought.

If only he could by some means amalgamate with the "heads" of the Zogo-le!

He well knew now that the hand of the mysterious cult reached into every island, every tribe, every hut in the Coral Sea. Apparently there was not room in Torres Strait for both Wongai and the Zogo-le.

If only he could link up with this infernal organization, then island after island, group after group, must inevitably fall to him. He was thinking only of himself, of his own interests and now devouring ambition. He did not realize the Zogo-le would be dead against the islands becoming amalgamated under one man's control. For such would mean the end of *them*. There was not room among these little islands for both dictator and Zogo-le. He frowned, pondering deeply. He had so much yet to learn—to do! And his "white queen" —he had failed to secure her. That little devil of a Scotch girl should be with him now, she should be at her duty rearing him sons to help him rule his island kingdom-to-be.

But another wet and another dry season were to come and go before he dared leave Badu on his second attempt to seize Barbara Thomson.

CHAPTER XXIX

BARZA THE SORCERER MUST REPORT TO THE ZOGO-LE

Dark the night. Quietness within the sorcerer's hut. Outside, not even a sigh from the reed whistles drooping from the taboo pole, no tinkle of a goa-nut rattle. The heavy scent of the surrounding foliage. A sibilant hiss—Barza jerked up his head with spiteful grimace. That accursed snake!

Its evil head raised menacingly above the opposite side of the clay fire-pan, its scales glistening black, its throat blood-red, reflecting the glow of the coals. Jet beads its eyes, glistening with malice.

Barza hated that snake; he knew it hated him. He concentrated at the snub-head as mentally he demanded, "Why did you smoke the Pipe of Death, Enoko?"

Again and again, with intense concentration he insisted until the snake shot out its tongue with an angry hiss.

Barza was baffled. So were the Zogo-le. They had never been able to determine why Enoko had smoked the Pipe of Death. Through what strange, what unaccountable means had he come to do it?

Thoughtfully, eyeing the snake, Barza began filling his zoob. This slithering thing had gradually become an obsession. He had tried to trap it, for if he could only hold it prisoner then he would always know where it was, it would be within his power and—he could experiment upon it. But it was as cunning as all snakes put together—no wonder, with Enoko's spirit within it.

He had tried to poison it again and yet again, by every means his cunning wits could devise

But the snake *knew. Enoko* knew!

Barza reached over, flicked a live coal from the fire for his zoob. With deft fingers lifted it up and placed it upon the tobacco hole in the zoob, then sat back and drew quietly at the mouthpiece. The reptile had not moved, as he had known it would not, since he had no immediate intention of attacking it. Its head motionless over the edge of the broad fire-pan. Hidden its lithe body, pressed to the clay sides of the fire-pan. Had he stealthily reached for a stick, had he made one hostile movement, it would have vanished.

Uncanny it was, with its devilish cunning, its "know" instinct, its coming and going when least expected, its definite antagonism.

It knew perfectly well tonight there was no trap below it, around it, above it. He had laid traps, cunning traps, below, around, above. Those above he had been cynically proud of. Particularly of one above. Up there in the darkness of the roof, a large fishing net spread out. One jerk at a hidden string and the net would fall and enmesh the snake.

But it would never come there, to its favourite place, when that trap, or a trap below it was set. It would glare and hiss from the starlight of the open doorway, or from a black corner of the hut, or from a rafter above.

It was getting on his nerves.

Suddenly, from full lungs he blew straight across at the snake. Angrily its head darted from the cloud of smoke. When the smoke dispersed the head rose again, hissing as viciously as the sorcerer's hot breath.

What was getting on Barza's nerves worst of all now was the snake's appearing and distracting his attention when he had deep thought work to do. It only appeared now at such times, and despite himself he again and again found his concentration affected by its presence. Puffing at his zoob, glaring across at the snake, he did not hear the cricket chirp for quite a time. When it was born into his consciousness he thrust the zoob aside with a smothered curse.

He chirped in turn and a Shadow entered the hut, made deference. At a sign he squatted down, gazing at the sorcerer from expressive eyes.

The snake had vanished.

This Shadow was the chief Maidelaig of Barza, chief sorcerer of Badu. And he was there tonight to carry the sorcerer's weekly report to the Zogo-le on Sacred Pulu.

Despite unseen life good and evil, the sorcerer's chief men travelled by night. For no man must witness the coming and going of secret messengers of the Zogo-le.

And Barza's carefully concentrated message was now clouded in his mind, the sequence disturbed by attention to that wretched snake.

Ah, yes! Enoko, through his spirit in his totem snake, was slowly getting even with his earth enemy, Barza.

His brow furrowed in deep concentration, Barza stared unseeing at the coals.

For the chief sorcerer on every island was accountable to the Zogo-le for very definite work. It was left to the lesser village sorcerers to hoodwink the people, to see things and gather information, and carry out the job of a village sorcerer according to their greatly varying degrees of knowledge. But the chief sorcerer's job was a very different matter.

Tonight Barza's job was a detailed account of all that had happened and was happening in Badu, Wabait, Upai, Tulu, Wadauibad, and Baigoa villages during these last ten days. And a general account of happenings in all other villages. He collected these latter by routine, brought to him by the Maidelaig of each village sorcerer. But for the main villages Barza was directly responsible. And it would be a black mark for him should coming events prove any of his information, and to lesser degree, any of his surmises, unreliable.

In this report he must give the movements, the proposed movements, the intentions of the chief Wongai, as affecting all Badu, and Mabuiag. His intentions as to Moa, Murralug, or anywhere. His relations with Kosabad, the chiefs Sagigi, Bagari, Wypali, Pituai, Kariam, Waur. With objectives of any scout work being done by foot or canoe. The progress of a certain little matter regarding Yellow Powder. What the chief Wongai is saying to the people. What the people are saying of him.

Similarly, the intimate actions, and expressed or believed opinions of Kosabad, Sagigi, Bagari, Wypali, and any other chief or head clansman in close contact with the chief Wongai. And of their people, and what their people are doing and saying and believing.

And what the chief Wongai in particular, then the chiefs, then the head clansmen, then the warriors, then the people are saying and— *thinking* about the Zogo-le.

In silence Barza the chief sorcerer stared at the coals, collecting his concentrated message together again. He had got it perfectly—before that cursed snake had distracted his attention, had the complete report ready in as few concentrated sentences as possible. For the Maidelaig messenger must have them letter perfect before he left on his swift journey through the night. He should have been on his way before now.

Curse that snake!

CHAPTER XXX

THE BANANA

The chief strolled home from the gardens one sundown to find the villagers crowded round visitors retailing with gusto the latest doings of the "Giant". A week ago, they were saying, he had slain five men and put twenty to flight. The brawl occurred when a canoe-load of warriors sneaked on the Giant while he was asleep as usual under his favourite tree on the beach. He was alone except for little Patma, who was sitting upon his chest swishing the flies from his hero with a palm-leaf. Little Patma only woke him just in time, had to tug his beard and bite his nose to wake him. The Giant lumbered up and swung his great club as his enemies rushed him—he was still half asleep when he killed the first man. When he killed his fourth he was really angry and roared amongst them, swinging his club. They fled, while the Giant smashed the head of a fifth man to pulp. That was the trouble—those five lovely heads wasted—all smashed to pulp.

Wongai listened quietly to these timid visitors, so awed by him that they barely raised their eyes. In their nakedness they displayed nothing of the culture that distinguished the men of Badu and other islands. Wiry hunters, but with an air of being hunted, as often they were. Wongai encouraged them, and they repaid him with story after story about the Giant, obviously their very great hero. And not only a hero in war. For oh, just couldn't he eat! They exulted with expressive gestures of the enormous quantity of food he could put away. Wongai, eyeing their skinny bodies, thought they could do with a good week's feeding themselves. He began reviving his idea of this giant as bearer of the War Gud of Kwoiam.

What a terrifying figure a giant would look dressed in that fearsome regalia, if only he really were like what these puny hero-worshippers made him out to be!

Wongai gave orders that the visitors were to be especially well entertained for as long as they cared to stay. Everyone was to look after them and—give them plenty to eat.

They stayed a week, enjoyed a royal time. When ready to depart Wongai loaded their canoes, shrewdly sending a huge present of choice vegetables to the Giant. With a pressing invitation for him and his people to come and visit him at Badu. He impressed on the visitors, quite unnecessarily, the bounteous food they had enjoyed from the wonder gardens. They were to tell the Giant that everything in the gardens was his, while there were abundant fish, turtle, crabs, and succulent dugong in the waters of Badu, and plenty of palms under which he could sleep in peace.

And a month later they came, not only the Giant but all his people, sixty timid folk in three canoes. For though fearful of visiting Badu, they were more fearful of being without their Giant. He was their only, their mighty protection. Without him they were lost, could not call their heads their own.

The Giant certainly would not have ventured on the hardship of that short, peaceful voyage had it not been for his month of dreaming of the wonderful foods on Badu. Those returning visitors had done their work well, while Wongai's present had truly whetted his appetite.

Wongai stared in amazement as the Giant stepped ashore, for this enormous mass of beef, bone, and whiskers was really a giant. Wongai wondered the canoe had not sunk under him. With his timid people clustered behind him he stood on the beach, his eyes, brown and limpid as a cow's, gazing in innocent surprise at this largest village he had ever seen. A mane of hair in black ringlets fell like a cloak down massive back and shoulders. A beard that birds could have nested in almost covered the enormous chest. His face was featured like an innocent boy's—but *what* a face! Cheeks like two cheeses, brown as berries, smooth and firm. Pouting lips hiding a cavernous mouth. But his belly—Wongai stared. It was a magnificent thing, something about it reminded Wongai of a lazily rolling wave of a quiet sea. Instinctively, Wongai was measuring that club, the stories he had heard about it he now believed. For it was a mangrove-tree, minus the roots and branches.

Recovering from his amazement, Wongai measured this giant. His first impression was of a vast chest and belly upon stumpy legs. But he saw now that the carcass must be at least two feet taller than he. And the head upon that thick neck squatting upon that great barrel of a chest seemed ridiculously small. But it was not, it was a large head. And the eyes seemed small. But when he gazed full at them they seemed larger and larger. Wongai was puzzled. The more he looked, the more deceptive in every way seemed this smiling human mountain.

Where were the giants of his forgotten childhood tales, those ferocious monstrosities roaring along to rend and devour!

When the Giant waddled trustingly up to Wongai the powerful renegade felt uncomfortably like a small boy. Only at such close quarters could he realize how broad and thick and unbelievably round this unbelievable thing was. For once Wongai, gazing up at those soft, smiling, questioning eyes, did not know just what to say, to do. He really was gazing up at a giant, but felt ridiculously as if it were a gambolling puppy coming to play

The Giant settled down at Badu village with the trusting innocence of a child delighted with strange and wondrous things. The people of Badu pressed food upon him, in uproarious mirth at the quantity he could eat. And how he delighted in *their* delight! After the first few days, however, they began to wonder how much he really *could* eat. So, in all seriousness, they tried him out, only to desist in alarm. They piled him with turtle meat, dugong, fish and crab, aided by yams, manioc, sweet potato, bunches of bananas, native sugar-cane, and whatnot.

The Giant merely kept on eating steadily and delightedly, laughing with the children as his great paunch gradually swelled and swelled. At last he would quietly lie back, snoring like a grampus as soon as his head touched the ground. He would snooze thus for several hours under his palm-tree, not feeling the children, merely snoring the deeper as they piled themselves upon his stomach. When by weight of numbers they inconvenienced him he would grunt prodigiously, heave that enormously strong stomach, and shake them off.

After a couple of hours' snooze, his beard would open as his mouth like a pit stretched wide in a yawn.

He would shake his great head and rumble and cough a bit as the children thrust a stick of native sugar-cane down the great throat. Then he'd heave himself up, roar with laughter with the squealing youngsters, reach out for a yam and start eating all over again.

After he had strolled through the big village and gaped at its wonders he seldom left the shady palm-tree he had chosen by the beach. He ate there, slept there, laughed there, lived there in peace and happiness, to the delight of the village youngsters. Never had they dreamed of a playmate such as this. There was always something new they could do to him. Often they had Patma in tears—poor little Patma, trying to protect his hero the Giant.

Many a time Wongai, at work or smoking the zoob on the platform of his house, would frown in puzzled wonder at gusty roars of laughter as the youngsters tickled the Giant's navel with a palm-leaf. Or tried how many coconuts they could balance on his bingy.

Wongai simply could not understand the Giant, that bovine mountain of guzzling humanity had him completely puzzled.

The Giant's people, timidly uneasy but becoming reassured day by day, presently left the Giant in the care of his faithful little Patma and worked like slaves in the gardens and fishing canoes. They earned their keep, and they did eat. Never had they known such wonderful gardens, never the weapons and traps, ropes and harpoons and lines with which to catch the big turtles and meaty dugong, the plentiful fish. On their own little isle they had to toil from dawn to dusk with much inferior weapons to secure the food to feed their beloved Giant, with a scrap or. two over for themselves. But now, for the first time in all their lives the Giant had food—and such wonder food! —more than ever he could eat, *and* they enjoyed the same. Willingly they slaved and ate and filled out day by day, the children growing pot-bellied in delighted mimicry of the Giant.

Wongai, sourly puzzled, grew disgusted by the Giant. He had expected to gain a killer, not a baby whale. How on earth such a guzzling, snoring, sluggish, overgrown mountain of roaring laughter could ever develop the energy to kill a man had him bewildered. But that the Giant had killed just over thirty warriors Wongai now knew to be fact. He had to be taken by surprise and do it before he knew he did it, explained his people in awed tones, or else he must be in a great rage. There was one thing that threw him into a rage immediately, they explained, and that was a good spear-thrust behind. He could not stand that, in fact he jumped very high, and roared, a terrifying roar. Fortunately, it was nearly always a spear-thrust in the buttocks that spurred him into action. For enemies were terrified of him and always sought to attack him from the rear.

"How about an arrow in the belly?" growled Wongai.

The people laughed. No bowman could shoot the Giant in the belly, they declared proudly, he was too quick. He knocked the arrow aside with hand or club, or a side-on, funny sort of movement with his belly. How he did it they did not know, and they were sure he did not know.

No bowman could shoot the Giant in the belly, it was *his* belly and he was very proud of it, he thought more of it than of anything else in the world. Many bowmen had tried to hurt it, but all had failed. When enemies came, the people were glad if they tried to hurt the Giant's belly for then the Giant became really angry and roared straight in amongst them, whirling his club.

Which information did not please Wongai over much. If the Giant had first to be goaded by a prod in the backside or a blow in the paunch before he would fight, then he would not be much use as a bearer of the War Gud of Kwoiam. The bearer of the Cud must be a born killer, eager for the kill even though there was no immediate killing to be done.

But Wongai soon had something on his mind that over- shadowed his disappointment in the good-natured Giant. And this was a killing matter, too. But a very, very different way of killing.

It was during the night silence when all things slept—or seemed to. So still and quiet that Sisi's skull hung motionless, its green eyes barely luminous as it leered down upon the chief Wongai smoking his zoob, staring at the glowing coals. No sound but occasional deep breaths of the sleeping wives, a plaintive sigh from Miria.

"Even in her sleep she finds something to whinge about," muttered Wongai. "I'd like to slit her throat."

Miria was toying with her old games, though very, very cautiously since her father the chief Wypali, had forcibly dragged her back to her lord. Miria would never forget the lick of the Cat upon her firm young body—she felt it when she sat down. But she hated most the giggle in the eyes of the women in the village. She would have loved to have scratched their eyes out. But there was nothing she dared do about it—the thought of that Cat was terrifying. No wonder she sighed in her sleep, for every time she turned over she "felt" the Cat—which gave her horrid dreams. She turned over now and whimpered, which brought a low growl from her bad-tempered lord, sourly thinking of the white girl castaway.

His hard face deep-lined as he thought and planned, his eyes slowly growing proud as he gazed at a bunch of bananas suspended from a rafter. Every family in Badu and other villages now had their bananas, to be eaten as they ripened in the huts. For in this short time Wongai, friend of Sida, God of the Crops, had brought a comparative abundance to the once so scraggy gardens.

Pride of accomplishment transformed his harsh face as he stared at this bunch—such bananas, massed thick round the parent stalk, golden yellow, swelling with richness, the few he could see tinged with rose reflecting the glow of the coals. Yes, appetizing they were, and up the shiny skin of one fat beauty was energetically crawling a long, thin insect. It paused, its tiny head pecking about. Then it began to squat, its head commenced to bore. Wongai's cheeks grinned good-humouredly as he puffed at the zoob. He admired the insect for desiring a feast of this rich banana, but certainly no insect could bore into that thick. healthy, protective skin. His expression slowly changed to intentness, to frowning disbelief as he bent close. For without a doubt that threadlike insect was disappearing *quickly* into the banana. More slowly now, as it ate its way in. Very slowly, as its tiny tail disappeared.

Wongai scowled in chagrin, almost in dismay. Surely this could not be the forerunner of an insect pest that might bring to nought all his labours, that would devour the fruits of his toil. Presently, as with increasing uneasiness he visioned all that might be, a little dark speck appeared from the banana—the insect's tail was wriggling out backwards—in a hurry!

And the thread of a thing came all out, swaying there clumsily, for all the world like a man clinging desperately to a tall chimney. Wongai stared with intent interest. The insect seemed struggling to get away, it couldn't, it swayed this way, that way, it couldn't crawl away, its head hung down backward, then half its body, slowly swaying, swaying, losing its grip until only the tail seemed to cling. It stiffened, softly fell to the floor.

Wongai straightened, staring down, staring at the banana.

The insect was dead.

CHAPTER XXXI

"SHADOWS" SEE THINGS

Wongai yawningly refilled his zoob, put a live coal to the bowl, puffed away heavy-eyed as if for his last smoke of the night.

Soon his questing thoughts began to take shape. No insect, he believed, could have bored through that thick, tough banana skin so quickly, wriggling straight into the heart of the banana. There *must* have been a tiny, invisible hole pierced deep into the banana beforehand. The insect by smell of juice had found that hole, then burrowed straight in. It had eaten. Wriggled out in agitated hurry-to die.

That banana had been poisoned!

Who had poisoned it?

Wongai, puffing dreamily, listened to the deep, slumbrous breaths of his wives.

There were other bunches of bananas tied to the rafters. But this was his, the chief's bunch. It was always the largest and fattest, hanging to one side of the fire-place where he sat at night, where all he had to do was to reach up an arm and pluck a banana at leisure.

It was *his* bunch that had been poisoned.

With a cold detachment he remembered back over the last two months. That feeling of lassitude, of "don't care". Slowly it had grown into a feeling of depression; he could not make it out, irritably he had tried to shake it off. But it had come again. He had wondered what was the matter with him. Lately, he had grown so irritable and depressed that even Kosabad and Sagigi, Bagari and Wypali had hesitated to approach him. And he was steadily growing worse.

He clenched knotted fists in violent self-control. He was ;growing ill, steadily worse and worse-because he was being slowly *poisoned!* But he must not go mad—he must reason this thing out—then fight it as the Zogo-le would fight—

Ah! The Zogo-le!

His eyes dilated, his brow corrugated in amazement. Slowly he relaxed—he must think it all out.

His standing order to his wives was that they must do duty by turn in the hut. While the other three worked in the gardens, she on hut duty must attend to the cooking, the sun-drying of fish and dugong steak, the stacking in place of fruit, vegetables, and tobacco leaf, the repairing of the domestic fishing traps, gathering of wood and water, care and repair of her chief's ceremonial regalia. So that by day one wife in her turn was always on duty in the hut.

Could one of his four wives have poisoned his bananas?

He thought of Petula.

Ah! She stirred uneasily in her sleep.

He had not given it a thought before, he remembered now! She had been very fond of Sisi. Perhaps she had never forgiven him for killing Sisi. Not that he cared one straw. But she seemingly had cared all the time. Miria was a vindictive little devil, but terrified of him since he had tanned her hide with the Cat. Petula was different, now he came to think of it, she had always kept herself apart, she was always sullen, but now he came to remember, she was the only really defiant one when it came to the point—he realized now that in a quiet, deadly sort of way she had defied him far more than the others whom he had raged at.

Yes! Petula was still fond of this death's head grinning just above him—thinking back, he remembered an occasional glance from her slumbrous, vengeful eyes. Thinking more deeply, he suddenly realized it was only Petula who attended the skull of Sisi, tended it with a wildcat ferocity that dared any of the other wives to touch it.

He ground his teeth in silent rage, then grinned sarcastically. It amused him to realize she was "in love with a death's head". But to attempt to poison—*him!*

He lay down the zoob, yawned with an outstretching of powerful arms, lay back upon his mat to sleep.

Yes, he knew *now* that Petula had been, was still fond, deeply fond of Sisi.

His half-closed eyes stared up and Sisi's skull leered down. How devilishly lifelike the painted cheeks, the grinning teeth, the luminous sockets, the gleaming eyes—he shivered despite himself.

He snored. But before he really slept, he had planned.

Next day, in a Quiet Place, he called together two of his Shadows.

Every sorcerer in every village on every island had his Quiet Place. And his Shadows—as Wongai had learned from Kosabad long ago.

And long since Wongai had found *his* Quiet Place. And his Shadows also.

So henceforth, night and day, no matter when: she was, in hut or garden, bush or canoe, by night or day, a Shadow would be *always* watching. No matter what she did, even if alone in darkest night, a Shadow would always *know*. If in daylight amongst a crowd, her every gesture, her every glance—a Shadow would always *see*.

And but a few days later a Shadow met Wongai in the Quiet Place.

And whispered that Petula, when she was alone in the hut, carefully pierced the ripest bananas on the great chief's bunch with a long needle.

"Ah!" murmured Wongai.

"The needle is grooved," whispered the Shadow, "and before it is used is touched to a film of coconut oil. Then dipped in the Yellow Powder. Then the needle is carefully pushed into the banana, left there just a little while, then gently twisted round as it is slowly pulled out. The Yellow Powder stays in the banana, but it is no longer yellow, for the oil and the banana juice turn it white, it is slowly absorbed into the banana, impossible to see even if the banana were broken right there. And impossible to see the hole made by the needle, for the skin closes up."

"And how *many* bananas?" snarled Wongai. "And for him who eats the bananas—how long?"

"Many bananas must be eaten," murmured the Shadow. "'Tis very slow, but—very sure."

"Where does she keep the needle, and the Yellow Powder?"

"In a little bag of sharkskin under the knob upon the middle lath under her sleeping-mat."

"Ah, and who makes this Yellow Powder?"

Wongai read his answer in the fear in the Shadow's eyes.

"Ah!" he snarled. "The sorcerers of the Zogo-le!"

The Shadow nodded, wordlessly.

"Watch her, day and night," growled Wongai. "Sooner or later you or *he* will find from whom she gets the Yellow Powder."

From the village came merry laughter, music, too, of reed pipe and drum, girlish voices in happy song.

For today was Lu-esa's wedding feast. A great feast, as befitted the favourite daughter of a chief.

Sweet and pretty was Lu-esa, happy smile, soft brown eyes aglow. Her light-brown skin so young and fresh, shapely limbs entwined with ornaments, her wedding skirts the envy of the village girls. Her hair brilliant with the pulsing wings of living butterflies, their delicate legs entangled in the mass of frizzy strands.

Kartoy! Ah well, Kartoy. So proud his chest could not swell out one bit more, so bashful he could hardly talk, boyish smile strained to a grin. His strong young body so massaged with coconut oil that his friends' arms still ached. His wedding skirt so wonderfully fitting, of gleaming creamy fibre. His one ornament his proudest—the badge of the Beizam, the Shark clan.

And now from the corner of her eye Lu-esa saw the great chief Wongai approaching among the palms to take his place beside her father Kosabad and the assembled chiefs.

Wongai! Chief of chiefs of all Badu, war-lord of Mabuiag, lieutenant to Sida, God of the Crops, friend of Kwoiam, God of War. Could any girl dream of a more wonderful wedding? Kartoy, her boy husband soon-to-be. Kosabad and Maletta, her beloved father and mother. All under the blessing of the great Wongai, chief of chiefs of all Badu and Mabuiag.

Shyly Lu-esa gazed across at Kartoy standing with his friends, proudly erect and motionless as the chiefs took their places.

Lu-esa, dreaming dreams.

The days, weeks, went by. Wongai as usual ate his bananas. But they were not really *his*. They were the bananas taken unobserved from the women's bunches—but *not* from Petula's. Strangely, Wongai seemed to get great pleasure every time he noticed his young wife, Petula, eating a banana. Not that the wives noticed Wongai's pleasure. He had noted that for some reason Petula always took her bananas from the farthest bunch in the hut. Wongai also knew something that none of his wives knew, no one knew but he. He knew that those bananas regularly ripening on Petula's bunch were regularly pierced by the needle that carried the Yellow Powder.

Wongai pierced those bananas himself. And enjoyed watching Petula eating them.

Sometimes, lately, she would become thoughtful, and steal a glance at him.

But always then, he looked sullen—and sick. She did not know he was laughing deep inside.

CHAPTER XXXII

THE GIANT OVEREATS HIS WELCOME

The chief Wongai thought it high time he did something about the Giant. The Giant, who was growing so fat he could barely move, or was too lazy to move. Who slept so deeply these warm afternoons that the children playing "jumps" up and down from his stomach to the ground could hardly wake him up. How he used to roar with laughter when he did awake to feel struggling lizards entangled in his beard, scores of little crabs hiding in his hair, to see a mound of earth upon his navel and a full sized plant growing therefrom! To the shrieking delight of the youngsters he would roar with laughter until his great belly upheaved in an eruption that sent earth and plant in a shower amongst them. Wongai scowled. He knew that if *he* had been a child he would have played jokes on the Giant in a way that would have made him roar in a different manner. Such touching ways he could think of, too. Grudgingly he forbade himself to put any diabolical idea into the minds of the children, for the Giant indeed would be a tower of strength if only he could imbue him with the lust of a killer.

Wongai loaded four war-canoes with warriors bedecked in the panoply of war, took aboard the Giant and the Giant's people, and sailed round Badu to Mabuiag. A crowd of cheering people met them; the Giant's people cowered before the savage warriors rushing into the water to manhandle the big canoes ashore. Cowered more with frightened glances at the grim isle of Pulu near by, the barbaric designs of the Kwod grounds, the smoke clinging and coiling from the Sacred Fires by the monstrous Zogo-house.

The Giant became an immediate favourite with the people of Mabuiag. Grimly Wongai thought that when they found out that the more he was plied with food the more he ate their generosity would weaken. For five days and nights the Mabuiag warriors willingly played warlike sports and dances to imbue the Giant with the martial spirit. Quietly watching, Wongai saw the Giant's people cowered and frightened crouching behind him, never certain for a moment as to when their heads were going to decorate the sarokag poles. But the Giant enjoyed everything with childish delight. These dances, these wonderful feasts, were all for *him*.

At last Wongai, in anger, had the Bearers of the War Gud of Kwoiam parade in full dress. And cowed indeed were the Giant's people to the roaring acclaim of the people, the chill of blood in the air at mere sight of the War Gud. But the Giant roared his delight.

Wongai had the Giant dressed up in the War Gud, but both dresses had to be used and even then they were not large enough to fit him.

But the sight of that enormous figure with that savage mask, those towering headdresses, that mighty club, brought an awed silence from all the people. The Giant clad thus looked truly frightful, not a warrior but knew that no man surprised would dare stand against him. The Giant, pleased as a child with a new dress strutted like a peacock, then whirled his great club with rollicking laughter. A roar of applause spread out over the water to echo across the Kwod grounds of Pulu. With this terrible figure to bear the War Gud of Kwoiam and with Wongai to lead them the men of Mabuiag and Badu would be invincible. Roar after roar of applause rolled across the water as the Giant did his stuff.

But Wongai frowned angrily. He saw that the pleased Giant was merely a child with a new toy, the idea of crushing enemies' skulls with that great club he was so lustily swinging was far indeed from his thoughts.

And it was so. Next day Wongai had a heart to heart talk with the Giant, told him he would take him and all his people to be for ever men of Badu if he would become a bearer of the War Gud of Kwoiam. He must, though, be prepared to fight at any moment. And Wongai strongly hinted that a big fight was brewing.

The Giant was eager to wear the War Cud, it would be great fun.

"But why fight?" he inquired plaintively. "It is much nicer to sit under the palm-trees in the shade and eat and sleep."

Wongai immediately took his men back to Badu. And they sensed his displeasure, began to growl at the quantity of food the lazy Giant was devouring. They made no allowance for the work his people did, they could only growl at what *he* ate.

The Giant's people, their instinct razor-sharp from their hunted lives, immediately sensed they had worn out their welcome, unobtrusively made for their canoes. But were dismayed, for the Giant had grown so enormously stout that his canoe quietly sank under him.

Just as well. For had these guests slighted hospitality so abruptly by slipping silently away as they intended, Badu would have declared them enemies for all time.

It was the howl of the children that now put the show away, the scores of children who had discovered their beloved Giant was about to sail away. Wongai and the Badu villagers strolled down to the waterway to see what all the hullabaloo was about. The Giant's people in terror were lashing their two largest canoes together with rattan. Though now in fear of their lives, no thought of abandoning their beloved Giant entered their heads.

He stood up to his middle in water, leaning on his club, a bewildered expression on his great round face as he laughed with cheery jokes at the howling youngsters, eagerly encouraging the elder ones as they splashed out to him with their arms full of yams and manioc and bananas.

And this gave Wongai an idea. The Giant and his people after a couple of months on their own barren isle, would look back longingly to those marvellous foods on Badu. And when that fat whale lost that enormous belly he might be prepared to come back and fight—when Wongai needed him.

So Wongai gave orders to load their canoes with food, with an invitation to return to Badu next time they felt hungry.

So the little crowd of very relieved folk sailed peacefully away, their Giant squatting amidships of two canoes lashed together, piles of food round him, his hoarse voice roaring farewell to the blare of the boos as he waved his club.

And the very next day, in the Quiet Place, a Shadow awaited his chief.

CHAPTER XXXIII

FURTHER ATTEMPTS TO SEIZE GI'OM

"So?" growled Wongai.

"Yesterday, at midday," murmured the Shadow, "*she* went to the well of Zurat for water, as is usual. A palm-leaf had fallen across the pool—it *told* her something. She filled her water bamboo, walked slowly back along the path. At the big fig-tree she glanced round. Then bent down and reached under a flange of the tree. Placed something in her skirt. Then carried her water bamboo back to your house."

"And then?"

"She took a sharkskin packet from her skirt. Lifted up her sleeping-mat, lifted the palm lath with the knot in it, and hid the packet in the hollow under the knot."

"Ah!" Wongai grinned. "A new supply of the Yellow Powder!"

The Shadow nodded.

"I knew her supply was low," said Wongai. "I am a strong man, but *They* must be worried at all the powder she needs."

"You are looking well again lately, my chief," murmured the Shadow.

"Yes," grinned Wongai.

"Yesterday at the well," whispered the Shadow, "I noticed your wife Petula is growing thin. She seems to be sickening."

They gazed into one another's eyes.

"You are a good Shadow." Wongai frowned. "You see many things but—do not see *too* much!"

For a moment they stared. Then the Shadow humbly nodded.

"And who put the little packet under the flange of the fig-tree?" hissed Wongai.

"Kaigas!" answered the Shadow.

"Ah! Maidelaig to Barza, the sorcerer?"

The Shadow nodded.

"Are you. sure he did not shadow *you?*"

The Shadow leered evilly.

Wongai nodded understandingly.

"You hate him," he muttered. "It was he who poisoned your father by order of the Zogo-le through Enoko. But do not slit his gizzard yet—you know what the Zogo-le will do to *you* should you make a mess of *our* business. Bide your time until I am ready. I will plan for you. Then you slice the liver out of your enemy the Maidelaig Kaigas, while I attend to

Barza, the sorcerer."

"As you say, so it shall be, my chief," murmured the Shadow, "but—I long for the day."

"It shall be the night," grumbled Wongai. And, nodding, walked away.

He knew definitely now that it was the Council of the Zogo-le trying to poison him through his Petula, revengeful wife of Sisi. Should she have succeeded in doing the job they would have found means to lay the blame on her and thus the organization would have escaped the wrath of the people.

"Yes," muttered Wongai furiously, "they'd have got away with it. But now I'll silence her and kill Barza, too—in my own sweet time. Then sit back and see what the Zogo-le dare do about it."

While grimly he waited for Petula to die his thoughts turned hotly again to the castaway white girl, dream queen of his island kingdom-to-be.

He knew her general movements, through the Zogo-le's system of keeping close watch through the sorcerers on the movements of the main chiefs of all the islands, then relaying back to the chiefs such news as the Council thought advisable for them to know.

The Lamar girl had sailed with the canoes of Boroto of Entrance Island. Boroto's canoes had helped make up the fleet of the chief Piaquai of Murralug. They had sailed on their annual voyage among the southern islands, then down along the Great Barrier Reef, taking largess of the sea in turtle and big fishes, in shells for cooking-pots, loading the canoes with basketfuls of sun-dried Torres Strait pigeons, feasting on the purple wongai plums. Heavily loaded, the fleet would return just before the start of the wild nor'-west season-Piaquai and his chiefs to the Murralug Isles, Boroto and his people to their little Entrance Island just off the shores of Murralug.

Wongai thought of a plan, laughed exultantly. And discussed the plan with Kosabad.

"You need spies, O my chief," answered Kosabad, "to bring you constant news of the chief Boroto and the Lamar girl. Who better than the Giant's people, who must be ever fishing, who are of so little account that no one bothers about them? Yet to live they must see and hear many things. While, for very existence' sake they must know a great deal about the movements of their powerful neighbours. And—they often fish in Murralug waters!"

So a canoe loaded with foodstuffs sailed to the happy Giant, he even lumbered up from his tree to meet the canoe as little Patma shrilled, "Oh food! Food! Plenty food!"

Willingly the Giant promised to watch every move of the chief Boroto and the Lamar girl Gi'Om, and report by fast canoe to the great chief Wongai.

Which meant that the Giant's best canoe-men must travel far afield with ticklish work to do, to suffer a sticky end should they make a mess of it, while the Giant would snore under his tree, dreaming of the next coming of a Badu canoe with "Food! Food! Plenty food!"

The nor'-west season was very near to breaking. Breathless days, brilliant sunlight, calms and squalls, sudden thunderstorms. And the expected news came to Wongai by the Giant's swiftest canoe.

Near Albany Island the chief Piaquai's canoes were slowly sailing up along the Great South Land, heavy-laden, home to Murralug. Boroto and the spirit girl Gi'Om were still with them. Wongai sailed secretly that night with one swift canoe and thirty picked men. In due course he arrived by Possession Island, where Captain James Cook had taken possession of the entire eastern coast of Australia some seventy-eight years before.

Cook writes:

> Having satisfied myself of the great Probability of a passage, thro' which I intend going with the Ship, and therefore may land no more upon this Eastern coast of New Holland, and on the Western side I can make no new discovery, the honour of which belongs to the Dutch Navigators, but the Eastern Coast from the Lat. of 38° S. down to this place, I am confident was never seen or Visited by an European before us; and notwithstanding I had in the Name of his Majesty taken possession of several places upon this Coast, I now once More hoisted English Colours, and in the Name of His Majesty King George the Third took possession of the whole Eastern coast from the above Lat. down to this place by name of New South Wales, together with all the Bays, Harbours, Rivers, and Islands, situated upon the said Coast; after which we fired 3 Volleys of small Arms, which were answer'd by the like number from the Ship.

Canoes sailing north past the tip of Cape York Peninsula *en route* to Murralug must pass close by Possession Island.

And one morning they came, a long line of heavily loaded canoes, anxious to be home.

Wongai watched them pass. In late afternoon he sailed in their wake. At Entrance Island Boroto's canoe would land, at home, while Piaquai's main fleet would sail the few miles farther on to Murralug.

Boroto and his loaded canoes would be deliriously welcomed by the hungry people. There would be a feast. But all who had manned the canoes would be dog-tired; would sleep soundly.

Wongai and his men landed stealthily during the small hours. Cooking fires were still burning in Boroto's village, shadows round them still gorging, but most lay stretched out round the fires, replete and asleep. From the beehive huts came sounds of deep sleep.

From the outer darkness Wongai grimly surveyed the scene. Beside him the hissing breaths, gritting of teeth of his few warriors, hounds straining at the leash. What a chance for heads! At a gesture they would have rushed in for the kill.

And it would have been a kill, too. But Wongai knew that within moments his thirty men would have been fighting for their own heads against hundreds.

It was not heads he wanted, it was the white girl. If he could but have been certain of the chief's hut he would have rushed it, seized her, and made a swift get-away. But he had a surer, safer plan.

With a scowl at his disappointed warriors he turned into the bush, they filed silently in among the trees behind the village. And soon came upon what the Giant's spies had sworn was there—well-trodden path leading to the village watering pool. Here, at dawn, would come dawdling the sleepy-eyed women to fill the water shells so that their lords and masters could drink. And Gi'Om, the Lamar girl, must come too, on her morning duty to carry back water to her husband, the chief Boroto.

Barbara Thomson's narrow escape has been told in *Isles of Despair.* Wongai himself ruined the ambush, by one incautious movement missed the startled girl by inches. She fled screaming while he and his men retired to their canoe, the war-cries of the Kowraregas ringing in their ears. Wongai, mad with rage, would have killed any warrior who had committed such a foolish blunder as he.

On the early part of the return voyage no man dared speak, fearing the black fury of the chief. Until a sudden cry of *"Lamar nar! Lamar nar!"* ("Spirit canoe!") banished Wongai's anger in cold dread. For the "Spirit ship" stood out plainly as gracefully she sailed out from behind a group of islands to the west. A three-master, in full sail.

Wongai gazed silently, fearful as his men, though his fear was not as theirs. They really believed the ship a spirit ship manned by Lamars, spirit men in human form. But Wongai, gazing away across at the big ship could picture himself swinging high up at that yard-arm, his long-cured ankle sores where the irons had chaffed stung again, a hiss of spray brought the hiss of the lash. Silently he cursed the ship, cursed all ships, coming more frequently now into this barbarous sea. And he had so much, so very much more to do before he could defy them.

"A few more blunders like the one I made this morning and I'll never do it!" he snarled to the waves.

Ship and canoe sailed parallel for several hours before the canoe vanished among the islands.

He returned to find Badu a beehive of rage and hate. Kabara and his Italagas had struck again, had raided Baigoa village in broad daylight and got away with eighteen heads, while exactly at the same time other Italagas had attacked Aubait village on Mabuiag and got away with twenty-two heads. Well planned, swiftly executed, and a triumphant get-away.

Wongai's canoe came sailing into the waterway to a blare of war-boos from both islands, the foreshores brown with people howling war-songs, the waterway lined with opposing canoes taunting one another come and fight. Warriors from Mabuiag pouring into Badu village yelling in berserk fury for revenge, even Wongai's blood chilled to the animal roar of rage as across the waterway the Moans taunted their enemies by waving the heads aloft, spiked on long bamboos waved by spearmen in the canoes.

Wongai saw that to give the order. would mean an all-in fight, but the advantage would be with Kabara's men. There could be no surprise. Badu and Mabuiag must attack across the waterway, the Moans and Italagas could fight on the water, or the beaches, could fight and retire on the shores, could fight and retire inland just as they wished, with all the advantages of counter-attacking a tiring enemy on their own well-known grounds.

Wongai refused to order the attack, to the bewildered disappointment of the allies of Badu and Mabuiag.

In the succeeding weeks, while he planned reprisals, he thought bitterly of the Zogo-le, certain the Zogo-le through their sorcerers had yet again betrayed him, had let Kabara know of his absence from Badu. This was not a straight-out war of Badu against Moa, this was the Zogo-le playing off Wongai against Kabara. Keeping both notorious chiefs busy, keeping the clans and peoples of both large islands well occupied, just swaying the balance of power. He glumly thought that at this rate, with such a skilled leader as Kabara against him, with the Zogo-le constantly undermining both, then it could be years before he subdued Moa. And he must quieten Moa before he dare set out to conquer the island kingdom he regarded now as his right, his and the girl's and his sons-to-be. He struggled to calm the fury within him, for bitterly he had learnt that anger defeated him. It was through anger he had lost that slip of a castaway girl in the first place. Anger more than once had clouded his reason and goaded him to an act that rebounded against himself.

With calmer thoughts came the growing certainty that he could not as yet defeat this far-spread, elusively perfect organization of the Zogo-le. If only he could make this organization his tool, instead of its being his master. He could then easily defeat Kabara, but—ah, what a time it would all take! Time!

Frowning, he lapsed into deep thought. Kabara! Why not *kill* Kabara?

He laughed aloud. What a fool he had been! If he could kill Kabara that would be the beginning of the end for Moa; No other chief among them had his power of uniting their tribes. together into dangerous fighting men. They would split up again into harassed tribes once Kabara was gone. And Wongai would have gained a jump ahead of the Zogo-le.

More! With his wits about him he would amalgamate Moa to Badu and Mabuiag! What *then* could the Zogo-le do about it? And he would have gained the big Western Group but for the Sacred Islets, as a firm foundation for his island kingdom to be!

As he sat in deep thought a runner came racing through the village shouting words that sent every man and woman scrambling for weapons.

"Lamars! Lamars! Lamars!"

But already it was all over. Seven unfortunate castaways from a wreck had landed on the eastern side of the island.

Already their heads were being carried in triumph to Badu village.

CHAPTER XXXIV

A KILLER SEEKS THE CHIEF KABARA

A night of beauty came—many such bless the Coral Sea. The night glow amidst tree and palm. Stars of silver and gold in a sky of velvet blue. Peace along the shores, the waterway a soft blue with colour it had stolen from the sky. And something warm and quite lovely, gliding among the palms. She hesitates a moment, starlight in her eyes. She listens, starlight plays upon her mop of flower-decked hair, a flutter of purple and gold is a living butterfly imprisoned in the fluffy tresses. Her short grass skirt and shapely legs melting in shadows, but starlight plays upon warm brown breasts and coloured corals bedecking graceful neck. She half turns, softly breathing, pretty face stubbornly impish as tensely she listens.

She had cause to be anxious. For if she were caught in her misdoing then something decidedly unpleasant would happen to her.

She shivered involuntarily, but glided on amongst deeper shadows.

She was Moala, petted daughter of Kabara chief of all the Italagas. And she was going to meet her lover.

It was forbidden. For Kabara, her father, had threatened that if ever he caught that faint-hearted Warawe making love to her he would—!

And, creeping through the bush towards the tryst, young Warawe hesitated a moment, shivered. For the powerful Kabara had made no bones about what he would do to Warawe should he catch him making love to that desirable daughter. A grim threat that Warawe knew would be carried out, knew he would never make love again. He hesitated at the thought, but there came to him the melting eyes, the warm lips, the tremulous warmth of Moala. Eagerly, but with almost painful caution, he crept on amongst the deepest shadows.

Kabara had nothing really against the handsome young Warawe, but he did against his father, Kaima, chief of a small inland tribe. For Kaima was lukewarm in his defence of Moa, he concentrated on saving his tribe and his own small lands. Whereas Kabara was fiercely anxious that every tribe of Moa should unite to defeat the dreaded Wongai and his warriors of Badu and Mabuiag. And Kabara fiercely classed every tribe, every man who thought otherwise, as enemies of Moa.

And thus he scorned Kaima, and through him Warawe his son.

But love dares any barrier, and Moala crept on to meet her beloved, almost as stealthily as earlier in the night she had crept from her sleeping-mat, hearkened to her father's deep breathing, crept from the hut, crept through the sleeping village, and out through the palisade where the watchers slept.

But down along the waterway the scattered watchers would not sleep. Should canoes shoot out from Badu, then the blast of boos would alarm the sleeping villages on Moa.

Moala made herself less than a shadow of the night, lest a hidden watcher see her.

Then, she saw—*him!*

A shadow—that slipped past her!

She stared back with panting heart, with an intensity that made her eyes faintly luminous. What was *he* doing? He had vanished towards the rebuilt village of Moa, her father's village. A warrior bathed in slippery coconut oil freshly wetted from his swim across the waterway. Only a belt round his waist holding a long, cassowary-bone dagger. But she had seen the scarlet band of Kwoiam across his forehead—what meant this killer from Badu who vanished toward the village?

It might mean a message of death from the terrible Wongai—a message for her father, the chief Kabara.

On the instant she was following.

Swiftly back to the village. The watchers still snored. Had he passed through? Or had she passed him? Noiselessly she hurried through the gloom and shadow among the big, beehive huts. And came to the largest of all, the chief Kabara's.

And saw *him!*

He was kneeling, head and shoulders inside the low, open doorway, moveless as he listened to the breathing. Then he moved, stealthily, stealthily; she knew he had located the deep breathing of her father. On hands and knees he would creep over her mother, her brothers and sisters. And then—

Now he was nearly within the hut. She knew that if she screamed he would plunge right into the hut and with three swift blows do his work.

She crept forward, knelt down behind him, took a deep breath, and then—

As her teeth fastened deep where it hurt most he howled and the hut shivered to his plunging as he shook her off and leapt away. She was flung across the hut floor amongst writhing bodies with clenched in her hand a long, cruel dagger.

When the sick and sorry killer returned to Wongai, the renegade sneered at his mutilation. For now Kabara would be alert against assassination. While in turn, Wongai could expect a visit from a killer of

Moa. He sneered at the thought. For would even a lone killer, a phantom of the night, dare attempt the life of the dreaded Wongai the Lamar, reincarnated lieutenant of Sida, God of the Crops, friend of Kwoiam, God of War? Weather and ceremonies permitting, he kept his people industriously at work enlarging the gardens, enlarging the canoes. It would be quite a time before Moa settled down to the old uneasy life of occasional raids, of fishing and gardening, of dance and ceremony. Meanwhile he would keep his people at work while he planned deeply, he would strike only when sure he could surprise Moa. And—he would not breathe a word beforehand. He scowled. It seemed at times that the Zogo-le had read his very thoughts.

Eventually his spies brought word of a great feast being prepared at Moa village. For Kabara, chief of all the Italagas, was giving his daughter Moala to wife to Warawe, son of Kaima, chief of Kogal.

Wongai wondered what all the fuss was about. Then he learnt that the girl had saved her father's life. He grinned sourly, then a trifle more humanly. And sent a message to the woe-begone killer—"Would he care to go across and give a marriage gift to the girl who had acted so sharply on her father's behalf? Or did he feel she had gained reward enough?"

The renegade had no time for failures, even though occasionally he had failed himself.

Meanwhile, Wongai's young wife Petula was feeling poorly. Listless, with dark rings spreading below her eyes, she seemed to have no energy but to sit and stare all day, stare questioningly at Sisi. She had almost to drag herself to work. And yet, except for this tiredness, she insisted she was not ill. Mek and Naina made her rich broths of turtle and fish and pigeon, but she did not seem to care whether she ate or not; the only thing she seemed to live on was bananas, she had developed an almost passionate taste for bananas. At times she would glance at her husband in a puzzled sort of way, as if trying to think something out, but just couldn't summon the energy. She would sigh, gaze up at Sisi, slowly eat another banana.

Wongai did not seem to notice; he would not care anyway.

But Wongai *did* care, though not in the way Petula thought. He was resentful of the time and care and trouble she was causing him in doctoring her bananas while avoiding his own—those she daily fixed for *him!* One careless slip, too, and he could easily put the show away. But he would not hurry her off to the Isle of the Blest, no fear, he got too much inner enjoyment watching her eat bananas. Besides, the longer she lasted the safer he was from the Zogo-le. While she lived, *they* thought *he* was eating the bananas! When she went, then—oh well, he'd have to be on guard against some new trick. He knew a lot of theirs now, and he had a few up his own sleeve.

It was one night while he was pondering thus that Miria ventured to try out the lie of the land. She had been a good girl for a very long time; she felt she'd scream if she had to be good much longer. So, with wary eye and a tingling at her sit-me-down she ventured a little joke across the fire with the other wives. With playful laugh, in hushed tones just loud enough for the brooding Wongai to hear, she wondered whether the great chief was thinking about his Lamar sweetheart.

"Isn't it wonderful," she giggled, "that the great chief who can conquer Moa cannot catch a slip of a Lamar girl! But then—the great chief is a fighter, *not* a runner!"

It took some little time for the light words to penetrate the brooding Wongai. As it dawned upon him that Miria was taunting him on failing to catch the white girl he gaped in frank astonishment. Then breathed deeply—his big hand groped under his sleeping-mat. Slowly that hand withdrew—clenching the *Cat*.

With one bound Miria had landed out on the house platform, with another she was down on earth racing for her father's village.

Years, ah! years ago, when I was collecting, the material for this story, the last of the old greybeards remaining would throw up head and hands in uproarious delight in recounting poor Miria's fortunately very few—it needed few—experiences with the Cat. She must have worked up amazing speed, if the old fellows' estimate of time and distance was correct—she must have broken world records in putting space behind her from Wongai's hut to her father's village.

And by their description of that devilish little Cat I couldn't blame her.

Wongai, longing for an opportunity to attempt again to seize the shipwrecked girl, planned long and deeply to organize an overwhelming attack upon the three main villages of Moa. And—the most important thing of all—the killing of Kabara, chief of all the Italagas.

To make certain this time, he determined to kill the redoubtable chief himself. But of all that was revolving in his mind he mentioned not a word. The Zogo-le would not know in time—unless they read his thoughts!

The Giant, his paunch gaily bedecked with a rope of flowering creeper, with one canoe-load of his people honoured Badu with a visit, to the hilarious welcome of the village children. Wongai greeted him affably, inviting him to eat, and yet eat. And the Giant patted his not-so-fat stomach and gurgled his delight.

The Giant's people had proved very capable scouts and spies, still keeping Wongai informed of the movements of Boroto and the shipwrecked girl, Barbara Thomson. Plaintively, with a reproachful smile, the Giant inquired of the great chief Wongai why he had not sent him any more good foods, just because the great chief had failed to catch that tomtit of a girl.

The Giant, of course, had put his great foot in it, but then a Giant cannot be all beef and all brain, too.

The "great chief" would have loved to have slit the Giant's throat, but as the Giant still could be of important use to him he smiled sourly and with a wave of the arm gave the most acceptable of all answers—a great big basket crammed full of food!

So again the Giant's grampus-like snores, his rollicking laughter came in throaty gusts through Badu village as he slept and ate under his favourite palm-tree. Again his cheeks began to develop the face of the moon, his stomach rising high and spreading as the youngsters jumped upon it in play or tickled his nostrils with a straw, his navel with a palm-leaf. The elder boys quarrelled over his murderous club until one afternoon in a scrimmage a lad cracked the skull of his brother.

Thereafter the Giant's people were commanded to keep the club hidden.

So the Giant grew fat again, boyishly happy, divinely contented. Dolefully indeed did he consent to return home when his anxious people urged him that certain signs assured them they were perilously close again to overeating their welcome.

Time went by. At last the chief Wongai was ready for the great attack.

CHAPTER XXXV

WHILE PEOPLE SLEEP

Preparations had long been in hand for the important ceremonies of the Ad Giz, always held on Mabuiag. This eagerly awaited event would last ten days, culminating in the Parade of Kwoiam. The great chief Wongai had promised that these ceremonies would be the greatest ever.

Loading of the canoes with good things for the feasts, furbishing of weapons and regalia, gay chatting of women as they plaited new grass skirts, threaded olive shells and berries, dog's teeth and shark's teeth for necklace and arm-bands to bedeck shapely limbs.

Girls spending long hours over their lovely hair with combs and ornaments of exquisitely carved tortoiseshell, feathers of golden paradise, green and scarlet of parrot, colourful flower and butterfly wings.

Young bucks massaging broad chests, strong bodies with coconut oil, trying on emblems of clan and degree.

But— hesitant whisper. There would be some bitterly disappointed ones. For the chief Wongai suspected an attack upon the waterfront villages when the warriors were absent at Mabuiag. So he had planned a trap for Kabara.

Warriors must remain behind to man this trap.

Scornful hilarity in the villages of Moa. For strangely, they learnt of this deep-laid trap of the hated Wongai. They would sleep well, in dreaming smiles at that trap inviting them to cross over and attack Badu.

On a brilliant day, to the bray of boos, laughter and song, fleets of gaily bedecked canoes sailed from Badu to Mabuiag.

But strangely enough, no trap had been laid, though all believed it so. The people would have been amazed had they known that the guard was only sufficiently strong to keep any prowling scout from poking his nose too closely into the Badu business ashore.

As observed from Moa shore, the Badu waterway villages seemed invitingly deserted. Didn't the Moans laugh! As if they were children to walk into such an obvious trap!

Cheerily they went about their business, expecting no danger until their enemies' period of the ceremonies should be ended.

At Mabuiag, one week of the ceremonies was over. Mabuiag was massed with people. The Kwod grounds freshly palisaded, the giant totems glaring under new paints, the carved Zogos each in its shrine along pathway or on hill or beach patterned with symbolic designs in shells, freshly decked with flowers. The taboo poles heavy with coloured streamers, moaning with rattles warning the uninitiated not to dare one step farther. The feast places crowded with people day and night, the dancing grounds throbbing to the drums, stamp of feet. In each village the sarokag poles leering out over the feasters and dancers, the singers and laughter makers, those who were awake and those who slept in exhaustion.

While across on Pulu incense-scented smoke rose heavily from the Sacred Fires. Distantly, weird figures in ceremonial dress and grotesque mask creeping among strangely builded rocks. Motionless circles, concentric rings, squares of standing and sitting sorcerers. Ghostly processions of initiates under flame and torch.

For upon Sacred Pulu the Zogo-le in ceremony were in full force, attended by the sorcerers and Maid-le and their attendant Maidelaig and initiates from many islands. Solemn now the preparations upon Kulka, making ready for the Parade of Skulls upon the last day—skulls legendary with beeswax noses and cheeks heavily painted, decorated with the brightest of shells and berries, and with brighter things, too.

Those strange, glittering, flashing things taken from the clubbed bodies of shipwrecked Lamars. And from abandoned wrecks of how many years? Some definitely centuries ago.

At close quarters Wongai now saw these "sun stones", as the islanders called them in awe. For, so generations of Zogo-le had told them, the sun stones had been sent them by the Sun God, delivered to them by the Thunder God when he wrecked the spirit ships in storms. Powerful magic indeed was imbued in the glittering stones of red and blue, yellow and green. Magic not of this world, so the people implicitly believed, for it was magic of the sun.

Wongai's eyes grew big as he saw the flashing stones, just one or two here and there among the barbaric regalia of the Zogo-le, and among the ornaments adorning a moon-faced tortoiseshell Gud.

Nomoa, chief of Mabuiag, told him of many wrecks on and near Ugar Island, some even long before their fathers' fathers' time; of strange Lamars too who wore "skin" like plates of the giant turtle, skin so hard that arrows failed to pierce it. Such Lamars had been difficult indeed to kill. One story of a wreck at dead of night when nearly all the tribesmen were away at the great ceremonies at Eroob. Some Lamars came ashore in a boat and hastily buried a little "thing". Then the Lamars fought against one another and killed one another. All except two, who were killed when the people in hiding sprang out and clubbed them. The remaining Lamars on the wreck sailed away in boats. Then the people dug up the "little thing" and broke it open. It was full of "sun stones", and heavy little yellow things. The Zogo-le took them all away.

Other such stories Wongai heard as he gazed on the Sacred Relics, dimly realizing that the history of this little sea, of brown men and even white went far, far deeper than he would ever know.

When the great day came the trophies, carried by the sorcerers and Maid-le, led by the Zogo-le in their awesome dresses and masks, would be paraded throughout Mabuiag. While at night those trophies recently taken in warfare would be presented to their proud owners to be set upon the village or family sarokag pole.

But today was the day of Kwoiam, God of War. That morning Bauri, the Zogo of Zogos, with Wongai, chief of chiefs of Badu, had led the warriors and people to the Hill of Kwoiam, there to pay homage at Kwoiam's tomb. The chief Zogo in his Zogo dress, Wongai in all his savagery as chief of chiefs followed by the bearers of the War Gud of Kwoiam, and the warriors bedecked, heavily armed, in fierce homage to their greatest hero, the War God, Kwoiam.

And now tonight the commemorative war-dances were in full swing, squad upon squad of warriors roaring songs of legend and conquest as their feet thundered in the stamp of the war-dances. A mass of sitting people encircling them, their voices again and again thundering adoration. Drums reverberating, flame of fires upon Pulu, flame too far out upon the placid waters from glowing fires of Mabuiag.

The culmination of this night was the appearance of the bearers of the War Gud led by the chief Wongai, followed in packed ranks by the protectors of the Gud. As Wongai came marching out from the centre of the circle squad after squad fell in behind him, each led by its fighting chief. As he came to the outer edge of the circle he turned to march round it. He would continue doing so while as squad after squad fell in it would take the appearance of a huge, circling snake. Wongai at the head with the War Gud bearers would continue gradually circling inward until finally the parade ground would be a circle of packed warriors surrounding the War Gud, the people working up to a frenzy of enthusiasm at the steady, growing thud of marching feet, the crescendo of war-song as squad after squad joined in.

It was just when the massed circle was complete, just before the final thunderous act, that *it* came.

A messenger panting into the firelight to blow urgent blasts from a war-boo—urgent warning of an attack. Then shouted, "Badu! Badu!

Kabara and his Italagas are attacking Badu!"

Instant silence, breath-taking after the uproar of a moment before. The messenger's voice again carrying clear over all.

"To spear and club! The men of Moa are attacking Badu!"

Wongai's voice roaring "To the canoes! To the canoes!"

And pandemonium as the mass writhed and pushed to spread as the outer circle was racing down to the beaches.

Warriors leaping to the canoes, canoes all along the main beach shooting out from shore followed by others and others, swiftly paddling, now towards Badu. It had all happened so suddenly.

When well clear of Mabuiag, Wongai halted the canoes in a clustering cloud round his war-canoe. He called for every chief to come close beside him. And then, in a tense silence, e spoke.

There was *no* attack on Badu.

But—he was now going to attack *Moa*. Wipe out the three main villages, Moa, A-dam, and Dualud by surprise pressed swiftly home.

He, Kosabad, and the War Gud and warriors were to attack Moa village, with Nomoa and Sagigi attacking A-dam, Bagari and Wypali attacking Dualud.

To land silently, creep to their objective, to attack at the same moment. Each force to swarm through the village gateway, to surround the huts, burst into them, only then to howl he war-cry.

When Wongai was certain each chief clearly understood his part in detail he ordered them return to their men, fully explain the plan, then sort themselves out into the three fleets. Then all pushed on in silence but for the dip of the paddles along the dark shore of Badu, making for the wide mouth of the waterway.

And the lovely phosphorescence dripping from their paddle blades shimmered like pearls—pearls as effervescent, as fleeting as the lives of men, women, and children peacefully asleep in the three main villages of Moa.

CHAPTER XXXVI

KABARA DIES FIGHTING

The attack struck Moa like the howl of a tropical storm—shriek of the war-cry, rush of feet, bursting of palm-leaf matting, crash of breaking framework as yelling warriors hurled themselves into the huts. Thud of blows upon convulsive upsurge of waking bodies, grunts, screams drowned in roar of animal sounds as hell broke loose.

Wongai had hurled himself into the chief's hut and plunged his knife into Kabara's body as he leapt from his sleeping-mat. Locked in each other's arms, thrashing over the floor against the heaving bodies of the startled family they snarled like ravening animals, biting at each others throats, gouging eyes, plunging convulsively as they rolled over the coals while the frantic family burst through the hut and down came the matting walls upon the fighters. Struggling there under matting and falling poles they knew not the blaze outside as hut after hut flared up in a hissing inferno of berserk slaughter. Clawing in blinded fury, they strained and panted until the blazing matting forced them break away, tortured by flames.

Leaping out into the choking air Wongai dashed bleeding hands across smoke-filled eyes as he sprawled over a dead warrior, his outthrust hand clawing a spear-shaft. Leaping up on the second, through stinging eyes he glimpsed. the writhing Kabara tearing the burning skirt from his waist. With one desperate lunge Wongai thrust the spear into Kabara's body then, gasping, jumped away from the flames, clawing at his burning skirt and blinded eyes.

The village was an inferno of shrieking men, women, and children struggling to leap the stockade, frantic victims to the swinging clubs, the thrusting spears, the whizzing arrows of the howling victors of Badu and Mabuiag.

The surprise had been devastatingly complete, panic immediate, the slaughter the worst in the bloodstained legends of Moa. Out under the cool trees from the smouldering remnants of Moa village, Wongai dressed his wounds with coconut oil while his warriors' voices thundered in the dreadful triumph song. Presently, excited messengers appeared running. The victory had been almost as complete at A-dam and Dualud.

The three main villages of Moa burnt to the ground, their inhabitants annihilated.

And—Kabara, chief of chiefs of all the Italagas, was dead.

For a week Wongai's men raged among the hills and dales of Moa, slaughtering all whom they could catch. The power of Moa was broken. No other chief like Kabara was destined to arise, Kabara who had held the tribes almost together. This was the beginning of the end for the people of Moa. From henceforth they would fight only as hunted tribes.

Wongai, the third day after the burning of the villages, was forced to return to Badu, where nasty wounds kept him laid up for several months. An ungrateful, savage patient to the ministrations of his four wives, and his own trusted medicine man. But a grimly satisfied man. For he had broken the unity of Moa—outwitted even the Zogo-le.

And Kabara was dead.

The great chief Wongai's power now would be widespread indeed. He would allow the tribes of Moa live in hunted dread for a few months, then offer them peace and alliance with Badu and Mabuiag. They would accept with great thankfulness. Then he would set out in force, secure in his base, seize that elusive girl castaway, bring her to Badu.

And then—

This renegade who had gone through and then accomplished so much, this renegade living the life of, and now the centre of life and intrigue in a tiny little world that thought "itself" the only life on this earth, did not know nor care that this was the month of January and that on 24 January 1848 James Wilson Marshall had found gold in the tail-race of Sutter's Mill, California.

What on earth would he have cared if by some miracle he *had* known? California was in another continent, thousands of miles away across a great ocean.

But when Marshall found gold overseas his discovery was not only to bring an unparalleled transformation in the development of barely known California. It soon was to affect another great, distant, empty continent—Australia.

Strange indeed how a single man can start a chain of events that may go all the way round the world.

Can even affect a lone renegade in an unknown sea, battling to make a kingdom of his own.

But such momentous matters were as far away from young Kartoy as the end of the world. For Kartoy was now a full-fledged warrior, he had returned from the fight at Moa with a head—her head.

And wasn't Lu-esa proud—she threw her arms round her warrior bold when he laid the trophy at her feet.

While another lass, a lass of Moa, was sad, so sad. Moala, daughter of the slain chief Kabara.

For Moala, wife of young Warawe, son of the little chief Kaima, was the only survivor of Kabara's family. Safe with Warawe in his father's little inland village.

But Moala's heart was sad—sad indeed.

A YOUTH OF MOA

CHAPTER XXXVII

TOO LATE FOR PETULA

Through the long weeks of his convalescence Wongai the chief lived in renewed dreams of his island kingdom, crazily anxious for action and the girl.

His fever of bad-tempered impatience did not help his wounds. But he had grim consolation.

His wife Petula—Petula was obviously sickening.

When they had carried the great chief home Petula had eagerly wished to attend his wounds. Angrily he had pushed her aside. He would not even let Miria attend him. Only patient Mek and Naina would he allow dress his wounds and look after him.

Petula had brightened up noticeably when he came home desperately wounded, watching him closely from her sleeping-mat after sundown brought her trudging back from the gardens. But when it became obvious that the chief would recover Petula lost interest, sinking back into despondency.

And Wongai, noticing all; chuckled inwardly. If only that poisonous she-cat knew it was *she* who was really sick; if only she knew how sick she looked, how sick she was! He ground his teeth in a snarling enjoyment.

But—he would eat no bananas—only at such times as Mek and Naina tempted him with bananas fresh from the gardens.

Petula, though, still ate bananas—lived on bananas. And now Wongai hated seeing her eat those bananas. For until such time as he recovered and had the hut to himself he could no longer "doctor" Petula's bananas.

In grim silence he awaited the time when he again could handle the Yellow Powder. Seeming to gaze at nothing in particular, fiendishly he watched Petula dreamily munching a banana.

Then the Giant, the hungry Giant and his people came again, the eager Giant confident of welcome because he brought news of the Lamar girl, Gi'Om. With his magnificent stomach, alas, but a shadow of its former glory he almost hurried into the village to deliver the news to the great chief himself.

The chief Boroto her husband, watched over the spirit girl jealously, explained the Giant, he never allowed her stay too long in the one place. Sometimes at Entrance Island, sometimes with his kinsmen the Kowraregas on big Murralug Island, sometimes away with him fishing for turtle and dugong, sometimes visiting his friends the savages on the

Great South Land.

The Giant's scouts brought other news at which Wongai frowned, the coming and passing of an occasional Lamar ship, those spirit people who in great ships came from the skies to vanish—where?

The Giant, once he had comfortably lined his capacious bingy with the first instalment of manioc and yam and banana and turtle and fish and crab, in a spirit of grateful camaraderie went to all the trouble to waddle up from the beach and pay the great chief Wongai yet another visit. Grunting up onto the house platform he squatted down with a gusty sigh, leaning back against a post that Wongai irritably hoped would give way behind him. Gratefully patting his stomach the Giant regarded Wongai with one great big smile, inquiring with tender solicitude after the welfare of the great chief. Wongai grunted. But the Giant prattled on in childlike confidence. He complimented Wongai on his great victory, then went on earnestly to inquire if all that trouble was worth it? Yes, he knew the warriors of Badu and Mabuiag had done a very great thing, had taken many, many heads, more than had ever been known taken in one battle in all the history of the islands before, even more than the great chief Kebisu had taken in his famed raid on the Two Brothers Island. But, boomed the Giant earnestly, was it really worth it, all that trouble, all that hard work? Look how near to death had come his friend, the beloved Mamoose of all Badu, friend of Sida, God of the Crops, who had come to earth again to teach his people how to make such wonderful gardens. What utter tragedy it would have been—what waste, had the great chief Wongai been killed!

And the Giant's big, limpid eyes misted; he gazed compassionately at the irate Wongai. All the islands would mourn, assured the Giant earnestly, should anything happen the great chief Wongai. And was it really worth it? Here on this wonderful island of Badu where such luscious vegetables and fruits grew as man never dreamed would grow before, where the seashore teemed with fish and crab, the reefs and sea-bed with crayfish and turtle and dugong! "Why, oh why," inquired the Giant in pained tones, "did not the men of Badu just fish and eat and sleep, then fish and eat and sleep?"

Wongai glared in exasperated rage, imagining just what he would like to do to this overgrown hulk of whalemeat, this overbloated belly of a sea-cow whose dream it was to gorge until it nearly burst, then lie back on the warm sand under the shade of a palm and listen to warbling birds until it snored itself asleep. Wongai simply could not understand the Giant. Wongai the chief, Wongai the felon, Wongai who had laboured in chains at the breakwater, the labour of Hercules, Wongai who had ground his bloody teeth under the searing sting of the lash, who had slaved at Kingston in that grim prison fortress amid scenes of horror, Wongai who had killed men, Wongai who had *eaten* men. In silence he stared at the boyishly smiling face, that great moon-face exuding sympathy, that overpowering paunch, the limpid eyes of this most puzzling thing he had ever met.

And a queer thought struck Wongai.

If only *they* had had him with them in the boat—they would all have been alive today! How the Weasel would have gloated over those fat hams!

As the Giant prattled innocently on, Wongai fought his growing temper. To think that he should sit helplessly here while this plaything of brats gabbled at him, this mountain of guts that chuckled to the warble of a bird, the tickle of a straw in that valley of a navel!

But the Giant was of too much use to Wongai. Smothering disgusted curses, he growled out an inquiry about Gi'Om.

But here the Giant yawned prodigiously. He had given his news. Until he grew hungry again he would take no further interest in that Lamar girl, it was his scout men in their light canoes who on long trips sought news of her for the chief of chiefs, Wongai—would continue to seek news of her for as long as the great chief cared. But she was of no other interest whatever to the Giant except as a heaven-sent procurer of food for him through the chief Wongai. On her island there were no wonderful gardens, nor on the Murralug Islands of her kinsmen. But on Badu, now—! "Let us talk about your wonderful gardens," murmured the Giant drowsily. "Now that is something to talk about!" and he licked sighing lips.

"Hadn't you better go and have a feed?" gritted Wongai. "It's a long time since you've eaten! Only about an hour ago—your guts must be thinking your throat's cut!" Silently he wished it were so.

A delighted smile made happy the Giant's face.

"I wouldn't have thought of it, great chief," he chuckled admiringly and, pulling himself up with a grunt, dropped to the ground and waddled happily away to his feeding tree followed by an exasperated spit from his great friend, the chief of chiefs.

"May it poison you," growled Wongai.

And instinctively glanced across the hut at Petula. She was crouching there staring across at him, a strange look in her eyes, eyes now with such deep rings round them. Even on occasions of her passionate defiance he had never seen such an expression in those eyes. Despite himself he glanced up at his bunch of bananas, then at her again. And looked away down at the village palms feeling such a strange feeling—he had never,

never felt guilty before—never been so snarlingly uneasy when he had been found out—had never felt this strange feeling before. He almost wished he had *not* poisoned those bananas.

After a while she rose, took her bamboo water container, and like a wraith went silently from the hut for water. He watched her vanish among the palms. How thin, how listless she had grown, how feverish those eyes. He had neither noticed so much, nor cared. But now—he wished she had more guts. Thoughtfully he reached out for his zoob, slowly grinding a tobacco leaf between his rough palms. Those bananas! He remembered now how often, how solicitously, she had tried to entice him with bananas when he was half delirious from those cursed wounds. He should not have cursed her so angrily, he might have put himself away—had he put himself away? Just what *did* that look in her eyes mean? Thoughtfully he smoked and—

The Shadow was beside him.

"She is by the Zogo-house with Barza the sorcerer," he whispered earnestly. "They speak fast, she as if in fear, he as if suspicious. I believe they *know*—she is returning now. Beware, O my chief."

Wongai nodded as the Shadow vanished. Moments later Petula came slowly up the path. She entered the hut without glancing at him.

Thereafter Petula offered her chief no more bananas. Nor did she eat any herself.

But it was too late for Petula.

CHAPTER XXXVIII

IN WHICH THE SPIRIT WORLD IS INVOKED AGAINST WONGAI THE CHIEF

Barza, the sorcerer, sat within his hut, gloom upon his brow.

Enoko, the sorcerer, had failed. Barza had sworn *he* would *never* fail! Had he?

Wongai, the chief, was in ruddy health. Petula his wife was—dying!

Barza had not yet dared let the Zogo-le know. And—their patience was strained.

But now—now that the chief Wongai had killed Kabara and there seemed nothing to prevent him attaining Moa—

Ah, but *Barza* was to prevent him! The Zogo-le believed that for long Barza had been slowly but surely poisoning the chief Wongai through Petula his wife, widow of the long-dead Sisi.

And Barza had thought so, too.

If *They* knew that he had failed! Now that the balance of power was upset and there was nothing to stop that dangerous chief from combining Moa with Badu and Mabuiag—!

Cold and dismal the night, black as the pit. Dreary pattering from rain-drenched leaves, creepy swish of wind-blown branches. Warm in the hut, the air musty from sodden vegetation and dead, dried-up things. Perhaps because of damp and humidity and warmth the eyes of the divination skull glowed eerily each time a draught sent it spinning upon the end of its suspension cord.

The Zogo-le! The Zogo-le now were urgent. Kabara was gone. And the chief Wongai, even though he was a reincarnation, must go, too.

Barza stared gloomily at the coals.

Kabara dead. Moa now at the feet of this accursed Wongai—should he have the sense to act.

The reincarnated devil had *proved* he had sense. And he could act, too.

Barza dared not tell the Zogo-le that by some inexplicable means he had failed. That Wongai had returned to health in riotous strength—that it was Petula who was dying.

No! Barza had not failed yet—he *dare* not fail.

That cursed snake—there it was again, its vindictive head swaying at him from the opposite side of the day fire-pan.

Barza spat at it. The snake hissed.

"*You* failed, Enoko," sneered Barza. "Fool not yourself that I shall fail."

The reptile hissed.

"Ah!" snarled Barza. "What does it feel like, Enoko, to live within the belly of a snake?"

The beady eyes stared vindictively, it licked leathery lips with forked tongue, seemed to swell out its crimson throat.

Morosely Barza stared at the thing, certain the spirit of Enoko was within it, gloating at him.

"And so," sneered Barza, "Enoko failed! Failed to poison the great chief, reincarnation of Wongai, friend of Sida. Found it difficult to poison a spirit man, eh, Enoko?

"But no excuses, Enoko, for though reincarnated the great chief lives but in earth life again. For the time. being he must live as we do, feel as we do, find joy as we do—can be made to *suffer* as we do. And in this knowledge the Zogo-le accept *no* excuse. Oh, well, Enoko failed. When we fail, we pay. Enoko paid. And yet, Enoko was so very, so devilishly cunning with poisons!"

In the stillness the snake's head almost imperceptibly swayed just above the edge of the fire-pan, its beady eyes fixed on the sneering eyes of the man. A gust of wind showered raindrops on the roof.

"How was it, Enoko?" asked Barza softly. "How was it that you came to smoke the Pipe of Death?"

Suspended high above the sorcerer's head the divination skull revolved slowly, baleful its glaring eyes in their luminous sockets of green.

"You hate the great chief, Enoko, and so do I—in *that* we agree—But you hate *me* also, Enoko, and I hate *you*. Which do you hate most, Enoko? The great chief Wongai? Or me?"

The snake hissed—twice!

"Ah! You hate both so viciously you could nearly burst out of your totem. How extremely annoying it must be to hate so intensely while helplessly imprisoned within the belly of a snake!"

He chuckled sneeringly—the snake hissed hatefully as if understanding every derisive word.

Barza laughed cynically, gloating across at the reptile.

"I shall not smoke the Pipe of Death, Enoko, *I* shall find some way out—Barza the Silent will succeed where Enoko failed, *I* surely will poison Wongai, chief of all Badu."

For a long time man and snake stared across at one another. "Poison!" whispered Barza broodingly. "It must be a poison that no one can tell—he must die by some natural way that the people will be certain was not brought about by the hand of man. Otherwise there would be uproar, even against the Zogo-le, for Wongai now is so very powerful and so beloved of Badu and Mabuiag—soon may be of Moa, too—which would upset the Zogo-le. Yes, Enoko, he must die, *will* die—but it must *not* appear by the hand of man. Otherwise I, too, Barza must smoke the Pipe of Death."

Silence again, the sorcerer thinking, thinking, the snake's head motionless, staring across.

"Ah, Enoko, it does me good to talk to you, to tell you things. For though you would dearly love to, *you* cannot now poison Barza the Silent through words that come out of his own mouth."

Thoughtfully he resumed. "Poison! And you, Enoko, you knew, you *know,* such cunning secrets about poisons. Whisper me, Enoko, help me though against your will, tell me how to poison *him*—it must be *soon* now—tell me *how* to poison the chief Wongai—*your* enemy—so he will surely die and no man can say man's hand has been laid against him!"

Silence but for the raindrops—motionless the snake.

"Ah! You will not tell. Cunning mongrel! You know that it must be either he or I—one of us *must* die and you will be rid of one enemy by just looking on. Well Enoko, *I* shall not smoke the Pipe of Death!"

Morosely the sorcerer lapsed into silence, his mind deeply probing the problem.

"Poison!" he muttered. "And you know so much about poisons, Enoko. Why, you are poison *yourself*—"

His lips parted, his eyes dilated with understanding. Then smacked hand to thigh with exultant chuckle.

"Ho, Enoko! *You* shall poison Wongai, chief of chiefs of all Badu, lieutenant to Sida, God of the Crops, friend of Kwoiam, God of War! *You,* Enoko, shall poison the great chief Wongai!" His face was wreathed in evil smiles.

"Why, oh why did I not think it before! It is *you* who shall poison the great chief, Enoko. You, through the fangs of your totem snake! And no man then can say that man's hand has been lifted against the chief. *You* kill your enemy and mine, too! *You* give Barza his triumph!"

With a spiteful chuckle he leaned towards the snake. "Why did I not think it before! Or—" thoughtfully he paused, then added in curious voice, "Or *was* it you who but now told me Enoko? Through your spirit mind to mine? Ah, no! You hiss—mongrel of a thing—you *never* would have told. So much the better, Barza. thought it out for himself. And you shall kill him, Enoko, whether or no."

He began refilling his zoob, smiling with the liveliest satisfaction, then suddenly, "Ah, now, Enoko, how clearly now I think!" He leaned towards the snake. "Listen, Enoko! You are going to do me a great service—unwillingly. In return, I am going to do you a great service—unwillingly. Only now do I understand why you have lingered so long within your totem, the snake. 'Tis because you failed in your biggest work, the task that would have gained you that coveted seat within the Council of the Zogo-le. You *failed* the Zogo-le. And, failing, your kazi[4] failed your spirit ancestor, failed your own ancestral Ad[5] And failing, failed the Ad Giz[6] right back to the Ancient days.[7]

"No, Enoko, no wonder your existence is within the bowels of a snake. It is fitting that your spirit now is held within its totem snake here where in earth life you lived and worked and planned so long—and made the last, the great failure. But now, Enoko, you will not fail, you will kill Wongai the chief and by so doing complete your work and thus liberate your spirit to fly back to Kibu in the skies at last."

Barza drew at his zoob, with almost a benign expression, gazing across at his enemy the snake. And he had implicit faith in every word he had spoken, for such was their belief. When the spirit of Enoko had seen his task accomplished he would be free to leave his totem snake. His spirit would then fly to Kibu Isle in the skies to be trained in his new life as a spirit man in earnest.

In deep thought Barza smoked, giving no more thought to Enoko's imprisoned spirit.

It was so simple. The snake was deadly venomous. How to cause the snake to bite the chief Wongai naturally, so that to all the people the terrible fatality would be snake-bite through natural causes? Woe to Badu and Mabuiag! For the great chief, alas was dead. Dead of snake-bite, as had died many a good but far, far lesser man before him.

Barza grinned. How he would torment that snake, Enoko's totem snake, and—he grinned cynically—through the snake, Enoko's spirit!

Hours before the snake was to bite the big chief he would tantalize it—*and* tantalize it. Finally he would torment it. Torment it until its beads of eyes blazed from its head, its black forked tongue would be lightning,

---

[4] His own personal spirit.

[5] The first, the ancient founder of his sept.

[6] The first God, God of the Very Beginning.

[7] That time after the Earth was formed, but after the mighty convulsions of nature, when the first spirit-gods descended to plant the Earth, to prepare it with trees and fishes and fruits, animals and birds, to prepare the seasons, to prepare all things upon it so as to make it habitable for the coming of Man.

its poison sacks filled to bursting with tortured venom. Until, when it writhed across Wongai while he slept, it would sink its fangs so deep that Wongai would have to tear it and his throat out—nothing would loosen its hold!

For hours Barza silently gloated. It was just after dawn that he half choked a yawn—he had not solved yet how to cause the snake to *bite* Wongai, so that it would appear so natural—a snake crawling into his house and across the body of the great chief as he slept.

Barza finished his yawn. Ah, well. That problem was simple, it would work its own way out. Then—

He stared towards the snake. Ah! The cursed thing had vanished!

He had suddenly remembered that during all these months he had failed to trap the snake!

He must first *catch* his snake!

CHAPTER XXXIX

IN WHICH THE YARD-ARM LOOMS PERILOUSLY CLOSE

Lu-esa was dreaming.

In the snug little hut Kartoy had built for her, under the big old palm-tree.

That was where she had told him she would love the little home to be.

She smiled tenderly—at memory.

Sitting on the thick, warm mats, watching Kartoy's midday meal simmering on the clay fire-pan, she was listening dreamily.

Yes—joyous song, anxious, though, with tender solicitude. The sun-bird singing—*speaking* to his mate.

Up in the flowering creeper on the big old palm-tree. In their dainty little nest-home. And *she,* Lu-esa knew, the mother sun-bird was sitting on three such pretty little eggs. Soon the babies would come, Lu-esa was expecting them any day. And so, too, she knew by his proudly anxious song was *he,* the sun-bird.

Kartoy's dinner was burning. Lu-esa was dreaming.

Lu-esa was going to have a baby.

The good old Giant grew fat again, his stomach bloomed in all its glory, a really heartening sight, a baby mountain growing up there under his favourite palm-tree. His hearty laughter daily rolled through the village as the children frolicked upon him before he fell asleep between meals. When he snored they stood on their heads upon and jumped up to and from his stomach, which appeared to aid his digestion.

Now and again, though, he would awake with a convulsive, rumbling "Wow!" to shrieks of merriment. This was when the little devils guided the whirling point of the heavy stone spinning-top "over the edge" and down into his navel.

The Giant's beautiful round paunch, massive as the belly of an ox, taut as a drum after dinner, was an ideal place on which to spin the top. The slumberer took but little notice of his tormentors save for a protesting sigh, a rumbling twinge, or a belly upheaval now and then. But as for the heavy stone top, when they guided the spinning point "over the edge"—

"I'd spin more than a top there for two pins," sneered Wongai to Kosabad. "I'd chuck a lump of honeycomb into it, then lead a trail to a meat-ant's nest."

"That would move him," smiled Kosabad, "in a hurry. Although the ants would sorrow to feel him go. For there's enough meat on him to feed all the ants in Badu throughout one wet season."

"If I didn't need the swine's scouts I'd ram food down his throat with his own club until he burst!" jeered Wongai.

Kosabad smiled complacently. "He certainly is making a hole in our gardens," he murmured, "but the work of his people more than make up for it—none of our men and women toil so hard as they. But when you have had enough of him, my chief, let me know and I'll see they quietly go."

"I've had more than enough of him," growled Wongai. "I'd like to fry his liver in his own fat. But his scouts are too useful. Feed him a week longer—then kick him to hell out of this."

"With his canoes loaded with food?" smiled Kosabad

"Yes!" snarled Wongai in exasperation. "Better let him leave with a good taste in his mouth, though I'd rather plug his throat with a coconut."

"He might swallow even *that!*" smiled Kosabad.

"Not the way *I'd* fix it!" growled Wongai.

During the following months Wongai, longing for an opportunity to attempt again to seize Barbara Thomson, took advantage, of the enthusiasm over the great defeat of Moa to redouble tribal energies in the improving of canoes, in additions to gardens, in improving weapons and tools.

Willingly the people fell in with the great chief's desires, though the warrior clans were puzzled, eager to turn the defeat of Moa into a rout. Any bright day now, in a spirit of tantalizing bravado as the feeling seized them, they would skim their canoes to the very foreshore of any waterfront village of Moa and with blast of the boo taunt the people to come and fight. A challenge ignored now, with the Moans completely dispirited by the annihilation of their three main villages and the death of Kabara.

Grimly Wongai allowed his warriors to enjoy their play, it would all serve to impress upon Moa what he had in store for them in the future should they still defy him.

He wished the lesson to sink in well; he did not desire to attack Moa, did not wish to weaken her tribes any further. Shortly, when the time was ripe, he believed he could make peace with Moa and amalgamate the big island with Badu and Mabuiag. What a triumph that for him against the Zogo-le. And—what a great step forward in the gaining of his island kingdom!

If only he had that white girl beside him now!

But all his work—his plans, too—was constantly to be held up by the demands of ceremonial life, by the seasons, by the stern necessity of constant fishing, and by the natural island indolence to loll about and laugh and play and dance when food was plentiful and no ceremonial duties demanded attention. He had long since realized that preparations for the various ceremonies occupied one-fifth of the time of all the people. He determined that once he had won his island kingdom he would break the power of the Zogo-le and eliminate all ceremonial life except that glorifying Kwoiam, God of War, of Sida, God of the Crops, and his lieutenant, Wongai. But he kept such plans wisely to himself.

In the meantime, while driving the people, he sent a canoe loaded with goodly foods to the Giant, ordering him to urge his best scouts constantly to bring him word of the movement of the chief Boroto and his wife, Gi'Om. And the Giant, hungry again, obeyed with gusto. Immediately he had eaten Wongai's gift, he sailed for Badu and eagerly confronted the frowning Wongai, little Patma, big-eyed, leading him by the hand, his head barely up to the Giant's knees.

Smiling, he pointed out that he could so much better carry out the great chief's orders if for the time being he made his headquarters at Badu village. For his people then no longer would be obliged to feed him. Wongai could feed him while all his people's energies would be devoted to securing news for the great chief. And of course his people would swiftly bring all news to their beloved Giant under the shady palm at Badu village.

And Wongai had to grin and bear it, gritting his teeth at the massive stern as, led by Patma's tiny hand, the Giant waddled back to his shady palm and the food awaiting there.

But in course of time the Giant's scouts brought word that the chief Boroto with a handful of picked warriors had sailed to visit his friends, the savages of the Great South Land. As was his cautious custom, the chief Boroto had taken his wife Gi'Om with him. The scouts added that Boroto was alert against any attack by which the dreaded chief Wongai might try to snatch his Lamar wife from him.

At which information Wongai leered sarcastically.

The news that Boroto had sailed for the Australian mainland gave him intense satisfaction—he was passionately anxious to seize the castaway girl so that she could be rearing him white sons while he gave undivided attention to forming his island kingdom.

Having now no cause to dread Moa, he became crazily anxious for action.

Familiar with Boroto's general movements through the Giant's scouts, he had planned and been waiting for this very move. He would make no mistake *this* time. Boroto was friendly with the Australian aborigines, from the tip of Cape York Peninsula, south to the mouth of the Escape River. Wongai knew this.

There was something else, though, he did *not* know. A happening that was to affect the development of Australia's north eastern coastline, even the fate of an escaped convict dreaming to form a little island kingdom of his own.

Only a few months previously the explorer Kennedy, battling his way up along the Cape York Peninsula, had been speared to death near the mouth of that very river, the Escape, when almost within sight of the relief schooner *Ariel,* chartered by the New South Wales Government.

The tragic fate of the noted explorer, followed by the great gold discoveries soon to come, was to hasten development of the far north, within a comparatively few years helping to bring the first outpost of civilization to the edge of the Coral Sea.

And a shooting expedition in search of a renegade called "Wongai".

But Wongai, chief of chiefs of all Badu, lieutenant of Sida, God of the Crops, friend of Kwoiam, God of War, schemed deeply, blissfully unaware of the future.

Eagerly he planned to seize the castaway girl. From Badu, wind and tides being favourable, in a night's sailing he could reach any point between the Cape and the mouth of the Escape. His simple plan was to intercept Boroto when he was returning to Entrance Island, and take the girl from him.

Leisurely he sailed, in three war-canoes fully manned with picked men. But he had hardly cleared the waterway when a scouting canoe from the Giant came skimming towards him. And the eyes of the messengers were nearly starting from their heads as they gabbled at him that a great Lamar ship of war was anchored by the Great South Land right opposite Boroto's aboriginal friends. And smaller "spirit canoes" cruised with her.

Wongai felt a stiffening of the scalp. Slowly he sailed on, feeling he should turn back.

CHAPTER XL

THE YARD-ARM

A man-o'-war—and anchored for quite a time! With two auxiliaries cruising among the Murralug Islands. What were they doing there? In a locality unmapped, practically unknown?

What *could* their presence mean?

Surely they were not seeking him! At long last had those forgotten authorities heard that he was living among savages—in the distant islands! Here-at the "end of the world"?

His eyes dilated to a stiffening at the neck—he could almost swear he heard the creaking of a yard-arm. Yet—slowly he sailed on—he *must* get that girl.

He had cause to be fearful, certainly he would swing if they caught him. And—they actually had heard of him, sternly discussed him, as their records show. Had heard of him as one of the most ruthless fiends that ever slit a throat. As an implacable murderer of castaways. Other stories of rumour and fact had come to their ears—tales from shipwrecked men—word passed from ship to passing ship. And now by chance had received almost reliable information of the very island upon which he lived. They—were seeking him.

Particularly Yule, and Lieutenant J. Sweatman of the *Bramble*.

Dr Logan Jack writes in his *Northmost Australia*:

> Lieutenant J. Sweatman, of the *Bramble*, connected the advent of Wini [Wongai] on Mulgrave [Badu] Island with the murder of a boat's crew belonging to a Sydney *bêche-de-mer* and tortoise-shell vessel, who, in June 1846, landed on Mulgrave Island, but rowed off to a sandbank on the appearance of suspicious symptoms among the natives. Four men were killed on the sandbank, while two others, who were in the boat, apparently escaped. "In my opinion," observes MacGillivray, "Wini's arrival on Mulgrave Island apparently took place long before the murder of the boat's crew. More, I think, than three years and a half must have been required for him to have acquired the influence, reputation and property referred to by Gi'Om; and this supposition accords with her phrase of 'many years'."
>
> Only two years ago, *i.e.,* before 1849, adds MacGillivray, two men and a boy, who had reached Banks Island [Moa] in a boat,

were murdered by the natives.

But meanwhile the man-o'-war was engaged upon far more urgent and important work than chasing an elusive renegade—surveying the channels and reefs along Cape York Peninsula and across Torres Strait, while seeking any possible survivors of the ill-fated Kennedy expedition.

H.M.S. *Rattlesnake*, twenty-eight guns, Captain Owen Stanley. Now anchored at Newcastle Bay just off the mouth of the Escape River. The little *Bramble*, and the *Asp*.

The *Bramble, Asp*, and the *Rattlesnake's* pinnace had been ordered away on a month's work to complete the survey of the western entrance of the Strait, and while there if possible to secure the white renegade believed to be living as a chief amongst the natives of Badu Island.

Meanwhile, the *Rattlesnake* carried on with her own work, slowly cruising while surveying along Cape York Peninsula, across Endeavour Strait, slowly cruised past Entrance Island, and on to Murralug, to Torres Strait. Then back again.

Watched with heart-breaking yearning by Gi'Om, wife of Boroto, chief of Entrance Island, otherwise Barbara Thomson, who now had been nearly five years a captive of the Kowraregas of the Murralug Islands.

Wongai's canoes kept dawdling along over a sunlit sea, his warriors puzzled at this sudden indecision. It was not like the Mamoose of all Badu, conqueror of Moa, to act so undecidedly. Wongai's mind was baffled by passion and worry. He should turn back, back to the safety of the hills of Badu. But something would not let him turn back, something was dragging him slowly but surely on against all his better judgment. That white girl castaway, he had desired her all this time for his great dream, in all his busy work and scheming he had had no idea how fiercely she had been built into his ambitions, she had been the least part of it that he had considered personally, but *now* he knew she was the main theme upon which his dream was built. Without her there could be no white sons, and without sons what the use of fighting to build up a kingdom? Since the days of the boat he had won far, far more than he could possibly have dreamed. of. But having won it all, it now seemed small. She was the incentive for him to go ahead and win incomparably more.

And now, when at last he was total master of circumstances and free to take her—this should happen—

A man-o'-war! With two smaller vessels of the Queen!

Suddenly, he growled orders to head a shade towards east. He would hang round the Giant's little islet awhile, think out what he should do, just prowl awhile and see how events were shaping.

For a few days, to the Giant's delight, they anchored off the islet, the Giant's men keeping a sharp look-out from the look-out knoll. Until one morning, without apparent reason, the great chief suddenly gave orders to sail.

The obvious thought had struck him that by some means the man-o'-war might hear of the castaway girl and rescue her. What more natural? Boroto and his men with the girl were still visiting their aboriginal friends on the shore of the Peninsula, in the very locality opposite which the man-o'-war appeared most constantly to be working. The girl must see the vessel, would try to signal, try to attract attention—

Wongai roared to his men to hurry.

They had just set sail when a shout from the look-out knoll beckoned them back as a watcher came running down to shore waving urgently.

A canoe of Badu was swiftly coming, the message-palm at the bows.

In black mood Wongai waited. And soon a light canoe appeared, urged by paddle and sail. Presently she drew alongside Wongai's war-canoe and young Kartoy leapt aboard in eager-eyed haste to tell the great news.

"O my chief, two Lamar canoes of war cruise the shore of Badu. They signal peace to your people. They try to coax us out to their canoes. But we are trying to lure them all ashore, as you have taught us. Their ships are but small, the spirit men aboard are but few though heavily armed with terrible thunder-sticks. Come in haste, O my chief, and plan for us that we may lure the spirit men ashore and kill them and take their war-canoes and the wonderful things in them!"

And Kartoy ceased with panting chest, eager for praise of his news, for the swift command that he and all listening were certain would come.

Wongai's blood ran cold. The two smaller vessels of war! Trying to gain touch with his men of Badu! Then they *were* seeking him, seeking him to swing at the yard-arm!

CHAPTER XLI

DESPERATE TROUBLE—DESPERATE PLANS

For long moments Wongai stood as if in a troubled dream. Silently his warriors waited. A sea-gull screeched overhead.

Ah, yes! If those searchers sent a boat crew ashore his men would fall upon them—he had taught them discipline, ambush and surprise. Sailors—probably the boat's party would be wiped out. That would mean that a stronger party would land in reprisal. Or, more likely, word would be hurried away to the man-o'-war. She would come, a strong punitive expedition would land, the hills of Badu would be combed for Wongai, that run-away convict who had had the unbounded temerity to order his warriors to oppose Her Majesty's Navy. Even should he escape, this time he would be a hunted man, they would return. His authority with natives must vanish under the muskets and cutlasses of Jack Tars, the Zogo-le would be swift to take advantage, would betray him, have him seized and handed over to the man-o'-war for spite and reward.

He turned to Kartoy.

"Make all haste back to Kosabad," he ordered earnestly. "Tell him to call the chiefs together quickly. Order them to avoid the Lamars *whatever* they do. For *these* Lamars are spirit men of war, many more are behind them, they come with great thunder-sticks stolen from the Thunder God, they are invincible—no man can stand against them. Tell Kosabad that if they land then the people must run to the hills. Tell the fishers to fish close by the shores so that they cannot be surprised. No man must be *caught* by the Lamars. For if any man be caught by the Lamars they will fill him with the Big Sick and return him to my people, and then all will catch the disease and the death wail will arise throughout all the tribes. Tell Kosabad to send a messenger of peace to Moa to warn them likewise. And to Mabuiag. And to all other peoples he can. Hurry back with my message, Kartoy, before my people foolishly attack these Lamars and bring woe upon us all."

Superstitious fear had wiped the eagerness from Kartoy's face as mutely he stepped back into his canoe. She put about, swiftly sped back towards Badu.

Wongai, in stubborn indecision, remained by the Giant's Island. Again and yet again he decided to return to Badu, only to remain where he was. For if "they" searched Badu then he would *not* be there. And if only his people kept clear of them then they would obtain no definite news of him, must finally sail away. No, he was safer here, they would not dream of his sheltering here among these barren little islets.

Some days later Kartoy returned smilingly to Wongai. The Lamar war-canoes had sailed away. They had tried very hard to gain contact with men of Badu, but always the people had fled before them, dreading the disease. The orders of the Mamoose had been obeyed.

As Lieutenant Yule of the *Bramble* reported upon his return to Captain Owen Stanley of H.M.S. *Rattlesnake*. He had completed the survey of the western entrance to the Strait, and had made every endeavour to get in touch with the people of Badu and Moa. But on every occasion they had avoided contact with him and his men.

MacGillivray writes in his *Narrative of the Voyage of H.M.S. Rattlesnake:*

> During the period of our stay at Cape York, the Bramble, Asp, and Rattlesnake's Pinnace were sent away to the western entrance of Torres Strait to finish the survey, and returned after a month's absence. The boats had held no intercourse with any of the natives except a small party of Kowraregas, the inhabitants of Mulgrave [Badu] and Banks [Moa] Islands having carefully avoided them.

MacGillivray writes of the crews' hopes of catching up with Wongai, the renegade white man. But, as events proved, the natives had obeyed his orders too well. Wongai again was fighting for his life against the threat of approaching civilization. And he was going to take some catching.

As Kartoy delivered his message, Wongai's eyes gleamed with a sneering satisfaction. If the navy men had been searching for him then they had failed. And—they had not learned a thing! Eagerly again his thoughts flew to the southward—and the girl. He would sail now and take her—before it was too late. She was still there on the mainland, he knew from the Giant's scouts. The man-o'-war had long since made friends with the aborigines, giving them much food and wonder things in return for information of some "lost Lamars" they were seeking. Boroto and his party still remained there in the breathless hope of begging toorook from the mighty Lamar ship. But their dread of the Lamars was still so great that they had not yet dared show themselves, though from hiding each day they watched and saw that the landing parties of the Lamars and the ship itself did the aborigines no harm.

Instead, the Lamars talked only of peace, and gave the savages many wonderful presents, presents that turned Boroto and his men green with envy; he could not tear himself away from the place, nor yet was he game to approach the great ship.

Wongai knew then that the white girl must have seen the ship, he guessed how she must be breaking her heart in an attempt to steal away from Boroto.

With an oath, he ordered his men to sail.

From the Giant's Island he was not a night's sail from Possession Island, where he had intended to lurk again while Boroto came sailing back from the Peninsula. But now he would be in grave danger of being cut off should those cursed warships still be surveying Torres Strait. He decided to make for the Mori Group. From Mount Adolphus he would have a clear look-out towards Cape York and Albany Island, either of which would then be but an hour's sail away. From Mount Adolphus Island he would send the scouts to the mainland to find out just exactly where Boroto was, what he was doing, and where was Gi'Om. Meanwhile he would be east of the warships, he could double back to Badu, to a whole chain of islands if needs must. He was certain his canoes could outdistance the warships in a chase, but it would be a far different matter if his retreat were cut off. Not only would he have to outmanoeuvre three ships, but they could call upon the swarms of Kowraregas of the Murralug Islands to aid them.

Just before daylight his canoes beached by Mori. After a hungry breakfast he urged the scout's canoe away on their job. Then he climbed Mount Adolphus. A beautiful day, sunlight bathing the Coral Sea. A cloudless sky, the blue water still as a lake. Gazing west, he could see the Cape coast running south to where it was hidden by the bluff, long bulk of Pabaju (Albany Island). It was in the Pass between that long island and the mainland that the man-o'-war was most often anchored on its mysterious mission. Gazing towards that brown island filled Wongai with memories. How long ago was it, when he had sailed round that island alone in the boat? He had nearly sailed up into the trap in the Pass. How long ago was it that he had sailed by that island, a famished outcast, half-crazy with freedom, fleeing as far as he possibly could from the haunts of white men, a desperado with the salt-bitten weals of the lash upon his back, still feeling the sores of the leg-irons round his ankles, memory seared by visions of those massive piles of masonry by Kingston—every stone cemented by sweat and blood. A half-crazed beast he was, seeking life, but—life with freedom.

Breathing deeply, he gazed carefully all round. Not a sail in sight, not even a canoe. He set a watch, while his men down below sought their fish-spears, joking like boys on holiday transported to new hunting grounds.

The following day the scouts returned—with breathless news.

Gi'Om, the Lamar girl, had run away from Boroto and was now aboard the great ship!

Boroto had gone mad. Had actually boarded the Lamar ship and pleaded with Gi'Om to come back to him. She had refused. It was true. Barbara Thomson, captive for so long among the Kowraregas, was now safe aboard H.M.S. *Rattlesnake*. At last had come her opportunity. A shooting party from the man-o'-war had landed close by where Boroto and his men were hiding. The girl slipped away then ran for it, just managed to reach the astonished navy men and throw herself at their knees.

She had been so long among the Kowraregas that for a time the officers believed her to be what she looked to be — a native girl.

Wongai received the news in cold dismay, staring dully at the messenger. He felt chilled. He seemed to be some other man, as he told Kosabad and Bagari long afterward. He seemed to be "thinking" from a long, long way away.

For a week he remained at Mount Adolphus Island because he could not decide what to do, felt incapable of action, knew not whether to "come or go". Every twenty-four hours his scouts brought him news. Boroto had sent for Piaquai, chief of chiefs of Murralug, and his wife Nakobad to come and plead with Gi'Om, their "daughter", aboard the great ship.

Piaquai had come with Nakobad, had boarded the ship, had spoken to Gi'Om. And the Lamars had not harmed Piaquai or his men. Instead, they had given them pleasant things to eat, given them presents of precious toorook.

And now there were many canoes from the Murralug Islands close round the great ship, others arriving every day.

It was so. For Captain Stanley's policy was to gain the confidence of and make friends with aborigines and islanders wherever possible, in the hopes of ensuring the safety of shipwrecked crews that might fall into their hands and to acquaint them somewhat with the future coming of the white man. As to the Australian aborigines on the coast, he was particularly desirous of friendly relations, still hoping for news of possible survivors of the Kennedy expedition. And now, as a great help to much closer understanding both with the islanders and the mainland aborigines, had come this fantastic rescue of the shipwrecked girl Barbara Thomson, a white girl living amongst savages when they thought the nearest white woman was nearly a thousand miles away. For the girl, of course, knew the language both of the islanders and the aborigines. And her willing help, as haltingly she regained the use of her own language, was greatly appreciated, as the naturalist, MacGillivray, related in his *Narrative of* H.M.S. *Rattlesnake.*

At last Wongai sailed by night for Albany Island, hazily groping for some forlorn hope to seize the girl. A girl who now was not guarded by savages, but by a man-o'-war. What wild schemes flitted through his crazed mind will never be known, but several greybeards of Badu told me sufficient, as handed down to them by their fathers, to get a line on his thoughts.

"The chief Wongai believed he would have to board the great ship in the dead of night," explained a greybeard, "crawl down below, and steal the girl. And even if he had, though it was a man-o'-war, his men would have followed him. His men would have followed the great Mamoose anywhere," added the old warrior proudly.

Wongai reasoned that if the commander of the ship allowed the girl's native husband and friends come aboard and speak with her, if he allowed canoes loaded with people come round the ship within speaking distance while she called back from the deck, then it should be easy to get within touch of her. The ship would be very efficiently guarded, of course. But there must be some very pressing reason why the commander was at such pains for so long to make friends with all natives possible. So that any native or natives by day could get within speaking distance of the girl, while privileged ones were allowed aboard to speak to her. She had actually taken Piaquai and Nakobad and others down below to a cabin the captain had given her. Easy then, through his scouts, to find out just where she slept.

By night, all canoes would be ordered away. A strict watch would be kept.

But naked men of Badu, their bodies oiled, were slippery shadows by night, especially the Killers. At home in the water, as on land. He could send two of his best men, the best night fighters on all Badu, to board the ship while others waited in the water near by. Like eels they could climb the ship, like eels squirm across the deck, find their way below, silently seize the girl as she slept, bring her on deck and leap with her to the water and their friends. They would swim her to a canoe and be away.

There were other schemes, *too* many schemes. He might even combine with Boroto's people, now that Boroto so anxiously desired to regain the girl. He could suggest a plan whereby Boroto's people could substitute a native girl for Gi'Om, the sorcerers of the Zogo-le knew of a drug that dazed, but did not prevent the victim from moving and walking. Such a drug could be given to Gi'Om in her cabin, and a native girl could remain while the dazed Gi'Om came up on deck with her friends and with them back to their canoe and away—to where Wongai's men would suddenly appear and take the girl from Boroto.

Oh yes, there were plans, plans, all manner of plans. With plans swimming in his mind Wongai sailed at last for Albany Island. From there he could look straight down upon the man-o'-war and work out some plan which *must* win the girl.

CHAPTER XLII

WONGAI'S DREAM FADES AWAY

Wongai held his canoes off the eastern shore of Albany Island as a golden sun popped up away over the Great Barrier Reef. And, unseeing, watched a beautiful sight.

The black bulk of the island dissolving in silver that merged into rose, then gold as the sun shot up to paint in fiery hues brown hill and sombre cliff. Beautiful indeed is the colour play as the golden sun soars from its bowl of fire "up over" the Great Barrier Reef.

So far they saw no sign of life. But Wongai would not land until well after daylight. This island was fairly well inhabited. Wongai's warriors despised the people as being little better than savages, but they had the numbers, and were on their own home ground. However, Wongai believed all the people would be away over on the western shore, waiting for the time when they could paddle across to the big ship.

And so it proved.

Again the wonderful luck of this outcast held good, as it had so magically during the last few years, and would for years to come.

Had he landed but a day earlier he would have run into a hornet's nest—not only all the local inhabitants, but a strongly armed working party from the man-o'-war, the last land task of H.M.S. *Rattlesnake* in these waters.

Wongai beached his canoes so that they could be launched instantly, leaving a strong guard. Warily then he and his men climbed steeply up, alert for surprise as they made for the highest point of the island.

And a surprise.

Making sure the place was deserted, Wongai walked slowly towards the strange sight his men had pointed out to him. The last thing he had ever expected to see out here, ever to see again. A civilized grave, newly railed. He read the inscription, "Here lies Thomas Wall and C. Niblet, late of the Kennedy Exploring Expedition."[8]

What was the Kennedy Expedition? And how had these men perished? With the strangest feelings he stared at the grave, the rails laid by men from H.M.S. *Rattlesnake* only the day before, the tombstone by Captain Owen Stanley.

---

[8] The men had been buried a short time before by members of the crew of the brig *Freak*, Captain Thomas Beckford Simpson, chartered by the New South Wales Government as a relief ship to the Kennedy Expedition.

He gazed across Albany Pass towards Newcastle Bay. And there lay the *Rattlesnake* in plain sight, canoes around her, many canoes drawn up on the little beaches opposite. For a long, long time he stared at this armed emblem of the thing he hated most—civilization.

The long, rugged western shore of Albany Island is faced heavily with cliffs. Long but narrow, it is a brown, barren-looking island. Straight across the Pass, across a mile of water-way, the little cliffs and hills, the little headlands and tiny beaches of the mainland stand out prettily from their tangle of forest and scrub. Down below, the blue waters of the Pass lie deceitfully peaceful until the tide turns, when it can awake into a fury of raging waters.

For several hours, from that highest point up on Albany Island, Wongai stared out over the Pass at that activity upon and around the man-o'-war across by the mainland shore.

Perhaps if he had realized that the officers aboard now definitely knew that his haunt was Badu Island he might not have been so self-possessed. For the rescued Barbara Thomson had confirmed the fact. But his mind was so clouded with the problem of how to get the girl that he did not give such an obvious probability a thought. Though he need not have been worried over-much, for Her Majesty's ships now had more pressing business on hand than hunting an escaped convict in these troublous water. As Wongai realized with the turn of the tide.. For there was sudden activity aboard, and a rollicking sea-chanty came clearly up to him.

They were hauling up the anchor, men were swarming at the yard-arms, sails unfurled.

The man-o'-war was sailing.

A lovely picture she made, sailing up the Pass between island and mainland with favourable wind and a growing tide fast splashing the tumbling waters into white horses. Wongai stood erect, a towering figure in his savage regalia close by the new grave of the explorers, his savage bodyguard round him, a wild figure with heart now turbulent as the troubled water below.

The turning tide, the white savage, the sleeping explorers, the man-o'-war sailing on.

Symbols of the changing times.

Something deep within him told him that the ship was taking his island queen that should have been—away from him for ever. And his island kingdom would vanish with her.

And so it was. For H.M.S. *Rattlesnake* on this fair day of December 1849 was sailing for the survey of the Louisiade Archipelago, then Sydney

Town and—home.

And the white girl high up on deck, with the mournful calls of her native friends ringing in her ears, watched in tearful silence such well-known scenes from the last dreadful years gliding past. Cape York, then the extreme Peak Point of the Great South Land, Possession Island, then her Boroto's Entrance Island, then Great Murralug Island of her "father", Piaquai, chief of chiefs of all the Kowraregas, then all the Murralug Islands upon which she had gazed and slaved for so long. And as the *Rattlesnake* turned east-north-east, heading for Eroob, thence the Louisiades, they handed her a telescope and long she gazed towards the vanishing Peak of Moa, the dimming hills of Badu.

She wondered then, for quite a time, where *he* was—the great chief Wongai, the reincarnation of the friend of Sida, God of the Crops, that savage who had terrified her even when she had thought she had no terror left.

CHAPTER XLIII

THE SORCERER'S LIFE FOR THE YELLOW POWDER

Wongai sailed back to Badu not caring, morosely dispirited. The bottom had fallen out of his world. *She* had gone. Never now would an astonished world discover an island kingdom ruled by a race of white kings.

He arrived home to find that his Petula, once the loved wife of Sisi the chief, had died the day before. He didn't care, was sullenly resentful that he did not even feel pleased. Serve her right. She had tried to slowly poison him, just because he had killed Sisi when Sisi had sought to kill *him*. Well, she had gone, anyway, though it did not seem to matter so much now—mattered not at all.

He had never been attracted by native women, though there were plenty here who were really lovely, and warmly attractive.

Sorely disappointed was the big chief, savagely morose. But others were troubled, too. Away back on the outskirts of the village, alone in his hut, Barza, the sorcerer, was worried indeed—he could not find the snake!

For several nights now he had waited—but the snake did not come.

Barza had solved the problem—it had come to him in a flash!—how to catch the snake. He wondered he had not thought of it long ago, it was so simple, would not upset any totem laws, would only annoy the snake.

Barza grinned cynically. What he was going to do with that snake would turn it into a writhing fury. Then at dead of night he would crawl into the chief Wongai's hut and throw the maddened thing upon his sleeping body. He could vanish from the hut even as it sank its fangs into the big chief's throat.

And only just in time. For either the chief or the sorcerer must die. If the big chief lived to unite Moa with Badu and Mabuiag then it would be Barza who would die. And, the Council of the Zogo-le had hinted, none too pleasantly, either.

Barza, chief sorcerer of Badu, was granted one last chance to carry out orders or—vanish from the ken of men.

And now Barza was ready with a plan that could not fail. But—he could not find the snake! It had not come these last two nights. Surely it must come tonight. With the unlit zoob across his knees, staring round the hut, he waited for the snake, urgently calling upon the spirit of Enoko to come.

While directly above him two beady eyes glared down, the tip of a forked tongue darting silently, viciously, from leathery lips.

Tightly coiled round the divination skull, the snake, its head pressed close down the skull's forehead, stared down upon the sorcerer waiting below.

The night following the mourning ceremonies for Petula, the Shadow appeared to Wongai, a question in his eyes. And the sulking chief remembered his promise with a quickening of savage interest.

"Kill your enemy Kaigas the Maidelaig," he snarled. "Kill that murderer of your father in any way you like—kill him tonight, and I will protect you even against the Zogo-le. And now, that snake in the grass, Barza! Is he in his hut tonight?"

The Shadow nodded.

"Ah!" sneered Wongai as his hand closed down for his knife. "Then I shall go and kill him—now! He need make no more Yellow Powder!"

And the Shadow eagerly departed, vengeance in his eyes.

Wongai quietly left his house and walked among the palms, through the sleeping village towards the path that led to the deep seclusion of the sorcerer's hut. And presently heard low moans that shrilled into cries of despair, slowly gasping away. He looked up at the shrouded taboo pole. It would take more than the moan through hidden reeds swaying in the breeze to turn *him* aside. For the first time since he had lost the white girl he felt a man again—he had pleasant work to do.

He halted a moment—not from fear. Grinning knowingly, he half bent to fasten sandals upon his big bare feet, sandals with a sole of shell sandwiched between layers of plaited rattan, sandals that could defy the splinter of death.

For he is a fool who, despite the taboo warning, creeps along the sorcerer's path in the dead of night. Sooner or later his foot must tread upon that which pierces deep—the needle-sharp splinter of poisoned bamboo.

Wongai walked silently on up the path, dark as the pit from the enclosing shrubs. He was grinning with eagerness, though no living soul could see. Noiselessly he stepped into a circle of starlight bathing the beehive-shaped dome of the sorcerer's hut He bent to the open doorway.

A choking gasp-horrid death rattle—

He crouched as if frozen stiff, fist clenched on knife, dilated eyes glaring at the dark opening.

Sound of a man convulsively writhing on a palm-leaf mat—awful gurgle of that choking death rattle.

He peered into the hut.

Coals glowed upon the clay fire-pan. Odour of death's heads, of smoke dried charms of fish and bird and reptile. And Barza the sorcerer convulsively writhing, choking horribly upon his mat.

No other soul in the hut. On hands and knees Wongai crawled in. Gazed down upon the distorted face, the swollen tongue, the foam-flecked lips of Barza. In the bulging eyes Wongai caught a gleam of hateful recognition as the sorcerer gasped his last.

Poisoned! Someone had poisoned Barza the sorcerer!

In bewilderment, Wongai stared around. *Who* had poisoned Barza the sorcerer?

And his eyes were fixed by the eyes of the snake, the vicious head slowly swaying just above its coiled body. It hissed at the man, its black forked tongue darting in and out.

The snake! Enoko's snake! Enoko's snake had bitten, had *poisoned* Barza the sorcerer!

Wongai found himself creeping from the hut with the cold fear of a guilty man. He who was a killer, who had *come* to kill, sneaking away like a guilty murderer! With his mind in a whirl, he crept along the path back to his hut. Crept inside and quietly lay down upon his mat.

CHAPTER XLIV

THE GAUNTLET TO THE ZOGO-LE

Gradually the shock cleared from his mind, to be shadowed by a sense of defeated anger. He had set out for revenge, and to throw down the gauntlet to the Zogo-le, deliberately to kill a chief sorcerer, hand to hand, not by poison or under the cloak of intrigue. He felt cheated of a long-cherished revenge, cheated again because he could not now taunt the Zogo-le. Had he killed their chief sorcerer it would have been up to them to have done something about it—had they dared!

He sat up, filled his zoob, smoked a while, calmed down. He had been biding his time to claim vengeance upon the sorcerer who believed he was slowly poisoning him. But it must have been his disappointment at losing the girl that made him want to tear someone to pieces and at the same time to openly challenge the Zogo-le. But what to do now?

They would know of course, would immediately recognize the symptoms of snake-bite. Barza killed by the fangs of a snake. Queer that one sorcerer should be killed by the other's snake, the snake was Enoko's totem, too.

Wongai leaned forward, staring sightlessly, mind alert to grasp the germ of a great idea. The snake! Enoko's totem! Their age-old superstitions! He, Wongai, the reincarnation of a spirit man! Yes, and other startling, but such positive beliefs. The spirit of a man often appearing to his friends, often returning to his old haunts, often, too, appearing in ghost or spirit form within his living totem of animal, bird, fish, or reptile! Enoko's totem snake haunting the hut of Enoko, the hut that Barza the sorcerer had taken over, Barza who had become the new sorcerer after the mysterious death of Enoko! Barza who had been the jealous enemy of Enoko. The totem snake of Enoko kills Barza the sorcerer, Barza the poisoner!

Wongai pondered deeply, then thumped one big fist into the other with a delighted oath, chuckling so mightily that Mek and Naina and Miria sleepily awoke.

At full daylight he called before him the village chiefs and heads of clans. The warriors and people followed on, wondering. Standing on his house platform, in deep, impressive voice he told how last night he had killed Barza the sorcerer, killed him because he had poisoned Petula, his wife.

"He tried to poison *me!*" added the big chief, and paused for the deep significance to sink in upon all those silent, startled faces.

"Yes," he resumed, "he might have poisoned me, Wongai, chief of chiefs of all Badu. And bitter indeed would have been Sida, God of the Crops, thunder upon the brow of Kwoiam, God of War, when I rejoined them in the land of shades high above Boigu, Isle of the Blest."

He paused, glaring out over those hundreds of upturned faces, those staring eyes.

He laughed, a low, rumbling, sarcastic laugh.

"The fool Barza," he shouted impressively, "the fool that thought he could poison *me*, Wongai, come from the skies! I could not stop him from poisoning my wife Petula because she was of earth life, as you are. But *no* human sorcerer could ever poison Wongai, lieutenant of Sida, God of the Crops!"

He paused again, then shouted, "I poisoned Barza the sorcerer through the totem snake of Enoko, the dead sorcerer!"

The indrawing of breaths was like a sigh in the palms.

"Yes!" shouted Wongai. "Know you too that long ago Enoko *also* tried to poison me. But it was I who sent Enoko to the land of shades. Then, through Sida, I charmed his spirit to enter into his totem snake and remain there until he should atone his crimes. Then, when the time was ripe—last night—I ordered Enoko to kill Barza through his totem snake."

Wongai paused, slowly glancing over them all, grimly smiling.

"The spirit of Enoko obeyed!" he shouted. "The fangs of his snake fastened deep in Barza's throat. And thus the poisoner died by the poison he had long meant for me!"

For long moments he stood there, ears attuned to the utter silence. Then in fury roared, "Barza the sorcerer poisoned my favourite wife— would have poisoned *me!* I am going to throw his carcass to the sharks. Come!"

He jumped from the platform and the excited people followed him back among the palms. But their chatter ceased as Wongai at the head of his men turned into the sorcerer's path. Fearfully, many held back as he approached the dreaded hut. He strode straight to the taboo pole, wrenched it down, flung it aside. Then crawled into the hut and dragged the dead sorcerer out by the heels.

"Carry him to the meanest canoe," he sneered, "and we'll poison the sharks!"

And the Shadows were the first men to step forward and lay hands on the dread body, timidly helped by those of the Shovel-nosed skate clan.

Under Wongai's fierce eyes the body was carried down through the village to the shore. Thrown into a dilapidated canoe. Then all canoes were manned and rowed to the channel of the sharks. Here the corpse was thrown overboard. Silently they watched the lashing of the water as the sharks tore the body of Barza to pieces.

Lu-esa's blood ran cold. Remembering that Kartoy, her warrior husband, had in sweetheart days dared this fate—for her!

Low whisperings in the canoes as they rowed back to the village. What had been happening among them all this time? Things that only Wongai—the Zogo-le—knew about! Happening under their very noses. An earth chief from the spirit world intriguing against the sorcerers, the Zogo-le against *him!* Two sorcerers killed—serve them right!—their great Wongai triumphant—of course, he always *must* be. For he had come from the skies, the beloved of Sida—he could command forces unknown to earth—unknown to human sorcerers—perhaps unknown even to the Zogo-le. Why, but why, should chief sorcerers of the Zogo-le have conspired against the life of their Wongai?

Deep within himself, Wongai was laughing. He had forced the Zogo-le to defend themselves, a problem they had never been called upon to face before: And how puzzled they themselves would be! He felt it would be a long time, if ever, before he had anything to fear from the Zogo-le again.

CHAPTER XLV

TIME WRITES "FINIS" TO MICE AND MEN

And there *did* come a murmuring among the people, spreading throughout all Badu to Mabuiag.

Why should the Zogo-le desire the life of the great chief himself, beloved of Sida, reincarnation of Wongai, who had done so very much for them, so much for all Badu and Mabuiag? Who had brought the seasons back again, built such wonderful gardens that now no man need hunger, improved so greatly the canoes, taught them real warfare, thrashed their enemies and defeated even Moa? Wongai the great chief, friend of Kwoiam, God of War. Did the Zogo-le really desire the death of Wongai? And why? Would they really dare—?

Wongai chuckled mightily, grinding his teeth, clenching vengeful fists.

The triumph turned to ashes in his mouth.

If only the *girl* was here. Moa across the waterway was his for the taking—the whole Western Group was his. And he believed he could now combine, on his own terms, with the Zogo-le.

If *only* the girl were here!

He settled down to the rounds of native life again, but the zest of life had gone, gone with the castaway girl in that accursed man-o'-war. He grew sullen, morose. Took less and less interest in the island world. His one abiding interest his beloved gardens.

And time dreamed on.

Time—which he sullenly believed had defeated *him*. Remorseless time, which rolls on with the destiny of nations, of civilizations.

Let alone of individuals.

The renegade Wongai, chief of all Badu, would not have cared a tinker's cuss had he known that a man named Edward Hargrave had returned to Australia from California.

But—Hargraves had answered the lure of gold, joined the rush to California after Marshall had found gold in the tail-race at Sutter's Mill. And that district, he swore, was exactly the same sort of country as he had seen out in the bush, back in Australia. He returned to Australia, hurried bush in New South Wales and there, at the junction of Summerhill and Lewis Ponds Creeks, found payable gold on February 12, 1851.

As Marshall had started the first gold rush that led to the phenomenal development of California, so Hargraves started the rush in Australia that in but a few years' time was to develop the empty continent into a nation.

This vast happening was to affect the fate of a renegade chieftain of Badu.

Explorers, land-seekers, prospectors, pushed out to all points of the compass. And never would the restless be satisfied until from east to west, from farthest south to farthest north they had trod the land from sea to sea.

Population followed them. In a very few years population was pouring west and—north! Bringing more and yet more ships to sail the Coral Sea.

Meanwhile, Wongai was hoist with his own petard. In a few years that he had dreamed about his island kingdom he had trained quite a large number of war-loving islanders, picked men from every tribe on Badu and Mabuiag. And he was to find, like many immeasurably greater men, that when you create a fighting force with an objective, even though it be but a few savage islanders, the time will surely come when you will, or be forced to, use that machine.

Wongai's chiefs and heads of clans, urged by the warriors, implored him to carry on the war against Moa in earnest. At last he consented, though unwillingly, it was something that might help him from brooding about the girl. And thus started years of island warfare that practically depopulated Moa Island.

Eventually a Government semi-military post was established at Somerset, on Cape York Peninsula, exactly opposite Albany Island, as advised by Lieutenant Jukes of H.M.S. *Fly*, later backed up by Captain Owen Stanley of H.M.S. *Rattlesnake* on the advisability of establishing a post on the mainland opposite Mount Adolphus Island, as a haven for castaways and a coaling station for the future, with the object of ultimately forming "another Singapore".

John Jardine, Police Magistrate and Gold Commissioner at Rockhampton was the first Government Resident appointed at Somerset, and a few years later was succeeded by his son Frank, who soon came in conflict with the renegade chieftain on Badu, ordering the Government cutter *Lizzie Jardine* to cruise cautiously off Badu and shoot Wongai if given the slightest chance.

And in jubilation the cutter's crew returned to say they had accomplished the job.

Jardine wrote to the Colonial Secretary of this "great news" with the liveliest expressions of satisfaction.

But—his men had *not* shot Wongai. They had shot an islander whose body was whitened with pipeclay in mourning for his brother.

After the shooting, the great chief Wongai disappeared. He was "dead" to whites and browns alike. But the Zogo-le knew where Wongai was.

His "dying" was probably the most cunning of all his cunning acts in life.

He lived to be an old, old man, to see the great pearl rushes that so suddenly flooded the lovely Coral Sea with "Lamar" ships. To see the taming of the sea chief Kebisu by Captain Banner, and later by H.M.S. *Basilisk*, to see the finish of what would have been his island kingdom overrun by whites. To see the coming of the "white religion" swamp the Zogo-le and the island culture of a thousand years until today the descendants of his islanders would laugh to scorn the very mention of the old beliefs.

Perhaps some day I may complete the story of Wongai, though to me it seems his story ended when he lost the castaway girl. Years ago, cruising the Strait and fishing out a little of Wongai's history here, a little there, I used to wonder how much of his dreams he would have succeeded in putting into practice had he managed to seize Barbara Thomson.

Quite a lot, I'm sure. I used sometimes to wonder the result of what would have been his biggest fight, the clash between him and Kebisu. For the sea chief and his men were fighters indeed, and while Kebisu ruled the seaway the ambitious renegade would have been kept gnashing his teeth on his large islands.

I believe time would just have beaten him in the end. Population creeping up into North Queensland, but above all, the pearlshell rushes.

Yes, maybe that will be a future book. Completing the story of Wongai, but more the romance of Captain Banner and the finding of the great pearlshell beds along the Warrior Reefs, the taming of Kebisu by the patient, far-seeing Banner and later by Captain (afterwards Admiral) John Moresby of H.M.S. *Basilisk*. And—ah yes, the last great fight of the Giant! Yes, that might be the story, the romance and tragedy, the uncontrollable march of progress that filled the Coral Sea with the eager pearling fleets. And the ending of what *might have been* Wongai's island kingdom.

www.ingramcontent.com/pod-product-compliance
Lightning Source LLC
Chambersburg PA
CBHW030928090426
42737CB00007B/361